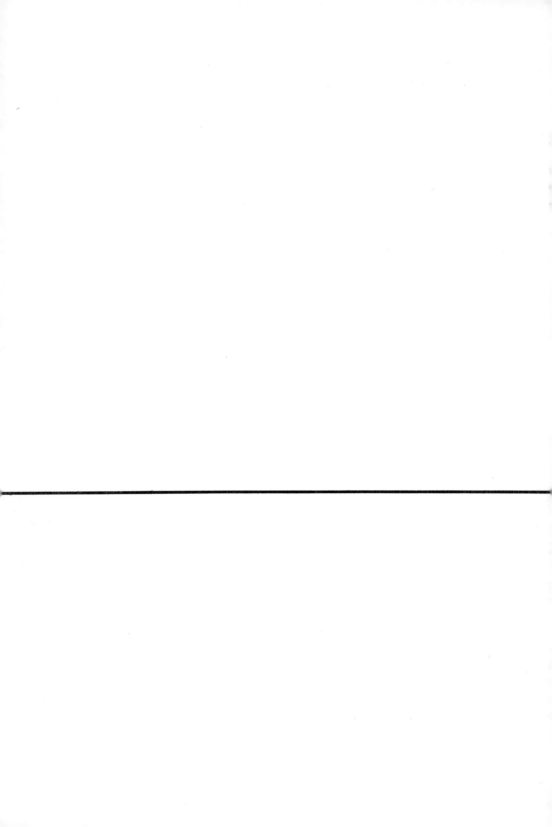

Soviet Policy towards

International Control

of Atomic Energy

JOSEPH L. NOGEE

UNIVERSITY OF NOTRE DAME PRESS 1961

Library of Congress Catalog Card Number: 61-10850
Manufactured in the United States

TO THE MEMORY
OF
MY MOTHER

PREFACE

THE PROBLEM OF INTERNATIONAL CONTROL OF ATOMIC ENERGY is distinctly propitious as a case study in Soviet diplomacy. Not only is it a problem that is now a closed subject, but it is one which permits examination of Kremlin policy on a vital issue from beginning to end. The choice between a national or international atom, so important in the middle and late 1940s, was a dead issue in the early years of the next decade: Soviet science and the cold war had permanently nationalized the atom.

Secondly, the topic is one that contains more than its share of the drama that is inherent in any problem of such magnitude. The Baruch Plan was almost as revolutionary in its political implications as the plan for controlled atomic fission—a formidable challenge which had to be faced. Whatever course of action Premier Stalin followed inevitably portended momentous consequences in view of the key position of the Soviet Union in world affairs.

Thirdly, a relatively complete body of documentary evidence on this subject is both available and accessible to the scholar at the present time. Almost without exception, the debates accompanying negotiations within the United Nations are a matter of public record. Because records of the highest Soviet policy-making bodies, if they exist, are not available to Western scholars, and because high-ranking Soviet leaders are notoriously delinquent in providing published memoirs, any analysis of the inside formulation of policy in the Politburo or Presidium is unfortunately forestalled. The public record of the United Nations' documents as well as Russian newspapers and periodicals, however, do provide an adequate picture of Soviet policy.

Part I of this book is devoted to as complete a statement as possible of the Soviet Union's atomic energy policy, presented in a historical context. I was particularly interested in discovering the precise Soviet objections to international control, specifically, whether the opposition was based on alterable or unalterable factors. I analyze this enigma extensively in Chapter Nine, Part II of this study.

In the course of writing the initial seven chapters, the consistent pattern of Soviet negotiating tactics gradually became perceptible. It was apparent that these tactics were directed toward more positive objectives than merely the digging of a grave for atomic energy control. These goals are discussed separately in Chapter Ten.

I am most indebted to Frederick C. Barghoorn and Walter R. Sharp of Yale University for their invaluable guidance at the time I undertook this study as a graduate student. John W. Spanier of the University of Florida and Stephen D. Kertesz of the University of Notre Dame aided invaluably by reading the manuscript and offering suggestions for clarifying the text and improving the style. T. C. Sinclair and James R. Jensen of the University of Houston generously adjusted my teaching schedule to maximize my free hours for the writing of this book. Moreover, I am grateful to my wife for countless hours of proofreading and numerous other tasks she performed in preparation of the manuscript. Finally, I acknowledge the services supplied by the staff of the Yale University Library, and secretarial and material assistance provided me by the University of Houston.

Joseph L. Nogee

Houston, Texas
April, 1961

CONTENTS

INTRODUCTION

INTERNATIONAL CONTROL OF ATOMIC ENERGY IS NOW A CLOSED
book of modern history. There may be some debate as to
when the last chapter was written: possibly as early as July,
1946, when the Soviet Union first rejected the Baruch Plan;
or in February, 1947, when Gromyko vetoed the "majority
plan" for international control of atomic energy in the Security Council; or even as late as the early 1950s when stockpiles of atomic weapons had been developed and integrated
into Western military defenses. But today international control of atomic energy is not a feasible objective of national
policy. Currently some part of the disarmament debate does
center around the problem of establishing a "cut-off" in the
production of nuclear weapons and even the transfer of
existing nuclear stockpiles to peaceful uses. To date, however, no one has proposed a plan by which even the production of nuclear weapons can be controlled. And scientists are
agreed that there does not exist a means by which hidden
stockpiles of nuclear weapons can be detected.

Atomic energy control has from the beginning been closely
linked to the problem of disarmament. The negotiations that
commenced in June, 1946, within the United Nations Atomic
Energy Commission had as their central purpose the elimination of one particularly potent weapon from every nation's
arsenals. This, of course, is a feature of disarmament. Theoretically and practically, however, the problem of interna-

tional control of atomic energy differed significantly from the problem of disarmament as the latter has been traditionally considered. Theoretically, disarmament and atomic energy control were solutions for two different problems. Disarmament has been concerned with the fundamental problem of war. Proponents of disarmament in modern times have worked largely on the assumption that men fight because they have arms.[1] Arms races have been looked upon as breeders of international tensions and fears which in turn ultimately breed wars.

In contrast, the movement for international control of atomic energy was primarily concerned with humanizing war by removing from national use the most terrible weapon science has ever created. Trygve Lie, in opening the first Atomic Energy Commission meeting, expressed the motivation which spurred atomic energy negotiations: "People all over the world demand that atomic energy shall be made to lighten the drudgery of their working days rather than fill their lives with fear." [2] The fear he referred to was not war itself but atomic destruction. In this sense the movement was essentially humanitarian, as were previous efforts in the 1920's to outlaw bacteriological, biological and gas warfare.

Had it been possible to maintain in practice the theoretical distinction between disarmament and international control of atomic energy, negotiations toward the latter might have fared better. Within a matter of a few years, however, atomic weapons became so integrated into the military arsenal of

---

[1] Hans J. Morgenthau, *Politics Among Nations* (New York, 1954), pp. 383-84. For a more concise theory of disarmament see Inis L. Claude, Jr. *Swords into Plowshares* (New York, 1959), pp. 296-302. The experience of disarmament efforts in the 1930s and since the Second World War has brought into question the assumption that arms are responsible for wars; but fundamentally disarmament efforts remain motivated by the desire to bring about conditions of peace. A second motivation for disarmament has been to reduce the cost of government due to the costliness of armaments. See Andrew Martin, *Collective Security: A Progress Report* (Paris, 1952), pp. 27-29, *et passim.*

[2] United Nations (hereinafter abbreviated to UN), *Atomic Energy Commission Official Records* (hereinafter abbreviated to *AECOR) No. 1. First Meeting,* June 14, 1946, p. 3.

first the United States and then the Soviet Union that, while the original motivation for control may have been humanitarian, it encountered the complete gamut of difficulties associated with disarmament. Just as political insecurity frustrated disarmament efforts in the interwar period, so did the mutual Soviet-American suspicion in the post-Second World War era frustrate agreement on control.

Agreement on atomic energy control was also made difficult by technological factors which did not exist in the case of disarmament. International control of atomic energy involved control over not only the military production of nuclear fuel but peaceful production as well. In the case of conventional weapons, generally, a clear distinction can be made between instruments for warlike uses and instruments for peaceful uses. Battleships are clearly not transports, and tanks are not related to trucks. Admittedly, the distinction is not always a sharp one; but a certain amount of violation of a disarmament agreement can be tolerated because no one weapon nor a small preponderance of many weapons is likely to prove decisive in combat.

Atomic weapons are different. Because of their immense destructive power, a small number of atomic bombs can be decisively used against an unarmed nation. Furthermore, nuclear fuel, once produced, can with relative ease be used for either peaceful pursuits or bombs. Thus in order to assure security from an atomic attack the most stringent type of control is required over all atomic energy production whatsoever. This feature of atomic energy control—the necessity for every nation to subordinate its peaceful as well as military production of atomic energy to international supervision—constituted the central Soviet objection to the Western control proposals.

To Western observers Soviet policy toward international control of atomic energy appeared to be quite negative. This judgment was derived from the refusal of the Soviet Union to accept the proposals of the majority or to propose a viable alternative plan of control. A good deal of Western frustration with Soviet policy (both its tactics and strategy) stemmed from an initial inability to realize that the Soviet leadership did not perceive the same threat as did the West in uncontrolled national atomic energy industries. To the Kremlin non-Soviet intrusion into the Soviet industrial structure constituted a far greater threat to its long-term stability and survival than an atomic arms race. Nor did Western diplomats and policy makers fully perceive the total nature of Soviet diplomacy. Indeed, from the point of view of achieving a control system Soviet diplomacy was negative. But in the larger picture of achieving foreign policy objectives other than control of atomic energy Soviet policy was remarkably positive. To isolate Soviet diplomacy on one issue from the totality of its foreign policy was as erroneous in the late 1940s and 1950s as it is now.

The present study begins in 1945 when the existence of the atomic bomb was first publicly revealed. It concludes with the debates of the eighth General Assembly in 1953. The terminal date of 1953 is chosen because it marks the approximate date when for all practical purposes atomic energy negotiations ceased.

While the focus of this study is Soviet Russia's policy toward international control of atomic energy, considerable attention is also given to American atomic energy policy. This attention is justified by the close interrelation between Russo-American atomic energy policies. Soviet policy was to a large extent a response to American policy. The Baruch Plan of 1946 was a challenge to which the Kremlin was forced to respond. In order to understand the response, it is necessary to have a clear idea of the nature of the challenge. Some attention too is given to Soviet disarmament policy, particularly after 1952 when the Atomic Energy Commission and the Commission for Conventional Armaments were amalgamated into a unified Disarmament Commission. But consideration of Soviet disarmament policy is limited solely to those issues that bore upon atomic energy discussions.

Part One

Negotiations, 1945-1960

1: LULL BEFORE THE STORM: FROM POTSDAM TO THE UNITED NATIONS ATOMIC ENERGY COMMISSION

AT EXACTLY 8:15 A.M. ON AUGUST 6, 1945, JAPANESE TIME, THE city of Hiroshima was engulfed in a fireball one and one half miles in diameter that killed or injured over 129,000 people and physically destroyed approximately 60 per cent of the city. Sixteen hours later President Truman gave the first official announcement of American possession and use of a bomb which had more power than 20,000 tons of TNT. "It is," he said, "an atomic bomb." Thus did the world learn of the spectacular new weapon created by Allied scientific knowledge and American industrial capacity. This explosion, and the one over Nagasaki three days later, heralded the end of the Second World War and the beginning of a new source of tension in international politics that was to loom large in the ensuing cold war.[1] History

[1] There are some learned apologists for the Soviet Union who believe that the dropping of the atomic bomb on Hiroshima in August, 1945, was a military-political act executed more to forestall Russian influence in the Far East than to save American lives. P. M. S. Blackett in *Fear, War and the Bomb* (New York, 1949) concludes that "the dropping of the atomic bombs was not so much the last military act of the Second World War, as the first major operation of the cold diplomatic war with Russia now in progress," p. 139. Cf. chap. X, "The Decision to Use the Bombs." For Soviet acceptance of Blackett's thesis see M. Rubenstein, "Proval Atomnoi Diplomatii Amerikanskikh Imperialistov" (Defeat of the Atomic Diplomacy of the American Imperialists), *Bolshevik*, VI (March, 1950), 42. For a more balanced and better

3

moved rapidly after the Hiroshima blast; on August 9 the Soviet
Union declared war on Japan; the following day a second atomic
bomb was dropped on Nagasaki and the Soviet offensive in
Manchuria was begun. On August 14 the Japanese government
capitulated.

Whatever the Soviet leaders may have really felt about the
role of the atomic bomb in terminating the Pacific war they were
quick to claim that Japan's sudden surrender resulted from the
joint efforts of the Allies—not the atomic bomb.[2] Until early
September there was, in fact, almost no public mention of the
atomic bomb in the Soviet Union. During August, 1945, a
mysterious silence reigned in the Soviet press as to the revolutionary nature of atomic destructive power and the damage done by
the bombs on Hiroshima and Nagasaki; nor was there any speculation as to the potential role of atomic weapons in future military strategy or as a source of power for industrial uses. *Izvestia*,
on August 7, 1945, revealed to the Soviet people for the first
time the existence of the atomic bomb. This anouncement was
a short *Tass* report, datelined Washington, August 6, of President Truman's declaration to the world that an atomic bomb
had been dropped on Hiroshima. *Pravda* the following day
duplicated this announcement. Neither report mentioned the
statements made by President Truman on international control
of the bomb. It was not until the beginning of September that
there appeared in the Soviet press any detailed comments on
the implications of atomic energy and not until the celebration
of the twenty-eighth anniversary of the "November Revolution" on November 6, 1945, that the first official government
statement on atomic energy was made.[3] Soviet official and unofficial taciturnity on the general subject of atomic energy was

---

documented account of this issue see Louis Morton, "The Decision to Use the
Atomic Bomb," *Foreign Affairs*, XXXV, No. 2 (January, 1957). See also
Michael Amrine, *The Great Decision* (New York, 1959), chap. VI.

[2] See "Observer" in August 16, 1945, issue of *Izvestia* and *New Times*,
September 1, 1945.

[3] Helen Corenetz, "Views of Pravada and Izvestia on International Control of
Atomic Energy." Unpublished Master's thesis, Columbia University, September
30, 1952, p. 3. *Izvestia* is the official organ of the Soviet Government; *Pravda*
is the official organ of the Russian Communist Party.

in marked contrast to the spate of news articles and commentaries on atomic energy in the Anglo-American press.

The Soviet Government in the person of Generalissimo Stalin first learned officially of the existence of the atomic bomb in the afternoon of July 24, 1945, at Potsdam. During the negotiations at Potsdam President Truman received word of the successful explosion at Alamogordo on July 16. In conjunction with Secretary of State Byrnes, he decided to inform Stalin about it and about the American decision to use the bomb unless Japan promptly surrendered. Stalin asked no questions about the bomb and surprised Byrnes by his general lack of interest. His only comment was that he was glad to hear of the bomb and hoped the United States would use it.[4]

Two explanations account for this apparent Soviet indifference to the implications of atomic energy during 1945. The first was the pressing nature of more immediate and equally important political problems of postwar reconstruction. In Germany the Allied Four Power Control Council was rapidly becoming deadlocked on the question of German reparations and economic policy; in Japan Soviet objections to the Far Eastern Advisory Commission precluded the execution of an occupation policy satisfactory to the Soviet Union and the United States; in the Axis satellites of Bulgaria, Rumania and Hungary lack of unity within the Allied Control Commissions was badly straining East-West relations. Secondly, it is probable that the Soviets had not fully decided on what kind of a policy to adopt toward the international control of atomic energy. They were not yet in possession of the technical information as to the construction of atomic weapons; nor had the United States, which did possess this information, announced its policy. There was nothing which compelled Russia to cross a bridge not yet reached.

It can be assumed that the egregious silence on the subject of

⁴ James F. Byrnes, *Speaking Frankly* (New York, 1947), p. 263. Byrnes adds, "I thought that the following day he would ask for more information about it. He did not. Later I concluded that because the Russians kept secret their developments in military weapons, they thought it improper to ask us about ours." See also Winston Churchill, *Triumph and Tragedy* (Cambridge, Mass., 1953), pp. 637-41.

atomic energy during 1945 and the first half of 1946 was an indication that the Soviet Government considered the subject to be of high importance and that it was determined to be very cautious in its pronouncements. Such was its caution that during the entire first year of the "atomic age" (July, 1945-June, 1946) the only official statement of Soviet policy toward international control of atomic energy, or any aspect of atomic energy, was the Moscow Declaration in 1945, in which it agreed to negotiate an agreement for international control through the United Nations. All other statements of Soviet thinking on the subject were reactions to and comments upon official and unofficial statements made in the United States and Great Britain.

UNITED STATES ATOMIC POLICY DURING 1945

Before President Roosevelt died he had entrusted Secretary of War Henry Stimson with primary responsibility for supervising the development of the atomic bomb. It was from Stimson that President Truman himself first learned on April 25, 1945, of the secret operations going on at Oak Ridge, Tennessee and Hanford, Washington.[5] In the months preceding the successful test explosion at Alamogordo, New Mexico, two questions were uppermost in the minds of those concerned with atomic policy: Should the bomb be used against Japan? What form of international agreements on future use of atomic weapons was possible and desirable?

To aid the executive in considering these matters, Secretary Stimson in April appointed an Interim Committee composed of leading government and scientific personnel. It was made responsible for recommendations with regard to the problems of both national and international control.[6] On June 1, before it

[5] Henry L. Stimson and McGeorge Bundy, *On Active Service in Peace and War* (New York, 1947), pp. 635ff.

[6] Statement by Secretary of War Stimson, August 6, 1945, in the State Department study, *The International Control of Atomic Energy: Growth of a Policy* (Washington, 1946), pp. 104-105. The members of the Interim Committee were as follows: Henry Stimson, Chairman; James F. Byrnes, Ralph A. Bard, William L. Clayton, Vannevar Bush, James B. Conant, Karl T. Compton, and George L. Harrison.

was still certain the bomb would work, the Interim Committee unanimously recommended that it be used against Japan as soon as possible.[7] Both Truman and Stimson concurred.

On the subject of international control of atomic energy there was far less certainty of opinion. No recommendations of the Interim Committee were made public. Even before the war in Europe had ended, it was apparent to Stimson that the critical questions in American policy toward atomic energy would be connected with the Soviet Union. He could see no assurance that the Soviet Government would agree to controls and was skeptical of the value of any agreement with the Soviet Union. Stimson's apprehensions were increased by his encounters with Soviet representatives at Potsdam, so much so that he advised President Truman to use the bomb monopoly to prod the Soviet Union into liberalizing its political system. Only under a democratic system, Stimson felt, could the agreements negotiated with the Soviet Union be relied upon. This policy which the Soviets were soon to label "atomic blackmail" was discouraged by Ambassador Averell Harriman, who persuaded Stimson that the Soviet leaders would regard any American effort to bargain for freedom in the Soviet Union as a clearly hostile move. In a memorandum to President Truman dated September 11 Stimson reversed his previous advice, recommending instead immediate and direct negotiations with the Soviet Government.[8]

Between August and November, 1945, the Administration gave little evidence of what it intended to do on the international plane to meet the atomic bomb threat to world security. Only one thing was clear: until there was an international agreement on control of atomic energy the United States would retain the secret of the bomb's production. On August 15, Presi-

[7] Eugene Rabinowitch, *Minutes to Midnight: The International Control of Atomic Energy*, Atomic Science and Education Series No. 1, published by the *Bulletin of the Atomic Scientists* (Chicago, 1950), p. 17. Scientific opinion in America on the advisability of using the bomb was mixed. A group of scientists who had taken part in the creation of the first bomb transmitted a report to the Secretary of War on June 11, 1945, urging that the bomb be not used. Known as the "Franck Report," this report stressed the argument that the use of the bomb against Japan would have a prejudicial effect on the achievement of international control of atomic energy after the war, pp. 13-15.

[8] Stimson and Bundy, *op. cit.*, pp. 636-41.

dent Truman directed the appropriate departments of the government and the joint chiefs of staff "to take such steps as are necessary to prevent the release of any information in regard to the development, design or production of the atomic bomb. . . ." [9]

In his statement to the nation revealing the nature of the bomb dropped on Hiroshima President Truman promised that recommendations to Congress would be forthcoming "as to how atomic power can become a powerful and forceful influence towards the maintenance of world peace." Speaking to the nation later that same day Secretary of War Stimson more specifically mentioned "international control" as a subject of study by the United States Government.[10] Three days later President Truman, again addressing the nation—this time on the results of the recently concluded Potsdam conference—introduced a new idea: that of a United States trusteeship over atomic weapons. "We must," he said, "constitute ourselves trustees of the new force—to prevent its misuse, and to turn it into channels of service to mankind." [11] It is doubtful that this or any other idea represented a fixed policy, although the idea of a trusteeship was repeated by President Truman in his Navy Day address on October 27 in New York City. When on September 21 the Cabinet met for a session devoted exclusively to the problem of the atomic bomb, the ideas of those in the Cabinet and government had not yet fully crystallized.[12] The central question of discussion was whether the United States should share the secret of the production of the bomb with the Soviet Union and under what conditions.[13] President Truman, characteristically, invited all at the meeting to submit their views in writing, after which he would

[9] Harry S. Truman, *Memoirs, Year of Decisions* (New York, 1955), I, 524.
[10] Statements by the president of the United States, and by the secretary of war, August 6, 1945, in *The International Control of Atomic Energy: Growth of a Policy*, pp. 97-105.
[11] *Ibid.*, p. 108. From President Truman's address to the nation on the Berlin Conference, August 9, 1945.
[12] James V. Forrestal and Walter Millis (ed.), *The Forrestal Diaries* (New York, 1951), p. 96.
[13] *Ibid.*, p. 96. Admiral Leahy for the joint chiefs of staff urged the administration to retain all known information on atomic weapons. Truman, *Memoirs*, I, 527.

make the decisions and pass these decisions on to Congress for
its approval.

By the time of Truman's message to Congress (October 3)
no decision had yet been reached on a policy for international
control of atomic energy. Several statements, however, did indicate the line along which the government might be moving.
Clear recognition was made of the fact that the essential theoretical knowledge upon which the discovery of fission was based
was already widely known and that the American monopoly
could not be maintained indefinitely. Truman spoke of the hope
of renouncing the use of the atomic bomb and using atomic
energy for peaceful and humanitarian ends. Foreseeing "a desperate armaments race" unless international arrangements were
made, the president felt that discussions must be initiated between governments even before the United Nations began
functioning.[14] Inasmuch as the first session of the General Assembly was scheduled to meet in January, 1946, Truman's
recommendation suggested a feeling of urgency on the matter.
His only announcement of specific action was the initiation of
discussions with Great Britain and Canada, "our associates in
this discovery."

In Great Britain the American policy, limited to maintaining
the secret of the manufacture of atomic weapons, was causing
considerable apprehension both within the government and with
public opinion. Relations between the Soviet Union and the
West were bad enough over occupation policy in Germany
and Japan and the postwar governments of Eastern Europe,
it was felt, without further alienating Soviet opinion because of fear of Western monopoly of the atomic bomb.[15] On

[14] See President Truman's message to Congress, October 3, 1945. Most of
this message concerned domestic control of atomic energy. In it the president
proposed the creation of an atomic energy commission with broad monopolistic
powers in the field of atomic development. The administration's views embodied in the second atomic energy bill (s.1717) introduced by Senator
McMahon on December 20, 1945, provided that any part of the act which
conflicted with any future agreement on international control of atomic energy
made by the United States would be null and void.

[15] See article by Mallory Browne in the New York Times, November 4,
1945. He quoted an editorial from the Daily Mail (London) which he said
typified the British attitude. Said the editorial: "A peace maintained because of

September 25 Prime Minister Attlee wrote a long letter to President Truman suggesting that they hold joint discussions on this question. Because Canada had also shared in the development of the first atomic bomb Prime Minister W. L. Mackenzie King was invited to take part in the discussions.

The result of these talks, which lasted from November 10 to November 15, was the first concerted statement of policy on atomic energy by the three governments which had taken part in the wartime development of the atomic bomb. President Truman and Prime Ministers Attlee and King agreed to seek international control of atomic energy through the United Nations. A three-power statement (the Truman-Attlee-King Declaration) was issued from the White House on November 15. It proposed the establishment of a special United Nations commission to prepare specific proposals for extending an exchange of scientific information, for control of atomic energy, for atomic disarmament and for effective safeguards against violations of a control plan.[16]

This statement of policy marked an abandonment of the idea of a "sacred trust." Also discarded was Attlee's proposal that the United Nations Security Council be entrusted with the scientific development of atomic energy provided the Soviet Union made a full and frank disclosure of its political objectives throughout the world. According to Attlee's plan, if the Soviets refused to make such a declaration, the United States, Great Britain and Canada were to retain the secrets of atomic weapons production.[17] Attlee's proposal, if adopted, would have given the Soviet Union more legitimate grounds for charging the West with "atomic diplomacy" than it had in reality. As it was, the three Allies made it clear that they were not lightly divulging

a dread power held in reserve by one nation would be a peace based upon fear—and that has no basis at all. Already the results of secrecy have been seen in the many recent intransigent actions of Russia."

[16] Truman-Attlee-King Statement, August 15, 1945. In *The International Control of Atomic Energy: Growth of a Policy*, pp. 118-20.

[17] See *New York Times*, November 12, 1945. Attlee's views on inspection as one form of international control are interesting in view of subsequent British policy. He then regarded inspection as impractical since it would involve the detailed investigative efforts of thousands of top-flight scientists.

the secret of the atomic bomb and this was enough to incur Soviet hostility.

SOVIET ATTITUDES TOWARD ATOMIC ENERGY: THE MOSCOW DECLARATION

From the first report of the Hiroshima blast until the Moscow Declaration in December, 1945, no official word of Soviet policy toward the future use of atomic weapons came from the Soviet Union. A virtual pall of silence hung over the Soviet press where the subject was concerned. Following the publication of a short digest of President Truman's statement of August 6 about the Hiroshima bomb, the role of the atomic bomb in terminating the Second World War became a closed subject for the press. Foreign correspondents in Moscow found that any suggestion that the bomb might have played a major role in forcing Japan to surrender was suppressed from their reports by Soviet censors.[18]

On the subject of atomic energy in general and its potential role in international politics a few articles in the Soviet press offered revealing hints as to what Soviet policy might be. In September one of the issues of *New Times* published the first lengthy Soviet comment on the atomic bomb.[19] It paid tribute to the Allied accomplishment in making "one of the greatest discoveries of modern science and technology." Then it criticized Western evaluation of atomic energy on three counts:

(1) Too much consideration was being given to the bomb as a revolutionary weapon in military science. ". . . the experience of the Second World War, and the unsurpassed victories of

[18] F. C. Barghoorn, "The Soviet Union Between War and Cold War," *The Annals* of the American Academy of Political and Social Science, CCLXIII (May, 1949), 2.
[19] See Modest Rubenstein, "The Foreign Press on the Atomic Bomb," *New Times*, September 1, 1945. *New Times* is a fortnightly periodical published by *Trud* in Moscow. It is generally devoted to international affairs and published in several languages. The commentators who write for *New Times* frequently also write for *Pravda* and *Izvestia;* so the journal can be considered authoritative. Modest Rubenstein, for example, is one of the several Soviet writers on atomic energy whose columns are published in *Pravda* and *Izvestia* as well as *New Times*.

the Red Army in particular, have clearly shown that success in war is not achieved by the one-sided development of one or the other weapon, but by the perfection of all arms and their skillful co-ordination."

(2) Some segments of the American press saw in the United States' monopoly of the atomic bomb a weapon with which to threaten other nations and establish United States domination throughout the world. Even more prevalent than arguments for this drastic use of the atomic bomb to achieve political gain, according to the author, were "arguments to the effect that the invention of the atomic bomb puts all international problems on a new footing, and that, accordingly, earlier Allied agreements, such as the San Francisco United Nations Charter or the Berlin Conference decisions, are 'out of date.' " Reference to the United Nations Charter in this context is important because it foreshadows one of the central Soviet objections to the proposed American (and later United Nations) plan of international control: the proposal to abolish the "veto" when questions of sanctions against atomic control violators were at stake. In opposing the elimination of the veto, the Soviets constantly reiterated that they were doing so in defense of the United Nations Charter. The Soviet claim (comparatively mild at this time) that the United States "brandished" the atomic bomb to secure political gain, grew in the ensuing years to staggering proportions under the label of "atomic blackmail."

(3) The American "yellow press" was full of sensational articles on the peaceful use of atomic energy. *New Times* cited with approval those who "warn against the illusion that atomic energy can be practically applied to industry immediately." [20]

[20] P. M. S. Blackett makes a similar summary of the contents of this article. Cf. *op. cit.*, pp. 161-62. He states that "Tendencies are noted in the American press to dampen hopes of the peaceful use of atomic energy, and mention is made of the fear expressed by American public utility companies at the potentiality of the new invention." In effect he sees the Soviets criticizing the United States for ignoring the peaceful uses of atomic energy; while, in fact, the gist of the Soviet criticism at this time was that certain groups in the United States were making unfounded, sensational claims for the possible uses of atomic energy. Actually, during 1946 Soviet criticisms were to change in the direction Blackett saw in 1947, but such was not the case with their initial criticisms.

The article expressed approval of the idea of international control of atomic energy but offered no suggestions as to who would exercise such control. One part of the article called for "an immediate agreement to establish international control by representatives of the Five Great Powers over the production and employment of atomic bombs." In another section of the article, however, approval was expressed of a suggestion in the *Manchester Guardian* calling for the United Nations to keep the bomb and the means to produce it. The author concluded his article with a general summary of the role of atomic energy for the future.

The utilization of atomic energy inaugurates a new era, one fraught with momentous and incalculable consequences in the subjugation of the forces of nature to man, a process which, under the social system which prevails in the majority of the countries of the world, assumes complex and antagonistic forms.

The practical utilization of atomic energy is one more striking demonstration of the fact that modern science and technology hold out prospects of unparalleled expansion of productive forces and of man's mastery over nature. However, formidable obstacles stand in the way of the utilization of these advances for the benefit of the masses. If atomic energy is applied on a big scale to industry, it would, owing to the predominance of capitalist monopoly, result in stupendous unemployment, in the permanent displacement of millions of miners and other workers, and in further enhancing the power of the monopolies, not to mention the awful peril involved if this formidable weapon should fall into the hands of aggressors.

The invention of the atomic bomb renders it still more imperative to mobilize all the forces of progress for the maintenance of enduring peace and reliable security for nations, big and small. At the same time it should be clear to all thinking men that this discovery cannot solve political problems, either nationally or internationally. Those who harbor illusions on this score are doomed to disappointment.

On the other hand, the discovery that it is possible to utilize the inexhaustible resources of atomic energy makes it likewise imperative to speed the organization on a broad scale of genuine international scientific cooperation which is one of the most effective methods of promoting mutual understanding among the freedom-loving nations of the world.[21]

[21] Modest Rubenstein, "The Foreign Press on the Atomic Bomb," *New Times*, September 1, 1945, p. 17.

One of the most salient features about the limited Soviet comments on atomic energy was the almost complete lack of objective analysis of the economic, military and political consequences of atomic energy. Publicly, at least, Soviet commentators failed to divorce the fact of the existence and nature of atomic energy from the fact that the only nation possessing it was a hostile or potentially hostile nation. Thus they never found it within themselves to express much enthusiasm about the discovery. Almost all their comments during 1945 were tempered by the malevolent uses to which this discovery could be put. At first no specific criticisms of the United States as the monopolistic possessor of the bomb were made; but following the deterioration of relations after the unsuccessful first meeting of the Council of Foreign Ministers in London (September 4-October 8), one theme began to emerge with consistent regularity: the United States was guilty of practicing "atomic blackmail" or "atomic diplomacy."

The first use of the term "atomic diplomacy" appears to have been in an article in *New Times* which purported to analyze world press reaction to President Truman's message to Congress on October 3. The article expressed neither a blanket approval nor condemnation of Truman's message. It looked upon Truman's speech as a compromise between the proponents of international co-operation and those who would pursue power politics. It concluded with the general theme that "history convincingly proves that the attempt of any country to attempt world domination with the aid of new weapons is doomed to failure." [22] Only by inference was the United States criticized. President Truman's Navy Day speech with its pronounced emphasis on trusteeship incurred more direct criticism. According to the Moscow radio those in the United States wishing to keep the secret of the atomic bomb from the rest of the world were "motivated by a desire to pursue power." [23]

[22] Colonel M. Tolchenov, "The Atomic Bomb Discussion in the Foreign Press," *New Times*, November 1, 1945, p. 17.

[23] *New York Times*, November 3, 1945. On November 5 D. Zaslavsky charged in *Pravda* that cynics in both the United States and Europe were following the "fetish of the atomic bomb" instead of believing in the possibility of permanent peace.

In the November 15 issue of *New Times* there appeared the sharpest attack yet made against United States foreign policy and what was believed to be the role of the bomb in that policy. It charged that "The atomic bomb served as a signal to the incorrigible reactionaries all over the world to launch a lynching campaign against the Soviet Union." [24] *Pravda* on December 9 claimed that there was in the West a clearly defined tendency to revise the Potsdam and Yalta agreements due to United States possession of the atomic bomb.[25] Exactly what revision the West sought was not specified. It was characteristic of the Soviet atomic propaganda throughout this period to be general in nature and avoid any specific charges or make any specific proposals.

The Truman-Attlee-King communiqué of November 15 urging international control of atomic energy under United Nations aegis was the first expression of a unified Western policy to end the threat of an uncontrolled atomic armaments race. It was directed primarily to the attention of the Soviet Government and constituted an open challenge to the Soviet Union to express its demands and state its policy. No comments from the Soviet Union were forthcoming. On Friday, November 16, radio Moscow reported the Three-Power declaration without any comment. In the press, however, there was no mention of the Truman-Attlee-King talks, not even the slightest hint that the secret of the bomb might be exchanged in return for Soviet-Western co-operation.

Just prior to the Three-Power communiqué Soviet Foreign Minister V. Molotov became the first member of the Politburo to comment publicly on the atomic bomb. At the twenty-eighth anniversary of the Bolshevik Revolution, before an overflowing crowd in the Hall of St. Andrew in the Kremlin, Molotov warned the West that "it is not possible at the present time for a technical secret of any great size to remain the exclusive possession of some one country or some narrow arch of coun-

[24] A. Sokoloff, "International Cooperation and its Foes," *New Times*, November 15, 1945, p. 15.
[25] *Pravda*, December 9, 1945.

tries." He then went on to promise the Soviet people that "we shall make up properly for all lost time and shall see to it that our country shall flourish. We shall have atomic energy and many other things too." [26] This statement provided such a rousing ovation from the audience that a signal bell had to be rung to quiet the tumult.[27] Molotov's remarks on atomic energy were interspersed within the general text on foreign and domestic affairs. The general nature of his remarks gave little hint as to what the Soviets expected of the West and would be willing to offer in compensation. What Molotov's remarks and the reaction to them did reveal was that to the Soviet people atomic energy was a subject of some concern.

Meanwhile, the date of the first General Assembly meeting (January, 1946) was rapidly approaching and there was still no indication whether or not Soviet co-operation would be forthcoming on the question of establishing a United Nations Commission for atomic energy. President Truman's message to Congress in October spoke of the need for concerted action even before the United Nations was in a position to handle the problem. His proposal to initiate discussions with Great Britain and Canada "and then with other nations" indicated a desire to con-

[26] *New York Times*, November 7, 1945.

[27] *Ibid.*, November 7 and 17, 1945. The long and stormy applause provoked by this remark attests to some degree of popular concern with the discovery of atomic energy. It would be difficult to measure Russian popular reaction to America's possession of the bomb during the latter part of 1945. The consensus of opinion among some foreign correspondents in the Soviet Union at this time was that America's possession of the bomb made the informed element of the populace uneasy. One correspondent was convinced by the popular gossip he heard in the fall of 1945 that there was widespread popular fear of the bomb. Barghoorn, *loc. cit.*, p. 3. The *New York Times* correspondent in Moscow, Brooks Atkinson, found the atomic bomb to be an edgy topic of conversation between Russians and foreigners. "There is," he said, "an intangible feeling of resentment—probably a mixture of uneasiness and injured pride." *New York Times*, November 25, 1945. An example of popular feeling on the subject is a poem published November 16 by one Kirsanoff. It was entitled "Tomorrow":

> "Let no atomic bomb
>   Remain a puzzle for us!
> The magic atom of uranium
>   We shall refill with creative soul."

New York Times, Nov. 17, 1945.

fer with the Soviet Union as rapidly as possible. As late as November 21, however, Secretary of State Byrnes stated in a press conference that he knew of no plans for bilateral talks with the Soviet Union in advance of the January meeting of the General Assembly in London.[28]

Early in December arrangements were made for a meeting in Moscow between the foreign ministers of the Soviet Union, Great Britain and the United States to begin December 16. The two central issues to be discussed were atomic energy and the establishment of administrative machinery for the occupation of Japan. Of the two the Soviets displayed more concern with the latter than the former. As the conference opened Secretary of State Byrnes suggested that the question of atomic energy be placed at the top of the agenda. Foreign Minister Molotov objected. At his request it was discussed last. When after about ten days the subject came up for discussions, Molotov revealed that the Soviet Government was basically prepared to accept the Anglo-American proposals as set forth in the Truman-Attlee-King communiqué.[29]

It was agreed that the "Big Three" (together with France, China and Canada) would sponsor a resolution proposing the establishment of an Atomic Energy Commission at the first session of the United Nations General Assembly in January, 1946. The wording of the terms of reference of the new Commission was identical to that of the Three-Power communiqué. According to it the Commission would make specific proposals:

(a) For extending between all nations the exchange of basic scientific information for peaceful ends;
(b) For control of atomic energy to the extent necessary to ensure its use only for peaceful purposes;
(c) For the elimination from national armaments of atomic weapons and of all other major weapons adaptable to mass destruction;
(d) For effective safeguards by way of inspection and other means to protect complying states against the hazards of violations and evasions.[30]

[28] *Ibid.*, November 22, 1945.
[29] Byrnes, *op. cit.*, p. 266.
[30] The Soviet-Anglo-American Communiqué, December 27, 1945. See *The International Control of Atomic Energy: Growth of a Policy*, pp. 125-27.

That part of the Moscow Declaration outlining the specific tasks of the proposed Commission constituted the heart of the agreement. Paragraphs (a) and (c) providing for proposals for exchanging scientific information between nations for the elimination of atomic weapons from national armaments embodied the heart of the Soviet demands. For the United States (and to a lesser extent, Great Britain), these provisions were the concessions felt to be necessary to secure achievement of paragraphs (b) and (d)—which provided for control of atomic energy and other safeguards including inspection. To the Western negotiators, implementation of paragraphs (a) and (c) without paragraphs (b) and (d) was inconceivable. Under no conditions would the United States at this time have agreed to any international system which compelled them to divulge the secret of atomic bomb production or destroy its atomic stocks, without a *prior* assurance that the Soviet Union would agree to such a control system as guaranteed that neither it nor any nation could secretly make and stock atomic weapons. Thus the order in which the objectives were listed was in no way indicative of the priority of objectives.[31]

As a guarantee to the Western powers that some form of control would precede revelation of atomic secrets and elimination from national arsenals of the atomic bomb, the Declaration provided that "The work of the Commission should proceed by separate stages, the successful completion of each of which will develop the necessary confidence of the world before the next stage is undertaken." This was the only paragraph to which Molotov raised serious objection. This, Molotov argued, was a matter to be determined by the Commission. Byrnes adamantly defended this paragraph, claiming that it went to the heart of the proposal as far as the United States was concerned. Whereupon Molotov withdrew his objection.

A second modification of the original United States proposals

[31] This interpretation of the agreement was unanimously held by the Congressional and executive leaders in the government. See Arthur H. Vandenberg, Jr. (ed.), *The Private Papers of Senator Vandenberg* (Cambridge, Mass., 1952), pp. 226-36; Tom Connally, *My Name is Tom Connally* (New York, 1954), pp. 289-90; Truman, *Memoirs*, I, 533-36.

sought by the Soviet foreign minister was an explicit understanding that the proposed Commission would be subordinated
to the Security Council with its veto privileges. Secretary
Byrnes and Foreign Minister Ernest Bevin accepted Molotov's
proposal and agreed to give to the Security Council the authority
to issue directions to the proposed Commission "in matters
affecting security." This concession was later defended by
Byrnes on the grounds that the Security Council bore the
primary responsibility for the maintenance of international
peace and security and the Security Council, unlike the General
Assembly, is in continuous session and has the power to take
action.[32]

In all, Secretary Byrnes was highly pleased with the results
of the conference. Where he had expected considerable Soviet
opposition to the Anglo-American proposals, agreement came
more quickly than with any other subject on the agenda.
Premier Stalin exuded satisfaction over the mission's success
at the Christmas Eve dinner given for the departing diplomats.
He paid special tribute to Dr. James Conant, one of the American scientists who worked on the Manhattan project, congratu-
lating him and his associates for having rendered a great service.
As Byrnes trudged through the heavy snow at the Moscow air-
port on December 28, he felt that at last Big Three unity was
re-established.

How illusory Byrnes' hopes and expectations were was
quickly revealed at the opening sessions of the General Assembly
held in London, beginning January 10, 1946. Instead of Big
Three harmony, acrimonious debate ranged through the auditorium and committee rooms of Westminster Hall, even where
no crucial policies were at stake. Mr. Paul-Henri Spaak was
elected president of the General Assembly (over Trygve Lie)
only over the determined opposition of the Soviet bloc. Debate
on the election of the nonpermanent members of the Security
Council brought forth accusations of lobbying, intrigues, and
charges of bad faith from both the Western and Soviet delegates.

[32] Byrnes, *op. cit.*, pp. 267-68.

Nor was the atmosphere less oppressive in the Security Council, where almost immediately upon its initial organization the Soviet Union lodged a formal complaint against the presence of British troops in Greece.

In marked contrast to the bickering on other international issues was the handling of the problem of atomic energy. The resolution proposing a United Nations Atomic Energy Commission which had been agreed upon in Moscow was put on the Assembly's agenda at its sixth plenary meeting. Following a brief debate the First (political and security) Committee approved it unanimously. On January 24 unanimity again prevailed when the General Assembly passed its first resolution creating the Atomic Energy Commission.[33] General Assembly resolution 1 (I) was worded exactly as that proposed in the Moscow Declaration.[34] The new Commission was to be composed of representatives from the same nations comprising the Security Council plus Canada when not on the Security Council. "This," said Soviet delegate Andrei Vyshinsky, "is the first important act of the joint efforts of the United Nations to ensure peace and security throughout the world. May this noble act be attended with complete and genuine success." [35]

The reason for the harmony surrounding atomic energy amidst the East-West discord on other political issues is clear: agreement on basic principles had already been established at Moscow. All that was required of the United Nations at London was to ratify this accord. Furthermore, the commitment made by the signatory nations was of the most general kind. At the very least they were obligated only to "deal with the problems raised by the discovery of atomic energy" through the organization of the United Nations. Beyond that nothing was mandatory. In principle, international control of atomic energy was approved; in principle, inspection was recognized as part of such

[33] UN, Department of Public Information, *Yearbook of the United Nations 1946-47* (New York, 1947), p. 66.
[34] See p. 17 above. For the text of General Assembly resolution 1 (I) see *ibid.*, pp. 64-65.
[35] United Nations, Official Records of the General Assembly, pp. 637-41 (hereinafter abbreviated to UN, ORGA), *First Session, Part 1. Plenary Meetings . . . Verbatim Record 10 January-14 February 1946*, p. 264.

control; in principle, the elimination of atomic weapons from national armaments was encouraged; and in principle, there was approved the extension of scientific information for peaceful purposes between nations—but all of this only in principle. The terms of reference for the Atomic Energy Commission were all qualified by the understanding that none of these principles were valid unless there was a specific agreement on the adoption of measures by both sides to implement all of them.

Even in the brief speeches on this resolution both the Soviet Union and the United States emphasized the elements which they considered most important. Vyshinsky, for example, speaking before the plenary session, warned of the importance of maintaining the primacy of the Security Council over whatever action on atomic energy might be taken.[36] Andrei Gromyko in the First Committee stoutly resisted any attempt to change the wording of the resolution from that of the Moscow Declaration.[37] Under no conditions did the Soviet Union intend to lose its freedom of action. For the United States Senator Tom Connally repeated the interpretation given by Secretary Byrnes in his report to the nation upon returning from Moscow in December:

As Secretary of State Byrnes said on 30 December after returning from Moscow, 'The four objectives set forth in the proposed resolution establishing the Commission are not intended to indicate the order in which they are to be considered. In particular it was intended and is understood that the matter of safeguards will apply to the recommendations of the Commission in relation to every phase of the subject and at every stage. Indeed, at the root of the whole matter lies the problem of providing the necessary safeguards.' [38]

Under no conditions did the United States intend to abandon its monopoly of atomic weapons until adequate assurances of control were given.

[36] UN, ORGA, *First Session, Part I. Plenary Meetings . . . Verbatim Record 10 January-14 February 1946*, pp. 263-64.
[37] UN, ORGA, *First Session, Part I. First Committee . . . Summary Records of Meetings 11 January-12 February 1946*, p. 8.
[38] *Ibid.,* p. 7.

The January speeches in London marked the last official word on Soviet policy until Gromyko offered the Soviet proposals to the Atomic Energy Commission in June. The Soviets were possibly even more inscrutable during the five months following the creation of the United Nations Atomic Energy Commission than in the five months preceding the Moscow Declaration.

THE ACHESON-LILIENTHAL REPORT

During the first half of 1946 there evolved in the United States a more systematic program designed to solve the substance of the problem of international control of atomic energy. Originating as the Acheson-Lilienthal Report, it was modified by the administration into the Baruch Plan and after presentation to the United Nations Atomic Energy Commission, Baruch's proposals were further modified into the United Nations majority plan. This program, in its various phases, served as the major challenge to the Soviet Union to respond with its own program.

As the first producer of an atomic bomb, the United States was expected to be the first power to propose to the world a specific plan for international control of atomic energy. President Truman's official statements comprising United States policy on this subject as of January, 1946, indicated a full awareness of the responsibility of the American government for such action. His statements, however, were almost all couched in general terms, viewing the subject more from a technical or legal point of view than a political one. In the first year following the defeat of the Axis powers, the gradual *refroidissement* in Soviet-Western relations indicated that a major political obstacle to an atomic agreement would be mutual distrust. The Truman administration had not only to contend with Soviet secretiveness but also with Congressional and public suspicion of the intentions of the Soviet Government.

During the fall of 1945 the problem of atomic energy vis-a-vis the Soviet Union was posed in the question, how much of the secret of atomic production should be revealed before any form of control is established? Privately sponsored suggestions ranged from proposals that the United States permanently keep the secret of atomic production to those urging that all information known to the United States be turned over immediately to the United Nations as a gesture of confidence and a means for fostering confidence. Nationwide and state-wide polls revealed that public opinion was overwhelmingly in favor of the former.[39]

This public suspicion or caution was strongly represented in Congress, particularly in the persons of Senators Tom Connally (Democrat) and Arthur Vandenberg (Republican), both leaders of their parties in Congress on questions of foreign policy. Neither had much faith in the diplomatic ability of Secretary of State Byrnes; both felt that he relied far too much on expediency in handling United States-Soviet relations.[40] Both Senators Connally and Vandenberg violently objected to the wording of the Truman-Attlee-King statement because, of the four stated objectives of the United Nations Commission, the exchange of information was listed as part one and the establishment of effective safeguards was listed as the fourth part. They and the Senate Committee on Foreign Relations were worried lest the United States Government reveal any of its secrets before the Soviets guaranteed some *quid pro quo* in the way of effective international control. Just prior to his departure for Moscow Secretary of State Byrnes consulted with the Senate Committee on Foreign Relations and members of the Special Senate Commission on Atomic Energy to inform them of the American

---

[39] *The International Control of Atomic Energy: Growth of a Policy*, p. 13. Even as negotiations with the Russians for international control began in June, 1946, the overwhelming majority of Americans felt that the bomb's secrets should be kept by the United States rather than turned over for United Nations control. *Public Reaction to the Atomic Bomb and World Affairs*, p. 2. This is a study conducted by a subcommittee of the Committee on Social Aspects of Atomic Energy of the Social Science Research Council. Mimeographed copies are distributed by Cornell University.

According to the *New York Times*, September 28, 1945, of sixty-one telegrams sent to senators and representatives about the atomic bomb fifty-five urged the government not to reveal the secret of the bomb to any nation. Most of the telegrams specifically mentioned the Soviet Union.

[40] Connally, *op. cit.*, p. 289; Vandenberg, *op. cit.*, p. 225.

proposals. The senators were greatly dismayed at the possibility of the United States abandoning its atomic monopoly.[41] Lacking confidence in Secretary Byrnes' assurances, the Special Senate Committee on Atomic Energy unanimously voted to ask for an immediate interview with the president. President Truman received them the following day, December 11, 1945, to be informed that ". . . the Senate's not going to permit an exchange of information before we get a control and inspection system." [42] In spite of President Truman's assurances that the wording of the Truman-Attlee-King proposals guaranteed control before an exchange of information, at least a majority of the senators remained "uneasy" about the wording of the proposed Moscow Declaration.

While James Byrnes and Ernest Bevin were negotiating with Molotov in Moscow, President Truman made the appointments of American delegates to the forthcoming United Nations session in London. Tom Connally was appointed American representative to the important Political and Security Committee which among other matters would be concerned with disarmament and control of atomic energy. Senator Vandenberg was made a member of the American delegation to the General Assembly. On hearing the first release of the Moscow Declaration, Senator Vandenberg was so dismayed that he seriously considered resigning as a delegate to the United Nations. He was convinced that the four subjects of discussion listed in the terms of reference of the Commission were parts of the "stages"

[41] Connally, *op. cit.*, pp. 289-90. Senator Vandenberg summed up the Congressional consensus at this meeting as follows:

"We agree that Russia can work out this atom science in perhaps two years; but we are unanimously opposed to hastening the day unless and until there is absolute and effective agreement for world-wide inspection and control. This is the crux. We want to banish atom bombs from the earth. But it is impossible unless Russia agrees to a total exchange of information, instead of hermetically sealing herself behind 'iron curtains.'

We are opposed to giving any of the atomic secrets away unless and until the Soviets are prepared to be 'policed' by UNO in respect to this prohibition. We consider an 'exchange' of scientists and scientific information as sheer appeasement because Russia has nothing to 'exchange.' It was our general opinion that we made little impression on the Secretary [Byrnes]."

Vandenberg, *op. cit.*, p. 228.
[42] Connally, *op. cit.*, p. 290.

of the Commission's work. He understood the phrase stating that each stage should be completed before the next was undertaken as obligating the United States to disclose information before effective safeguards were established. Senator Vandenberg's doubts were shared by many senators.[43] Again President Truman sought to assure the senator and Congress that under no conditions would the United States reveal information about the bomb until adequate guarantees on controls were established. As to the wording of the Moscow Declaration President Truman reiterated that it did not require the proposed Commission to take the four subjects of discussion as "stages" in the order recited. Rather, each stage of disclosure would be accompanied by adequate arrangement for security. Vandenberg appeared to be satisfied.

Between negotiations at Moscow and representation in London, Secretary of State Byrnes made a short report back to Washington. Before leaving for London on January 7, 1946, Byrnes appointed a five-man special committee, headed by Undersecretary of State Dean Acheson, "to study the subject of controls and safeguards necessary to protect this Government." [44] In part this was done to allay Vandenberg's and others' suspicions, though such a committee would have been necessary in any event to devise an American plan for presentation to the anticipated United Nations Atomic Energy Commission. As an aid in analyzing and appraising all the relevant facts necessary to formulate a set of proposals the committee on January 23 appointed a Board of Consultants chaired by David E. Lilienthal. Beginning its work in February, the Board of Consultants worked almost continuously, spending most of its time in the attic of an office building in downtown Washington. After about a month the Board took its report to the Acheson Committee which, at the Dumbarton Oaks estate in Washington, prepared the final form of the report. It was transmitted to

[43] Vandenberg, *op. cit.*, pp. 232-33. See article by James Reston, close friend of Senator Vandenberg, in the January 7, 1946, issue of the *New York Times*.
[44] *New York Times*, January 8, 1946. In addition to Dean Acheson the committee included John J. McCloy, Dr. Vannevar Bush, Dr. James Conant and General Leslie Groves.

President Truman on March 21 and made public on March 28.[45]

Many commentators have noted the fact that the Acheson-Lilienthal Report was truly a revolutionary document. It was revolutionary for the United States in suggesting a self-abnegation of military power that was unrivalled in the world at the time. Its implications for international politics were revolutionary to the extent that it proposed ending national sovereignty over and the internationalization of potentially large segments of every nation's economy. So revolutionary were its proposals, that even should it have proven acceptable to the Soviet Government, there was considerable doubt that a similar acceptance would have been accorded by the United States Senate and House of Representatives.

David Lilienthal and his consultants were primarily concerned with the kind of control system demanded by the science of atomic energy production. Psychological, sociological and political factors which would shape the control system were considered only in a general sense. It was assumed that all nations throughout the world, even in a state of political tension and hostility, would react approximately in the same manner to the conditions imposed by the terrible destructive power of the atomic bomb and the technological requirements to create the bomb. No specific attention was given to the growing tension between the Soviet Union and the United States, the incompatibility of Soviet and American political objectives in Europe and the Far East, the role of atomic weapons in this conflict, nor to the political "operational code" of the Soviet governing elite.

Rather, attention was focused upon the scientific and technological aspects of atomic energy production. The organizational plan recommended by the report followed logically from the scientific conclusions. These scientific conclusions became the basic assumptions of the Baruch and subsequent United Nations plans. Later Soviet criticisms of the United Nations majority

[45] The other members of the Board of Consultants were Chester I. Barnard, Dr. J. Robert Oppenheimer, Dr. Charles Allen Thomas and Harry A. Winne. According to Truman the report fell into the hands of the press "by some unauthorized means." Truman, *Memoirs, Years of Trial and Hope* (New York, 1956), II, 8.

plan in the Scientific and Technical subcommittee of the United Nations Atomic Energy Commission involved disagreement not only with the conclusions drawn from these assumptions, but with the assumptions themselves. As the authors of the Acheson-Lilienthal plan saw them, the most salient facts which determined the nature of international control were as follows:

(1) "The only scientific evidence worthy of regard makes it clear that uranium is indispensable in the production of fissionable material on a scale large enough to make explosives or power. Uranium is the only natural substance that can maintain a chain reaction. It is the key to all foreseeable applications of atomic energy."[46] From this fact it concluded that there must of necessity be established absolute control of uranium and the most effective means to insure such control would be "adequate safeguards regarding raw materials." It found this control problem narrowed by the fact that uranium deposits exist in high concentrations "only under very special geologic conditions which would seem to mean that the areas which need to be surveyed, to which access must be had, and which would ultimately have to be brought under control, are relatively limited."[47]

(2) Atomic explosives are identical with atomic fuels required for the production of atomic power for nonmilitary purposes. In other words, the separation and refining plants producing nuclear fuels can be considered as instruments of war production or peaceful power production, depending entirely only on how the end product is used. "Assume an international agreement barring use of the plutonium [an isotope of treated uranium

[46] A second element used in atomic energy production is thorium, but "Thorium cannot maintain a chain reaction, either itself or in combination with any other natural material than uranium . . . but with a fairly substantial amount of uranium to begin with and suitably large quantities of thorium a chain reaction can be established to manufacture material which is an atomic explosive and which can also be used for the maintenance of other reactions." *The Acheson-Lilienthal Report,* Department of State Publication 2498 (Washington, 1946), p. 13.

[47] *Ibid.,* p. 14. Very slight changes in the wording of the quotations in the text of the Acheson-Lilienthal Report have been made to facilitate the presentation of the ideas in the *Report.* The citations following are contained in pp. 2, 6, 21, 23, 26-29, and 31-49.

used as a nuclear fuel] in a bomb, but permitting the use of plutonium pile for heat or power. No system of inspection, we have concluded, could afford any reasonable security against the diversion of material to the purposes of war."

(3) A corollary of the above fact is the recognition that control of the atomic bomb reduces primarily to control over the nuclear fuel in the bomb. The actual casings and detonating mechanisms for atomic bombs can easily and quickly be made in small factories. A ban on the building of the outer casing of the bomb could constitute only a minor element of effective disarmament.

(4) At present separation plants for U-235 (*e.g.*, Oak Ridge, Tennessee) are "huge and bulky in the extreme." While this will "quite probably" always be true, "this is not a law of nature."

(5) There exists a process by which uranium 235 and plutonium can be denatured; "such denatured materials do not readily lend themselves to the making of atomic explosives, but they can still be used with no essential loss of effectiveness in reactors for the generation of power . . ." Installations which used material both denatured and insufficient in quantity for the manufacture of bombs could be regarded as "safe." On the other hand, those installations using or making large amounts of uranium not denatured, would be regarded as "dangerous" from the point of view of control.

(6) There is no adequate military defense against atomic weapons.

(7) The United States monopoly of atomic weapons is only temporary. "It is recognized that the basic science on which the release of atomic energy rests is a world-wide science . . ."

These then constituted the basic scientific framework which defined the scope and limitations of an effective international control system for atomic energy. Nuclear devastation, argued the Board of Consultants, was too great a threat for an international control system to rely solely upon "inspection and similar police-like methods." Fear of surprise violation would, in their estimation, break down any confidence if treaty obligations and good faith were the only assurances upon which to rely. "As a result . . . we are clear: that every stage in the activity, leading from raw materials to weapons, needs some sort of control, and that this must be exercised on all of the various paths that may lead from one to the other; that at no single point can *external* control of an operation be sufficiently reliable to be an adequate sole safeguard; and that, for effective control, the controlling organization must be as thoroughly informed about the operations as are the operators themselves."

As the most effective means of such control the Acheson-Lilienthal plan proposed the creation of an international agency (referred to as the Atomic Development Authority) "with exclusive jurisdiction to conduct all intrinsically dangerous operations in the field." In particular the plan proposed giving the Authority four important powers: (1), ownership or effective leasing control over the world supplies of uranium and thorium; (2), authority to construct and operate all atomic reactors and separation plants; (3), unlimited research activity; and (4), inspection of all activities not under direct managerial control.

A distinction was made between "dangerous" and "safe" activities. The latter referred to uses of atomic materials for peaceful purposes on a sufficiently small scale to be incapable of generating fissionable fuel. These were to be under national control, essentially independent of the Authority. They included such activities as the use of radioactive tracers in medicine and research and relatively small scale power projects from "denatured" uranium 235 and plutonium. Power reactors, for example, which by their design, construction and operation could be safely built by individual nations would be subject only to "reasonable supervision" (presumably inspection) by the Atomic Development Authority. Reactors of this type would make it possible to open up the field of atomic power production to national or even private enterprise.

But even this noninternationalized sector of the industry would have to be limited by political considerations. There was always the possibility that an aggressor might suddenly seize the stock-piles, refining plants and reactors within its boundaries and con-vert them to weapons use. As a protection against this contingency the concept of "strategic balance" was devised. According to this plan the Atomic Development Authority would distribute atomic facilities throughout the world in such a fashion that no one nation will be able to seize atomic facilities without other nations having similar facilities and materials within their own borders and consequently not being in a disadvantageous position. Security considerations and not economic ones thus would determine the distribution of atomic power plants throughout the world.

In transmitting the final report to Secretary of State Byrnes the Acheson Committee emphasized its expectation that the re-port was not to be considered a final plan so much as a frame-work within which Congress, the public and the Executive were to consider a solution of the problem of international control of atomic energy. It would be realistic to assume that another reason for publishing the report in March was to sound out world opinion and the Soviet Government in particular. Hereto-fore, in the United States the idea of international control of atomic energy was generally associated with some form of inspection. With the Acheson-Lilienthal Report a revolutionary new idea of control through international ownership and manage-ment (*i.e.*, operational control) was introduced. Even though not designated official United States policy in March, 1946, the Soviet Union must have known it was being given a fairly realistic preview of coming attractions. Undoubtedly during the three months before the convening of the first session of the United Nations Atomic Energy Commission, there was con-siderable planning within the Soviet Government of both its own proposals and its response to the anticipated United States plan.[48]

[48] Frederick Osborn, United States delegate to the UNAEC during 1948 be-lieves the Soviet proposals of June 19, 1946, must have been planned long in

Whatever discussion was provoked in the Soviet Union by the Acheson-Lilienthal Report was done solely within the confines of the Politburo. As in the case of the Truman-Attlee-King declaration, no press discussion followed publication of the Acheson-Lilienthal Report. The few references to atomic energy in the Soviet press between March and June, 1946, did not augur well for Soviet receptivity to at least one of the central elements of the American plan, the proposal to entrust the Atomic Development Authority with almost monopolistic development of atomic energy all over the world. On at least two occasions the Soviet press printed references to atomic energy which emphasized the tremendous potentiality of atomic energy for the development of the Soviet Union's peacetime economy. On March 14, 1946 *Pravda* told the Soviet people that atomic energy would play a large role in the new Soviet Five-Year Plan.[49] This would raise the question as to what extent a government already known for its secretiveness and suspicion could permit an international body to exercise considerable authority over even a segment of its economy. The last Soviet publication on the subject before Gromyko presented the Soviet proposals to the Atomic Energy Commission in June, 1946, indicated the seriousness of the above problem. Modest Rubenstein in the June 15 issue of *New Times*[50] attacked "modern capitalism" which hampered the peaceful utilization of new productive forces (*e.g.*, nuclear energy) because of the innate contradictions inherent in capitalism. He also criticized the idea of converting the United Nations into a world state "whose mission it will be to save the world from atomic war." Such a world state, argued Rubenstein, would in effect be American domination of the world. "The florid talk about a 'world state' is actually a frank plea for American imperialism." The Soviet author

---

advance as indicated by the speed with which they were offered. Frederick Osborn, "Negotiating on Atomic Energy, 1946-1947," in *Negotiating with the Russians*, Raymond Dennett and Joseph E. Johnson, eds. (Boston, 1951), p. 215.

[49] *Pravda*, March 14, 1946. See also *Izvestia*, March 24, 1946, article by Sergie Vavilev on the potential peaceful uses of nuclear energy.

[50] Modest Rubenstein, "The Atomic Age as American Scientists Picture It," a review of the book *One World or None* by Dexter Masters, Katherine Way, *et al.*, *New Times*, March 15, 1945.

failed to define what constituted a "world state" but on the eve
of the opening sessions of the United Nations Atomic Energy
Commission these comments could, with menacing ease, be
applied to the anticipated United States proposals.

2: THE FIRST DEADLOCK: THE ATOMIC

ENERGY COMMISSION IN 1946

SECRETARY GENERAL TRYGVE LIE SET JUNE 14, 1946, AS THE DATE
for the first session of the United Nations Atomic Energy Commission. By May 28 all twelve nations entitled to representation
on the Commission had appointed their representatives. For the
United States President Truman selected Bernard Baruch, aged
but highly respected "elder statesman." Baruch's appointment
had been announced by the president on March 18 shortly
before publication of the Acheson-Lilienthal Report. Baruch
himself had no direct hand in the formulation of the report,
but he and his advisers[1] contributed to the formulation of
American policy by transforming the Acheson-Lilienthal Report
from a working paper to a set of systematic proposals. The only
provision, but an important one, added by Baruch was that
concerning the elimination of the veto in cases of sanctions
against atomic control violators.[2] As its representative the Soviet
Government chose Andrei Gromyko, its permanent representative to the Security Council. By June, 1946, Gromyko had already achieved a world reputation for his vetoes and walkouts in
the Security Council. He was a tough negotiator upon whom the
Soviet Government could rely.

[1] Bernard Baruch chose as his alternates and advisers John Hancock, Ferdinand Eberstadt, Herbert Bayard Swope and Fred Searls.
[2] Truman, *Memoirs*, II, 10.

Only Bernard Baruch among the representatives of the five major powers on the Commission was not also a representative or alternate representative in the Security Council. None had sufficient scientific or technical training to qualify as specialists in atomic energy, a clear indication of the paramount political nature of the problem. On the other hand, the negotiations in the Atomic Energy Commission were unhampered by the specific political problems currently plaguing the Soviet Union and Western world.[3] In the summer of 1946 the world's attention centered on Paris, where the peace conference was struggling with treaties for Italy, Rumania, Hungary, Bulgaria and Finland. On the very day of the opening session of the Atomic Energy Commission, Secretary of State Byrnes was leaving Washington for his eleventh trip across the ocean in less than a year. While Baruch and Gromyko were parrying each other's arguments in New York, their respective superiors were doing likewise in Paris.

Both Baruch and Gromyko arrived at the opening sessions of the Atomic Energy Commission, held in the Hunter College Auditorium, at New York City, fully prepared to present their governments' cases. The speed with which the proposals were presented and the tenacity with which both sides held their positions indicated that considerable forethought had been given the issue. As representative of the host nation and then sole possessor of atomic weapons, the United States delegate was given the opportunity to present the first set of proposals.

Bernard Baruch's now famous speech opening the United Nations Atomic Energy Commission debates confronted the Soviet Union with a direct challenge. Coming immediately to the point he expressed what was felt would be the central Soviet objection to the American plan and attacked it. "The

[3] There were some senators who felt that the United States should demand a definite agreement between the United States and the Soviet Union on the European peace treaties before entrusting American secrets to any form of international control. Senator Eugene D. Millikin, for one, felt that the future work of the United Nations Atomic Energy Commission and the outcome of the Big Four Foreign Ministers meeting in Paris would be closely interrelated. *New York Times,* June 16, 1946.

peoples of these democracies . . . hate war. They will have a heavy exaction to make of those who fail to provide an escape. They are not afraid of internationalism that protects; they are unwilling to be fobbed off by mouthings about narrow sovereignty, which is today's phrase for yesterday's isolationism." Baruch then went on to propose the creation of an International Atomic Development Authority along the lines envisaged by the Acheson-Lilienthal Report. Such an authority would be entrusted with all the phases of the development and use of atomic energy, starting with raw materials and including:

(1) Managerial control or ownership of all atomic-energy activities potentially dangerous to world security. (2) Power to control, inspect and license all other atomic activities. (3) The duty of fostering the beneficial uses of atomic energy. (4) Research and development responsibilities of an affirmative character intended to put the Authority in the forefront of atomic knowledge . . .[4]

Only after an adequate system of control, including the renunciation of the bomb, had been agreed upon and put into "effective operation" would the United States cease to manufacture atomic bombs and dispose of its then existing stock. Again anticipating the Soviet position, Baruch made clear the United States position that a treaty merely outlawing possession or use of the atomic bomb would not be adequate. "Before a country is ready to relinquish any winning weapons," Baruch was frank to announce, "it must have more than words to assure it." Such assurance, argued Baruch, could only be realized if there were a clear agreement that any violator would be summarily and effectively punished—before the violator was able to obtain a decisive, atomic-supported, military superiority over its rivals. As seen by the American government, sanctions against a violator could not be entrusted to the Security Council under its voting procedure because any of the permanent members, or a lesser nation supported by a permanent member, could veto sanctions. Therefore, on the question of sanctions against a violator of the control treaty, there must be no veto. Of all the elements in the American proposals, Baruch placed the greatest

[4] UN, *AECOR, No. 1. First Meeting, 14 June 1946,* pp. 10-13.

emphasis on the elimination of the veto. "It would be a deception," he said, "to which I am unwilling to lend myself, were I not to say to you and to our peoples, that the matter of punishment lies at the very heart of our present security system."[5]

The Soviet Union was afforded its opportunity to respond at the second meeting of the Atomic Energy Commission on June 19, 1946. Actually in presenting the Soviet proposals Andrei Gromyko did not "respond" to the American proposals. Baruch's proposals were in fact never mentioned at all. Gromyko's speech had undoubtedly been prepared long in advance and Soviet diplomats were not permitted the flexibility to comment on policy statements before clearance through Moscow.

As had his American colleague, Gromyko limited himself to a general statement of principles governing a future control system over atomic energy. He began by stressing that "There can be no effective system of peace if the discovery of atomic energy is not placed in the service of humanity and is not applied to peaceful purposes only." Accordingly, "as one of the first measures to be carried out," the Soviet representative proposed "the conclusion of international agreements forbidding the production and use of weapons based upon the use of atomic energy for the purpose of mass destruction." As far as they went, these statements of principle were fully compatible with the United States proposals, which agreed that the ultimate use of nuclear energy must be for peaceful ends and which favored prohibition.

Gromyko then went on to make two statements which were markedly incompatible with the American plan. First, he asserted that agreement on prohibition *"should be followed* by other measures designed to introduce means of assuring the observance of . . . [prohibition, including] the setting up of a system of supervision and control to see that the conventions and agreements are observed, and measures concerning sanctions against unlawful use of atomic energy." A declaration of prohibition should *precede* the establishment of a control system. What appeared in effect to be a difference in timing only—because in principle both the Soviet Union and the United States conceded

[5] *Ibid.*, pp. 5-6, 9.

the necessity of prohibition and control—was looked upon in the United States as a difference on a question of substance. Secondly, Gromyko directly attacked the American position on the veto question. He asserted the Soviet Government's determination to resist all attempts to eliminate or modify the veto. "Efforts made to undermine the activity of the Security Council, including efforts directed to undermine the requirement of unanimity of the members of the Security Council, upon questions of substance, are incompatible with the interests of the United Nations . . . Such attempts should be resisted." [6]

The Soviet representative then asked the Commission to adopt two specific resolutions. The first one provided for the conclusion of an international agreement outlawing the production and use of atomic weapons. It included the following articles:

(1) The high contracting parties will forbid the production and use of a weapon based upon the use of atomic energy, and with this in view, take upon themselves the following obligations:
 a) Not to use, in any circumstances, atomic weapons.
 b) To forbid the production and stockpiling of weapons based upon the use of atomic energy.
 c) To destroy within a period of three months from the entry into force of this agreement all stocks of atomic energy weapons whether in finished or semi-finished condition.
(2) The high contracting parties declare that any violation of Article 1 of this agreement shall constitute a serious crime against humanity.
(3) The high contracting parties, within six months of the entry into force of the present agreement, shall pass legislation providing severe punishment for the violation of the terms of this agreement.[7]

Secondly, Gromyko proposed the establishment of two committees. One would be a committee to work out recommendations for the exchange of scientific information; the other committee would elaborate a control system for atomic energy production. Among the kinds of information which the scientific exchange committee would seek to disseminate would be knowledge of the: (1), scientific discoveries connected with atomic

[6] UN, *AECOR No. 2. Second Meeting, 19 June 1946,* pp. 24-25, 30. Italics added.
[7] *Ibid.,* pp. 26-28.

fission; (2), technological processes involved in producing atomic
energy; (3), industrial organization to utilize atomic energy; and
(4), forms, sources and location of atomic energy raw materials.
While the scientific exchange committee was elaborating its
proposals the control committee would concurrently be examining specific measures for insuring the observance of the outlawing
of all weapons of mass destruction including a system of sanctions for violators.[8] In short, the Soviets were asking the
Western powers to prohibit the bomb first and then study the
means of insuring the prohibition.

By the conclusion of its third plenary session the full Atomic
Energy Commission membership had expressed its official reactions to both the Soviet and American proposals. Approval of
the United States plan in principle was voiced by the representatives of Canada, Great Britain, Brazil, China and Mexico,
France, Australia and Egypt. Only Poland endorsed Gromyko's
proposals. Mr. E. N. van Kleffens of the Netherlands expressed
no preference as between either the United States or Soviet plans.
If there was felt any pessimism as to the incompatibility of the
two plans, it was not expressed. Alexandre Parodi (France)
expressed, somewhat negatively, the general feeling toward syn-
thesizing the Baruch and Gromyko proposals when he said,
"it would seem that they [the United States and Soviet pro-
posals] are nevertheless not entirely irreconcilable on the points
where they are not in perfect harmony." [9]

The obliqueness of Parodi's comment accurately reflected the
preponderance of "unknowns" over "knowns" in the Soviet
position. Soviet pre-Atomic Energy Commission silence was
transformed into extreme cautiousness during the initial discussion. Gromyko's proposals of June 19 have frequently been
described in the Western press and by the Soviet representatives
themselves as the "Soviet plan"; but they really constituted no
plan at all. Not, if by a plan, one comprehends a systematic

[8] *Ibid.*, pp. 28-29.
[9] UN, *AECOR No. 3. Third Meeting, 25 June 1946*, p. 39. See also pp. 44,
47-48.

and comprehensive procedure for action. Gromyko's "plan" was, in fact, the enunciation of three or four basic principles which guided Soviet policy (promotion of peaceful development of atomic energy, prohibition of atomic weapons, agreement on international control, and the retention of full sovereign freedom of action) plus proposals for the further organization of the Atomic Energy Commission to deal with the problems of control and the exchange of scientific information. On the exact form of international control, Soviet statements were deliberately vague. No mention was made of an inspection system; nor of the ideas of international ownership of raw materials; nor of international managerial controls of metallurgical and chemical refining plants which transform raw uranium and thorium to a fissionable fuel; nor, lastly, of a licensing system to distribute nuclear fuel to industrial nations. In short, though the Soviet Union expressed itself in favor of "supervision and control" it gave no indication of the form that control should take. This refusal to go into details must be assumed to be deliberate because of the advance notice of the American proposals which was afforded by the publication of the Acheson-Lilienthal Report in March.

The very refusal of Gromyko to condemn these features of the American plan (inspection, international ownership of mines, managerial control of refinement plants and licensing agreements) afforded some degree of optimism for future negotiations. It could be argued that agreement on inspection, ownership, managerial control and licensing was being withheld for use as a bargaining point in achieving agreements on banning the bomb and retaining the veto. And to those who held this view, such an exchange of concessions was feasible insofar as the declaration of prohibition and the question of the veto were peripheral to the central problem of control.[10]

---

[10] Among those who held this view were many of the Chicago scientists who had worked on the atomic bomb at the Argonne National Laboratory and the University of Chicago. To them the whole question of the veto was irrelevant. They felt that once a good system of control was established any violations could be detected and the free world could take whatever action it felt neces-

An amalgamation of the two sets of proposals was now in order. To expedite matters Herbert Evatt suggested the formation of a working committee to be composed of the same membership as the Commission itself. Gromyko agreed only on the understanding that the working committee consider all the proposals advanced, not just the Baruch plan. The working committee in turn appointed a subcommittee which between July 1-11 held five informal meetings in a converted ballroom of the Henry Hudson Hotel in New York.

The five meetings, intended originally as explorative sessions, immediately brought into sharp focus the major differences between the Soviet position and that of the majority. The first meeting began on July 1, 1946, with a determined attempt by Ferdinand Eberstadt (for the United States) and Herbert Evatt (chairman and representative for Australia) to elicit from Gromyko what, if any, methods for international control of atomic energy would be acceptable to the Soviet Union. Gromyko steadfastly evaded making any commitments. Herbert Evatt asked Gromyko point-blank whether he favored the establishment of an atomic development authority. Gromyko replied that "it was not of the first importance to decide this question." His steadfast position was that "long debates about the control of the atomic weapon could not be afforded unless a convention outlawing it was signed *immediately*." Ferdinand Eberstadt pushed the question further: Would the USSR representative regard the establishment of an atomic development authority as a second step? Gromyko replied ". . . this question should be considered later." When the subject of inspection was brought up, Gromyko asked how a system of inspection

---

sary without the legitimizing sanction of the Security Council. See Rabino-witch, *op. cit.*, p. 47. This attitude toward the veto was held by some American political figures, most notably Henry Wallace. See his letter to President Truman on July 23, 1946, *New York Times*, September 18, 1946. See also Walter Lippmann's article in *One World or None*, by Dexter Masters, Katherine Way, *et al.* (New York, 1946). Lippmann proposed that sanctions against an atomic violator need not be limited to the Security Council. Under Article 51 of the United Nations Charter a known violator of the control agreement could be suppressed as a legitimate means of collective self-defense. See also Quincy Wright, "The United Nations Charter and the Prevention of War," *Bulletin of the Atomic Scientists*, III, No. 2 (February, 1947).

could be reconciled "with the sovereign rights of states." [11] His clear implication was that it could not.

However disappointing Gromyko's unwillingness to discuss methods of control was, it was not entirely unexpected. During the three-month interval between publication of the Acheson-Lilienthal Report and convocation of the Atomic Energy Commission, no mention of atomic control had been made by the Soviet Government. This unofficial silence was made official policy by the totally vague references to control made by Gromyko on June 19. Temporarily at least, the Soviet Government was apparently determined to postpone any further discussion.

Having begun by interrogating the Soviet representative and failing to elicit adequate responses, Baruch and his staff proceeded to unfold in more detail the United States plan. They were determined not to permit Gromyko's stalling tactics to frustrate the work of the Commission. In time either the Soviets would have to agree to the majority position or propose alternatives. Failure to do either would condemn the Soviet Union before world opinion as implacable obstructionists to international control. Therefore, on July 2, 5, and 12, Eberstadt submitted three memoranda outlining in detail the operation of a control system envisaged by Baruch's original proposals.

These three memoranda revealed a widening gap between the positive position of the United States toward a strong control system and the ultra-cautious attitude of the Soviet Union. If inspection was looked upon by Gromyko as an infringement of sovereignty, then the functions and powers of the proposed Atomic Development Authority must have appeared to him as a total submergence of national sovereignty. As advocated in the first United States memorandum the Authority would be granted the following powers:

[11] UN, *AECOR Special Supplement Report to the Security Council* (Lake Success, N.Y., 1946), Annex 3, p. 70.* This was the first of the three reports of the Atomic Energy Commission. It will hereinafter be referred to as the *AEC First Report.* The quotations taken from Annex 3 are from the summary records of the subcommittee's meetings. No verbatim records of the subcommittee were kept. *See also pp. 70-73, 75, 83, 87.

(1) To obtain and maintain complete and exclusive control or ownership of all uranium, thorium, and other material which may be a source of atomic energy wherever present in potentially dangerous quantities, whether in raw material, by-product, processed, or other form;

(2) To conduct continuous investigations and surveys of sources of atomic energy throughout the world, in aid of the proper exercise of the foregoing and the authority's other functions and powers;

(3) To acquire, construct, own and exclusively operate all facilities for the production of U-235, plutonium and such other fissionable materials as may be specified by the authority; and to maintain supplies of fissionable materials adequate to fulfill the purposes of the authority;

(4) To define and determine, in the manner set forth in the charter, any other facilities or activities in the field of atomic energy which would be dangerous unless controlled by the authority, and to supervise and have complete managerial control of all such activities and facilities;

(5) To have unhindered access to, and power to control, license and inspect all other facilities which possess, utilize or produce materials which are a source of atomic energy, and all other activities which utilize or produce, or are capable of utilizing or producing atomic energy;

(6) To have the exclusive right of research in the field of atomic explosives;

(7) To foster and promote the nondangerous use and wide distribution of atomic energy for beneficial purposes under licenses or other suitable arrangements established by the authority; and

(8) Subject to the provisions of the treaty and charter, to have power to take other necessary action and to issue rules and regulations.[12]

The very scope of these powers considerably reduced national freedom of action in developing atomic energy. At the same time a whole new category of possible serious offenses constituting a threat to the peace was added. Bernard Baruch in his opening speech to the Commission had clearly outlined the range of actions to be prohibited to any nation. These included not only possession of an atomic bomb or fissionable fuel suitable

[12] Memorandum No. 1 submitted by the United States representative on the Atomic Energy Commission in the *AEC First Report*, Annex 4, pp. 94-95. For amplification of the meaning of these powers see Memorandum No. 2 submitted by the United States representative . . . , pp. 97-102.

for use in a bomb, but also the seizure of any property belonging to the Authority or the wilful interference with the activities of the Authority. Any one of these would be considered action threatening the peace.

Ordinarily—that is, under the United Nations Charter—serious offenses constituting a threat to the peace would be handled by the Security Council. But any of the permanent members of the Council could block action to counter such offenses with the veto. Violations of an atomic control treaty constituted too serious a threat to national security to trust to the vagaries of Big Five harmony. Consequently the United States insisted upon guarantees that a violator would not be able to block action by a veto. In its third memorandum the United States frankly stated its objection to the veto:

> The controls established by the treaty would be wholly ineffectual if, in any such situations, to be defined in the treaty, the enforcement of security provisions could be prevented by the vote of a State which has signed the treaty. Any other conception would render the whole principle of 'veto' ridiculous. It is intended to be an instrument for the protection of nations, not a shield behind which deception and criminal acts can be performed with impunity. This in no way impairs the doctrine of unanimity. No State need be an unwilling party to the treaty. But every State which freely and willingly becomes a party to the treaty, by this act, solemnly and firmly binds itself to abide by its undertakings. Such undertakings would become illusory, if the guarantee against their breach resided solely in the conscience of the one who commits the breach.[13]

As a further guarantee that an offender of the control system would not go unpunished, the memorandum added a new interpretation of Article 51 of the Charter. Article 51 secures the right of individual or collective self-defense by the member states of the United Nations in the event of an "armed attack." A new definition of aggression was called for:

> It is . . . clear that an 'armed attack' is now something entirely different from what it was prior to the discovery of atomic weapons. It would therefore seem to be both important and appropriate under present conditions that the treaty define 'armed attack' in a manner

---

[13] Memorandum No. 3, *ibid.*, Annex 4, pp. 108-109.

appropriate to atomic weapons and include in the definition not simply the actual dropping of an atomic bomb, but also certain steps in themselves preliminary to such action.[14]

Ferdinand Eberstadt forcefully confirmed Baruch's warning that the United States would never agree to prohibiting the weapon until *after* the control system had been agreed upon and put into effect. Nothing as simple as a convention outlawing atomic weapons, argued Eberstadt, was going to solve the problem confronting the Commission.

The five meetings of the subcommittee brought to a close the first phase of United Nations negotiations on atomic energy. Their purpose had been no more than to ascertain what areas of actual or prospective agreement existed toward regulating atomic energy for peaceful use only. All discussions were informal, and no notes were taken. As far as it was intended to go, the work of the subcommittee was a success. It had explored the Soviet and American proposals though not reconciling their differences.

Following these exploratory discussions the representatives decided to reorganize the committee structure of the Commission in preparation for more intensive negotiations. Four new committees replaced the subcommittee and working committee. A Scientific and Technical Committee was made responsible for studying the scientific and technical questions involved in a control plan. A Legal Advisory Committee was established to examine the legal aspects of the relationship between a possible control system and the United Nations. Primary responsibility for examining all questions associated with the control plan itself was entrusted to Committee Two. Committee One would coordinate the work of the three other committees. On each of the four committees were representatives of the twelve nation-members of the Atomic Energy Commission.

Throughout the remainder of July discussions continued in Committee Two. With the completion of the discussions in the subcommittee, both the Soviet and Western positions had

[14] *Ibid.*, pp. 109-110.

been clearly revealed and a process of reconciliation was in order. In spite of the wide gap between the two sets of proposals, the only part of the American plan officially rejected by the Soviet delegates was the part eliminating the veto on questions of sanctions. However, before a reconciliation of plans could take place, more would have to be known of Soviet ideas for supplementing their convention outlawing atomic weapons with measures of control. Toward such an elaboration the majority delegates directed their efforts in Committee Two.

As resolutely as he was pressed, so did Gromyko steadfastly resist enlarging upon the Soviet plan. On July 24 at the second session of Committee Two, Gromyko made a major speech condemning the United States plan. He singled out for attack that part of the third United States memorandum which provided for a new organ to control atomic energy and the elimination of the veto on questions of sanctions against violators of the control. His argument ran thus: The United Nations Charter made no reference to particular weapons of aggression. As a problem of international peace and security, atomic weapons could easily be interpreted as coming within the general authority of the Security Council to take action against their misuse. Therefore, full power of control should be lodged only in the Security Council. Did not, after all, the General Assembly in January establish the Atomic Energy Commission to assist the Security Council by making recommendations? Furthermore, if the method of voting on atomic sanctions were changed to a procedural vote on recommendation of a new control authority, the new authority would be entirely autonomous from the Security Council. Even assuming that the member nations of the United Nations could change the Charter, would such a change be advisable? In arguing for the negative, Gromyko touched upon the fundamental Soviet objection to the proposed control authority: infringement of national sovereignty. He found it impossible to reconcile the powers of the proposed authority with the principle of sovereignty of states. He reminded his listeners of the importance attached by all the states at San Francisco to national sovereignty and insisted that any violation of this principle "would have far-reaching and negative consequences, not only on the Organization's [United Nations] activities, but maybe for its very existence." Consequently, Gromyko concluded, the United States proposals "in their present form, could not be accepted by the USSR, either as a whole or in their separate parts." [15]

Gromyko's rejection, even though looked upon as tentative by some, quenched much of the optimism of those delegates who had hoped for a rapid agreement on a problem which they considered urgent. Two days later, in Committee Two, Gromyko let it be known that Soviet rejection of the United States plan was not the only—or even the worst—bar to agreement confronting the Commission. He suggested that further negotiations were useless unless the committee recognized the necessity of and began making preparations for, a convention outlawing atomic weapons. Without such a convention, he said, it would be practically impossible to consider the control of atomic energy "even in the initial stage of the Committee's labors." He made it clear that a convention outlawing the use of atomic weapons must be accompanied by a cessation of the production of atomic weapons. In other words, Gromyko was threatening to refuse even discussion of control unless a condition was met which the American delegation considered impossible.

A determined effort was made in Committee Two to elicit from Gromyko (1), the means by which the Soviet Government believed its method of control would insure that no nation would secretly manufacture atomic weapons; and (2), how the control authority could effectively curb a nation found to be illicitly producing atomic fuel. In response to the peppering of questions thrown at him, Gromyko again insisted that fundamentally there was no difference between atomic and nonatomic weapons.

This question . . . was applicable not only to atomic energy, but also to the general activities and the very existence of the United Nations. He [Gromyko] asked where was there a guarantee that

[15] *AEC First Report*, Annex 5, pp. 117-18.

the aims of the United Nations would be reached. The only guarantee lay in the genuine desire of all Members of the United Nations to co-operate, and this was the only means of reaching peace and security. He said that the importance of inspection as a means of control of atomic energy had been exaggerated, that inspection could not guarantee peace and security between the nations, and that inspection would violate the principle of State sovereignty.[16]

The only specific types of guarantee that he could suggest which would not violate the principle of sovereignty were (1), the enactment of national legislation providing severe penalties for individual violators of the control treaty; and (2), international action by the Security Council, including sanctions.[17]

To the majority of delegates these were no guarantees at all. National punishment of individuals offered no assurance that the nation itself would not engage in illegal activities. It was considered totally unrealistic that any individual, particularly in the Soviet Union, would have either the means or motivation to build atomic weapons. Only a nation could engage in such a pursuit and who, it was asked, would punish it? Certainly not the Security Council, argued the majority, if the aggressor nation happened to be one of the permanent members, or be supported by any one of the Big Five. Alexandre Parodi, whose Gallic logic pursued Soviet delegates through many a United Nations committee room, observed that according to Gromyko's reasoning, it could be concluded that regulation of atomic weapons was useless inasmuch as the members of the United Nations had renounced war.

The diplomats, having thus failed to establish a common ground, temporarily retired in favor of the scientists. Basically, the American plan was derived from the scientific and technological facts of the production of nuclear energy. As described in the Acheson-Lilienthal Report these facts constituted the assumptions upon which the Baruch Plan was built. The Acheson-Lilienthal Report had described the intimate link between science and politics. Presumably, if the Soviet Union would recognize the validity of these scientific assumptions, it

[16] *AEC First Report*, Annex 5, p. 124.
[17] *Ibid.*, Annex 5, pp. 124-25.

might be more amenable to a "workable" control plan. At least, if the Soviet representatives did acknowledge the validity of the facts upon which the Baruch Plan was created, it would be more difficult for them to condemn the American plan outright. Committee Two, therefore, on July 31, voted to request the Scientific and Technological Committee to report on the question of whether an effective control of atomic energy was possible, together with an indication of the methods by which the committee believed this could be achieved. Commencing in August, the scene of negotiations shifted to the American Institute of Physics on 55th Street.

THE WORK OF THE SCIENTIFIC AND TECHNICAL COMMITTEE AND THE ATOMIC ENERGY COMMISSION REPORT

Between August 1 and October 7 the Scientific and Technical Committee met eighteen times in informal session. All meetings were held behind closed doors where the representatives were able to speak freely without officially committing their governments. Communication was made easier, too, because at the onset it was unanimously agreed that only the scientific and technical aspects of the problem would be discussed. Problems of a nontechnical or political nature were considered within the jurisdiction of other committees. Each of the delegation on the committee was headed by a scientist. Professors D. V. Skobeltzyn (a physicist) and S. P. Alexandrov (a geologist) represented the Soviet Government.

In the private discussions of the committee rooms Professor Skobeltzyn, head of the Soviet scientific delegation, displayed a co-operative, energetic and even courteous attitude while he spoke as a scientist. He let it be known from the beginning, however, that he could not approve any recommendations which would be political in nature. Therefore, he cautioned the committee against making any deductions from the technical facts at its command. Rather, he suggested, the committee should limit itself to preparing a report covering a "general" system of control. Each of the representatives should be free to draw his own political conclusions from whatever statements would be contained in the committee's report.[18] With this limitation, the committee successfully accomplished its mission in less than a full calendar month. Its final report, written as a cooperative effort of all the members, was ready for official approval by the end of August, though formal unanimous approval was delayed until September 26.[19]

Behind the facade of unanimous approval of the committee's report lay the continuing struggle of East and West for justification of their respective control proposals. Baruch and his advisers strongly believed that his June 14 proposals followed necessarily from the technical and scientific facts of nuclear energy production. If the Soviet delegation could be made to acknowledge these nonpolitical facts, perhaps they would move closer to the American position on control. It is not surprising that the evaluation of the problem of control in the committee's final report was almost identical to that of the Acheson-Lilienthal Report. Their sources of information were the same. The information upon which the United Nations Committee based its reports was nonsecret, previously published information supplied by the United States.[20]

However similarly the Scientific and Technical Committee

[18] *AEC/C.3/W.3* and *AEC/C.3/W.13*. All Atomic Energy Commission working documents are designated AEC/. The symbol after the first slash (/) indicates the particular committee. In this instance the third committee (C.3) was the Scientific and Technical Committee. The symbol after the second slash indicates the particular meeting or session of the committee. Thus the W.3 in this instance would reveal that the document was a record of the third meeting of the committee.

[19] The delay was required by the Soviet delegation in order to receive clearance to vote for the report. *AEC/C.3/W.18*.

[20] A footnote in the committee's report reveals the source of its information as follows: "The main body of information is contained in the . . . report by H. D. Smyth, entitled 'Atomic Energy for Military Purposes,' 1945. Additional information is contained in 'A Report on the International Control of Atomic Energy' prepared for the United States' Secretary of State's Committee on Atomic Energy, 1946 (Lilienthal Board Report), and in the press release of the United States Department of State, 9 April 1946. Articles and announcements have also been published in the *Physical Review* and in other scientific journals. Useful summaries will be found in the two volumes of 'Scientific Information Transmitted to the United Nations Atomic Energy Commission by the United States Member,' dated 14 June 1946 and 10 July 1946." *AEC First Report*, Part IV, p. 21.

and the Acheson-Lilienthal Board may have viewed the nature of nuclear production, Soviet acceptance of the report did not imply acceptance of the same conclusions as deduced by the majority. Even as the United Nations Committee neared completion of its report, Skobeltzyn observed that one could find in it many reasons why the Soviet "plan" of control should be accepted. As a guarantee that nothing in the report would prejudice the Soviet proposals Skobeltzyn added a reservation to his acceptance. Because the information at the disposal of the committee was "limited and incomplete" the Soviet Union would consider "the majority of the conclusions" as "hypothetical and conditional." [21] Consequently, the final conclusion of the committee had to be watered down to the minimal statement acceptable to all. It concluded:

With regard to the question posed by Committee 2, 'whether effective control of atomic energy is possible,' we do not find any basis in the available scientific facts for supposing the effective control is not technologically feasible. Whether or not it is politically feasible is not discussed or implied in this report, nor is there any recommendation of the particular system or systems by which effective control can be achieved.[22]

Although negatively expressed, the committee did agree that control was feasible. It furthermore cited the several danger points in atomic production where control was most important. Going from the lesser to the greater danger points, it agreed that control must begin with mining operations. Skobeltzyn himself, who commented rarely on any of the aspects of control, remarked that "it was clear to all that the mines [producing uranium] should be controlled." [23] Next in the process of nuclear fuel production was the extraction of ore-concentrates and the making of uranium and thorium compounds. Somewhat less bulky than unrefined ore these products had to be carefully watched lest diversion for military use take place. At this stage of production, too, preparation of the metal from the uranium

[21] *AEC First Report*, Part I, p. 6.
[22] "First Report on the Scientific and Technical Aspects of the Problem of Control," *ibid.*, Part IV, p. 37.
[23] *AEC/C.3/W.7.*

or thorium compounds, would have to be safeguarded. The locale of such control would be the chemical and metallurgical plants. Lastly, the highest measure of safeguards would have to be applied to the separation and extraction plants and reactors, where the final products—uranium 235 and plutonium—are made.[24]

Specific measures of control as "ownership," "managerial control," "licensing," "inspection" were not found in this report. No description of the type of safeguards to be established at each danger point was mentioned since this was felt to involve larger considerations of international policy. There was, nevertheless, agreement that at more advanced stages of production, as the nuclear fuel becomes more concentrated, diversion became increasingly a more serious problem. Fewer subsequent operations, less time and fewer plants were necessary to produce weapons. It followed from this that the later stages of production required increasingly stringent safeguards.

In addition to illegal diversion of fissionable fuels, the committee took into consideration the possibility that a nation bent upon aggression might openly seize all the atomic facilities within its territory. As in diversion, seizure was looked upon as a more serious menace when stocks of nuclear fuel, rather than raw ore was involved. Weapons could be produced most quickly and in relatively small plants with stocks of concentrated nuclear fuel. The committee confirmed the findings of the

[24] "First Report on the Scientific and Technical Aspects of the Problem of Control," *AEC First Report*, Part IV, p. 33. The Report stressed that "Production of nuclear fuels is the crucial stage in the operation. Both separation plants for the production of uranium enriched in U-235, and the reactors and extraction plants for the production of plutonium or U-233 deliver nuclear fuel, which, under proper conditions, may be used directly for the manufacture of atomic weapons. According to the published statements available to us, the installations necessary for weapon manufacture are relatively small, and the time required is relatively short if the necessary highly skilled personnel is available and the procedure is known. If therefore the strictest standards are not taken to prevent the material in the installations producing nuclear fuel from being diverted, the danger is extremely serious." *Ibid.*, pp. 33-34. More than any other single finding of the committee this one explains the essential difficulty of obtaining agreement on the control of atomic weapons. In order to control effectively the production of nuclear weapons, it becomes necessary to control the complete output of nuclear energy, peaceful as well as military. See also pp. 25, 30, 35.

Acheson-Lilienthal Report that the facilities for fabrication of the bomb mechanism were small and inexpensive. As a remedy against the risks that any one nation could seize a large quantity of fuel in a single seizure, the committee recommended a "wide geographical dispersal of stocks and plants and the restriction of stocks to minimum operating levels . . ."

In the concluding section of its report, the committee summed up the basic facts of nuclear production which would determine the type of plan for any effective control.

> The substances uranium and thorium play a unique role in the domain of atomic energy, since as far as we know these are the only raw materials from which the nuclear fuel required for the development of atomic energy can be obtained. There is an intimate relation between the activities required for peaceful purposes and those leading to the production of atomic weapons; most of the stages which are needed for the former are also needed for the latter . . .
>
> With respect to mining operations, which are of special significance as the first step in these activities, it appears hopeful that safeguards are not too difficult. Particular attention should be paid to the installations in which concentrated nuclear fuel is produced, since the product lends itself immediately to the production of bombs. Unless appropriate safeguards are taken at each of these stages, it will be difficult to ensure that no diversion of material or installations will take place.[25]

Soviet willingness to "go along" with the committee report was, as noted above, tentative and certainly not enthusiastic. But it marked the first substantial form of agreement between the Soviet Union and the United States since both nations had agreed at Moscow to work toward international control through the United Nations. Two orders of problems yet remained to be solved. First, specifically what type of safeguards at each of the steps of nuclear production would be required to guarantee security? Second, what group or agency would maintain these safeguards and what powers would be entrusted to that authority?

Having achieved a qualified success with informal, closed

[25] *Ibid.*, pp. 36-37.

meetings, the representatives, at the suggestion of General A. G. L. McNaughton (Canada), decided to take on the first of the remaining problems—that of specific safeguards—by a continuation of such procedure in Committee Two. The results of these sessions could then be debated in formal session. The committee agreed to discuss safeguards for (1), uranium, thorium and mines; (2), concentration plants; (3), refineries; (4), chemical and metallurgical plants; (5), primary reactors and associated chemical separation plants; (6), isotope separation plants, and (7), secondary reactors.

Between October 15 and December 13, Committee Two met informally in nineteen sessions. The delegations were all advised by technical specialists. In addition testimony was heard from experts from the United States, Great Britain and Canada. By the middle of December, a "First Report on Safeguards" had been drawn up which proposed a plan of safeguards for each of the seven crucial activities necessary in the production of nuclear fuel. Consistent with its past activities before the full Atomic Energy Commission, and in its various working committees, the United States again took the lead in making specific proposals. Seven out of the ten witnesses who testified were Americans. Most of the memoranda and technical papers were supplied by the United States delegation.[26]

Also consistent with its past activities, the Soviet Union took a relatively passive role in the discussions. During the initial meetings tremendous optimism was created when Professor Alexandrov unexpectedly proposed that control of atomic energy must begin at the most basic stage—unmixed mineral resources—and called for a world-wide report on mineral resources. At a subsequent session on October 22 he denied being

[26] See *ibid.*, Annex 8, pp. 140-41 for the names of the experts who testified. Two of the papers supplied by the United States delegation were entitled, "Control Measures in the Mining and Metallurgical Recovery of Uranium and Thorium Ores" (*AEC/C.2/9*, appendix 2) and "Control of Thorium . . ." (*AEC/C.2/W.8*) Among the American scientists and specialists who gave expert testimony were Harry A. Winne, W. E. Kelly, Dr. Charles A. Thomas, and Dr. George T. Felbeck. *The International Control of Atomic Energy: Policy at the Crossroads*, Department of State Publication 3161, General Foreign Policy Series 3 (Washington, D.C., 1948), p. 45, fn. 4, and p. 47, fn. 8.

interested in specific figures but spoke of the importance of knowing how uranium deposits were registered in different countries, what methods of mining uranium were in use, and how losses of mined uranium were evaluated.

Alexandrov's suggestions received public attention through a United Nations press release dated October 21. It created a considerable stir. What Alexandrov proposed was actually quite modest and certainly, by United States standards, almost a *sine qua non* in any system of control. Implied in Alexandrov's proposals, however, was the existence of a *control agency* which would make the specified inventory of world uranium resources. No Soviet proposal heretofore had specified the powers which a control agency would exercise.

Public and official optimism quickly faded when on October 25 Andrei Gromyko issued a statement reinterpreting Alexandrov's statements in Committee Two. According to Gromyko, Alexandrov actually said:

The question of the raw materials could not be left without attention. Information on this subject was insufficient. This had been recorded also in the scientific and technical committee's report. Therefore, while approving the program of our work it will be necessary to leave the question of studying the raw materials on the agenda.

The Soviet delegation considers the national control to be sufficient and, therefore, it might be possible to extend discussions on safeguards in the line of national controls.

The delegations have competent experts, who are sufficiently experienced for a more profound consideration of the question, even without receiving any additional information from their Governments.

"All other statements published in the press in connection with Professor S. P. Alexandrov's remarks," said Gromyko, "do not correspond to the realities." [27] The "realities" of the Soviet position remained their continued opposition to a strong control organ, if not any control organ, strong or weak.

Committee Two's "Report on Safeguards" was discussed formally in meetings on December 18, 19 and 26. This report

[27] *New York Times*, October 26, 1946. See also *ibid.*, October 22, 1946.

did not purport to constitute a plan for control of atomic energy; rather, only the basic elements which would have to be considered in any systematic plan. Specifically, it avoided considering the organizational aspects of a full plan. That feature was being considered separately by the parent Atomic Energy Commission in plenary session. Its one conclusion relating to organization was the general one that "a single international control agency must be responsible for the system of safeguards and control." [28]

Two sets of safeguards were prescribed in the committee's final report. One set concerned the prevention of diversion of nuclear fuel from known mines and plants producing nuclear fuel. The other sought to avoid clandestine production of nuclear fuel. In its proposals to prevent diversion the committee followed the report of the Scientific and Technical Committee in distinguishing between several phases in the production of nuclear fuel. For each phase, specific safeguards were recommended as follows:

(1) Findings for mining and milling of uranium and thorium:

Adequate safeguards against diversion from declared mines and mills are possible by a system of inspection, including guards, similar to normal managerial operating controls, provided that the inspectorate has unrestricted access to all equipment and operations and has facilities for independent weighing, assay, and analysis.

(2) Findings for refineries and chemical and metallurgical plants:

Adequate safeguards against diversion from declared refineries and chemical and metallurgical plants are possible by a system of inspection, including guards, similar to normal managerial operating controls, provided that the inspectorate has unrestricted access to all equipment and operations and has facilities for independent weighing, assay, and analysis, and provided that it has the right to require the plant to be shut down for purposes of clean-up and accounting at appropriate times and to require efficient operating procedure.

[28] "First Report on Safeguards Required to Ensure the Use of Atomic Energy Only for Peaceful Purposes," *AEC First Report*, Part V, p. 43. The following quotations taken from this report are contained in pp. 48-49, 51-53, 55-57, and 59.

(3) Findings for isotope separation plants:

At present, it is not possible to place reliance on the method of obtaining a material balance of uranium isotopes in the case of isotope separation plants. This is one of the important reasons why there must be internal control of such plants by a director or manager, and why the management must be established by and be responsible to the international control agency. Even if the material balance could be greatly improved, the inherent danger of the operation would still require management by the international control agency.

(4) Findings for nuclear reactors and associated chemical extraction plants:

a) At present, it is not possible to place reliance on the method of obtaining a material balance of plutonium in the case of reactors and associated chemical extraction plants. This is one of the important reasons why the chemical extraction plants and, in some cases, the reactors should be subject to internal control by a director or manager and why the management must be established by and be responsible to the international control agency. Even if the material balance could be greatly improved, the inherent danger of the operations would still require management by the international control agency.
b) The safeguards required for the control of reactors will depend on their size and design and especially on their content and possible rate of production of nuclear fuel. The safeguards available to the international control agency should include licensing and inspection, supervision, and management of the operation of reactors. In addition, close supervision of the design and construction of reactors is essential in all cases.
c) Periodic inspection, together with licensing, is an adequate safeguard in the case of small research reactors and their associated chemical plants, unless their total content of nuclear fuel or potential rate of output in any area is of military significance.
d) Adequate safeguards for chemical extraction plants associated with all except small research reactors are only possible through management by the international control agency.
e) Adequate safeguards during the preparation of high grade or pure nuclear fuels in a suitable form for insertion in secondary reactors, and during the storage and shipment of such fuels, are only possible through management by the international control agency.

Precautions against clandestine activities differ from those against diversion in that the former are directed against suspected illegalities utilizing undeclared plants, while the latter are concerned with declared facilities. In order to guard against possible clandestine production of nuclear fuel, the report made the following recommendations:

(1) The right of authorized personnel of the international control agency to direct access and inspection, subject to appropriate restraints, and the right to travel without restraints, is essential in the detection of clandestine activities.

(2) The international control agency would need periodic reports from States on categories of information directly related to the production and use of atomic energy. Certain ancillary information would also be desirable.

(3) Aerial surveys, combined with ground surveys and direct inspection, are essential in some circumstances for the detection of clandestine operations.

That part of the committee's recommendations providing for aerial photography and ground surveys met with particularly strong objection from Professor Alexandrov. In his estimation, these provisions touched more on economic and other spheres, not at all related to atomic energy, than on the question of the detection of clandestine activity in the mining and refining of uranium. He, therefore, refused even to take part in any of the discussions concerned with aerial and ground surveys.[29]

By the middle of December the various working committees of the Commission had completed studies on all the major aspects of atomic energy control, except the political problem of what group or agency should exercise the controls and what powers of enforcement should be given to the control authority. In other words, the basic elements of a control plan had been established by the majority, but no systematic plan embodying these elements had been drafted. At its sixth meeting on November 13, the Atomic Energy Commission decided that it would submit a report to the Security Council by December 31, 1946,

[29] *Ibid.*, p. 60, fn. 1.

including a set of recommendations based upon its deliberations to that date. The Soviet delegate abstained in the voting on the grounds that choosing a terminal date was inadvisable in view of the fact that the scope of the Commission's work was unknown.

Even before Committee Two had completed its studies, the United States took the initiative in the parent Atomic Energy Commission to present a formal plan of control for adoption as part of the Commission's final report. On December 5 Bernard Baruch introduced a resolution containing a series of specific items to be included as "General Findings" and "Recommendations" in the report to the Security Council. They provided for the establishment of a "strong and comprehensive" international control agency, whose decisions would govern the operations of national agencies for atomic energy. And they clearly specified that the rule of unanimity, "such as found in certain cases in the Security Council," should have no relation to the work of this agency.[30]

Soviet opposition to the United States' December 5 proposal was instantaneous. At the December 17 session Gromyko attacked the provision eliminating the veto as a "breach of the [United Nations] Charter." He condemned the plan for lacking a convention prohibiting the production and use of atomic weapons; he criticized that part of the plan permitting the agency to engage in atomic armaments research. Knowing that a scant fourteen days remained before arrival of the Commission's self-imposed deadline, Gromyko attempted to kill the proposal by delaying actions. He asked for additional time to study the plan and argued that the proper course would be to have a committee study it before the Commission took a decision. Failing in that, Gromyko sought to extend the length of time between meetings of the Commission. In response to his request for a time extension, Baruch remarked: "There may be more delays; time goes by and years pass, and then nothing is done." The Commission met as scheduled.[31]

[30] UN, *AECOR Supplement No. 3*, Annex 4 (AEC/15).
[31] UN, *AECOR No. 8, Eighth Meeting, 17 December 1946*, pp. 111-12, 119-20.

At the following Atomic Energy Commission meeting on December 20 Gromyko pressed his request for a postponement of discussion "for six or seven days" to a formal vote. "I very much regret," he said, "that . . . it [postponement] may rather disturb [your] tranquility during the Christmas holidays." By a vote of ten to two, the delegates decided against disturbing their holiday tranquility. Similarly, a Polish move to transmit the United States resolution to committee was defeated.[32] This temporarily ended Russian and Polish active opposition to the United States plan.

Realizing that the plan was moving toward its inexorable fate of adoption, the Russian delegates began a new tactic: passive resistance. From December 20 until the end of the year the Soviet representatives purposefully abstained from any participation in further debates or voting. When at its ninth meeting (December 20) the parent Commission approved in principle the United States plan, Gromyko neither voted against nor abstained: he wished merely to be recorded as not having taken part in the vote. In the December 27 meeting of Committee One, when the United States proposal was examined paragraph by paragraph, the Soviet delegate, Alexandrov, continued his silence. At 6:45 Alexandrov raised his hand, and a tense silence ensued, in expectation of a statement from him. No speech came: all he wanted was notation in the record that he had taken no part in the discussions.

Final approval of the first complete Atomic Energy Commission Report to the Security Council was scheduled for the tenth and last meeting of the Atomic Energy Commission in 1946. Gromyko opened the debate, thereby breaking the barrier of silence that shrouded the Soviet delegation. He asked for a further "item by item" study of the United States proposals but failed to press his request to a formal vote. His criticisms left it clear that the United States plan remained unacceptable. However, Gromyko made two points which indicated that the Soviet Union did not consider the door to future negotiations

[32] UN, *AECOR No. 9, Ninth Meeting, 9 December 1946* [sic] pp. 139-40. The date printed on the title page of this document is December 9, but it should read December 20.

closed. "In spite of the serious defects of the proposals of the
United States representative," he said, "the Government of the
USSR has no objection to discussing these proposals in detail."
Secondly, Gromyko agreed that "It is indisputable that control
organs and organs of inspection should carry out their control
and inspection functions, acting on the basis of their own rules,
which should provide for the adoption of decisions by a majority
in appropriate cases." [33] "In appropriate cases" remained yet to be
defined. It was clear that one such case not considered "appropriate" would be sanctions against a violator. Nevertheless, this
concession toward a majority rule within the proposed agency
was one of the few positive statements toward control emanating
from Soviet Russia. In the final vote on the first Atomic Energy
Commission report, Gromyko, along with Mr. Lange of Poland,
abstained. All others approved the report.

As finally approved on December 31 the first report of the
Atomic Energy Commission to the Security Council included the
two important reports of the Scientific and Technical Committee and Committee Two. It also contained a section of recommendations. These recommendations closely followed the ideas
and wording of Bernard Baruch's December 5 resolution, which
in turn constituted a spelling out of his original proposals made
before the Commission on June 14. They provided for the
creation of a "strong and comprehensive international system of
control" of atomic energy. Among the recommendations was a
provision for the prohibition of atomic weapons and the "disposal" of any existing stocks. Also the control authority should
govern the operations of all national atomic energy agencies.[34]
Lastly the report stipulated that the control treaty should "provide for a schedule for the completion of the transitional process

[33] UN, *AECOR No. 10, Tenth Meeting, 30 December 1946*, pp. 146-47.
(Italics added.) This concession had actually been made earlier by V. M.
Molotov in a speech before the First Committee of the General Assembly.
[34] This recommendation was qualified by the following: "In carrying out its
prescribed functions, however, the international control agency should interfere as little as necessary with the operations of national agencies for atomic
energy, or with the economic plans and the private, corporate, and State
relationships in the several countries." *AEC First Report*, Part III, p. 18. The
full recommendations are on pages 17-19.

over a period of time, step by step, in an orderly and agreed sequence . . ."

The Commission had concluded that, technically, atomic energy control was possible. Whether or not it was politically feasible was another question. While Atomic Energy Commission diplomats were negotiating unsuccessfully in New York, their superiors were carrying on parallel negotiations in Paris at the Peace Conference. The failure of Gromyko and Baruch to reach agreement is not at all surprising when viewed alongside the failure of Molotov and Byrnes to compromise their nations' immediate political objectives in Europe. Not that the Paris Conference failure caused the deadlock in New York. Events in Paris no more circumscribed the New York negotiations than did the Atomic Energy Commission deadlock determine the peace treaties' fate. Rather, both deadlocks stemmed from the same basic causes: incompatibility between American and Russian political objectives and mutual suspicion. In essence these are the causes of the "cold war"—a term then not yet current in international political parlance. So both the Peace Conference and Atomic Energy Commission failures can be looked upon as children of the cold war.

At Paris, conflict was generated by the questions of Trieste, the control of the Danube, and reparations. On the question of atomic energy, the United States' determination to preserve and extend its atomic weapons supply until a foolproof control system was in operation, was in conflict with the Russian desire to bring about destruction of the American stockpile or neutralize its political influence. The obverse of this conflict was the Russian determination to develop its own weapon as rapidly as possible and the American desire to prevent the development of a Soviet stockpile by limiting weapons research to an international agency. In a more general sense, all these objectives can be described as a conflict between the drive of the Soviet Union to expand its area of influence in Europe and Asia and the determination of the United States to resist that expansion.

Mutual distrust was a natural concomitant of this conflict.

Distrust within the United States was intensified by the revelations of the Report of the Royal Commission on atomic espionage in Canada. Among the Soviet agents exposed in Igor Gouzenko's testimony was Dr. Allan Nunn May, who had access not only to the highest Canadian atomic secrets, but also to work done in the United States.[35] For its part, the Soviet Government professed difficulty in reconciling the Bikini Tests held in early July, 1946, with the American proposals for control before the Atomic Energy Commission. "If the atomic bomb at Bikini did not explode anything wonderful," wrote Boris Izakov in *Pravda*, "it did explode something more important than a couple of out-of-date warships; it fundamentally undermined the belief in the seriousness of American talk about atomic disarmament."[36] Into this atmosphere of mistrust two plans were projected, each of which presumed a high degree of confidence to be successful. Prohibition without controls, as proposed by the Russians, assumed that no nation would covertly build atomic stockpiles. A strong control agency, envisaged by Baruch, presumed that the majority of the agency would promote the development of national atomic energy programs according to nonpolitical criteria.

During the summer of 1946, while political agreement was in a stalemate, the Soviet Union and United States were compelled to explain and justify their position before world and domestic public opinion. Until agreement on substance was reached, neither nation could afford to neglect the propaganda value of the Atomic Energy Commission negotiations. For the United States and the Western powers, this problem was much simpler than for the Russians. Their justification was fully conveyed in the reports of the several Atomic Energy Commission committees which culminated in the first report. The first Atomic Energy Commission report not only proposed a fully developed

[35] *Report of the Royal Commission . . . to Investigate the Facts Relating to and the Circumstances Surrounding the Communication, by Public Officials and other Persons in Positions of Trust of Secret and Confidential Information to Agents of a Foreign Power*, June 27, 1946 (Ottawa, 1946), p. 451. See pages 447-57 for a detailed description of Allan Nunn May's activities.
[36] Boris Izakov, "Bikini," *Pravda*, July 3, 1946.

plan, but gave to its proponents the advantage of representing the majority view. The Soviet Union, on the other hand, in justifying its position before public opinion, had to contend with two troublesome aspects: (1), the Russian proposals were less concrete, more general than the Baruch Plan; hence in rejecting the more positive United States plan, the Soviet Union was placed in a negative position; (2), numerically the Soviet "group" was constantly a minority—usually of two, sometimes of one—hence was always in the position of "bucking" the majority.

Russian press and journal articles sought to overcome these propaganda obstacles by constant reiteration of the Soviet statements and speeches and presenting a minimum amount of information on the Western position. The Russian people first learned of the Baruch Plan on June 16 when *Pravda* published a six-paragraph announcement of the United States proposals. No part of Baruch's speech was printed. Nor were any details of the plan given. All that the Soviet people were told was that the United States had proposed establishing a control agency over "every possible kind of activity in the sphere of atomic energy." [37] More space, in fact, was devoted to procedural maneuvering within the Commission than the substance of the discussions. No comment was made on the proposals. On June 21 *Pravda* printed in full Gromyko's speech of June 19 before the Atomic Energy Commission. Still no word of comment was added.[38] Two days later *Pravda* gave the Soviet proposals contained in Gromyko's June 19 speech in outline form. Again no comment was given.[39]

On June 24 the Soviet press began its attack on the Baruch Plan. It continued throughout the summer, paralleling Soviet charges in the United Nations Atomic Energy Commission. In its endeavor to discredit the proposals before the Russian people the press attacked them as being motivated by two sets of pernicious motives, one negative and one positive. On the one

[37] *Pravda*, June 16, 1946.
[38] *Ibid.*, June 21, 1946.
[39] *Ibid.*, June 23, 1946.

hand, the United States had no intention of abandoning its monopolistic control over atomic weapons; rather, it sought to preserve and extend its monopoly. At the same time, it sought to promote United States "hegemony" in world politics by using the weapon as a threat.[40] Both objectives were inherent in the Baruch Plan. As proof of its claim that the United States would never reveal atomic secrets, *Pravda* cited the American insistence that the control plan be put into operation in stages. This would leave the United States complete freedom to determine when *it* would reveal its atomic secrets and halt atomic production. "The Baruch Plan . . . tries to avoid this fundamental issue [*i.e.*, prohibition of atomic weapons] by resorting to vague and confused promises without specifying any definite date of fulfillment. This plan is an attempt to consolidate the monopoly of the United States in the manufacture of atomic weapons and to make it possible to continue research in atomic explosives on a still wider scale." [41] Nor could it be otherwise because of the powerful trusts and cartels which produced the atomic bomb and are the bomb's real owners. These trusts include Westinghouse Electric, General Electric, Dupont de Nemours among others. "The Baruch Plan proposes to transfer all authority in this field to an international monopoly organization and to introduce the system of licenses customary with monopolies of this kind. This would mean, as we know from much past experience with international capitalistic monopolies, that the peaceful utilization of atomic energy would be either prevented or greatly hampered." [42] One of the major functions of this international "supertrust" would be to gather information on the existence

[40] *Ibid.*, June 24, 1946. For a more detailed indictment of America's use of the atom bomb in its foreign policy see M. P. Tolchenov, *Problema Vseobshchevo Sokrashcheniya Vooruzhenii* (The Problem of a General Reduction of Arms) (stenograma publichnei lektsii prochitannoi 19 Dekabrya 1946 goda v Lektsionnom Zale v Moskve) (Moscow, 1947), pp. 17-23.

[41] Modest Rubenstein, "Monopoly Trusts Control Atomic Energy," *New Times*, July 15, 1946, pp. 7-9.

[42] *Ibid.*, p. 9. The article also claimed that these monopolies had secret connections with German cartels such as I.G. Farbenindustrie, Krupp and the Schering Chemical Trust. Rubenstein claimed as his source of facts an article by Lucien Castet in the Paris newspaper *Liberation*. See also *Pravda*, July 3 and July 24, 1946.

of world-wide sources of uranium and thorium which would be made available to the United States.[43]

While the United States opposed control for selfish domestic reasons, continued the Soviet press, it sought at the same time to use its monopoly as a threat to the independence and freedom of other nations including the Soviet Union. It was guilty of the vicious policy of "atomic diplomacy." When American leaders spoke of preserving atomic weapons for "defensive" purposes, they really had aggressive intentions in mind. Atomic weapons for defense, *Pravda* argued, was impossible because of the very destructive nature of the weapon. "The invention of the new atomic weapon with its huge destructive force, is capable of bringing upon mankind incalculable destruction . . . this weapon is not designed for use on the front line . . ." Its large radius of destruction would cause death to one's own as well as enemy troops. The atomic bomb was designed chiefly for application against the enemy in the home-front as was demonstrated in the Pacific war. "From this it follows that the greatest threat of atomic weapons is against peaceful populations." [44]

Further evidence of American aggressive intentions was seen in the element of the Baruch Plan to eliminate the veto on atomic sanctions. "The Baruch plan . . . aims at breaking down the fundamental principles of the United Nations Organization, and, in the final end, at scrapping the Charter." [45] Without the veto, the United Nations would be used "to isolate" the Soviet Union and all socialist countries. Only the principle of the unanimity of the major powers could provide for the co-existence and collaboration of peaceable and democratic states, no matter what their ideology or social organization.[46]

As its solution to the problem of atomic energy control, Soviet spokesmen reiterated one demand: immediate prohibition of atomic weapons and destruction of existing stocks of atomic weapons. "No one can deny that the proposal of the Soviet

[43] *Pravda*, July 14, 1946.
[44] *Ibid.*, June 24, 1946. Also *ibid.*, July 14, 1946.
[45] Modest Rubenstein, "Monopoly Trusts Control Atomic Energy," *New Times*, July 15, 1946, pp. 7-9.
[46] *Pravda*, July 14, 1946.

delegate for a draft convention to prohibit the use of atomic weapons and an international agreement prohibiting the use in war of bacteriological weapons and poisonous and suffocating gases and liquids, conforms to the interests of all peace-loving people and serves the cause of universal security." [47] Arguing in very general terms, Soviet spokesmen insisted that only an immediate prohibition would guarantee the world the security it sought.

At this stage in their discussions Soviet spokesmen equated prohibition with a declaration of prohibition; for no specifications were offered as to guarantees that such a prohibition would be observed by all nations. No suggestions were proposed for methods to investigate suspicions that a nation might covertly be building an atomic stockpile. Gromyko's June 19 proposals had specified that prohibition "should be followed" by "other measures" designed to insure the effectiveness of a declaration of prohibition. But nothing more was said in the Soviet press than had been said in the United Nations either as to the nature of these "other measures" or as to when they would be introduced. In the fall of 1946, Joseph Stalin permitted himself to be interviewed by two newspaper correspondents, eager to ascertain more details of the Soviet plan for prohibition and control. Stalin told Alexander Wirth (Moscow correspondent of the *Sunday Times*) that the use of atomic bombs would be prohibited.[48] On October 23, almost a month later, Hugh Baillie

---

[47] Tolchenov, *Problema Vseobschevo Sokrashcheniya Vooruzhenii*, p. 14.

[48] *Pravda*, September 25, 1946, "Interview with Alexander Wirth on 17 September 1946." The full question and answer as printed by *Pravda* was

> *Question:* "Do you consider that the factual monopoly of the United States with regard to the atomic bomb is one of the most prevalent threats to the peace?"

> *Answer:* "I do not consider the atomic bomb such a serious force as some politicians are inclined to think. Atomic bombs are intended to frighten the weak-nerved, but they cannot determine the fate of war inasmuch as the atomic bomb is totally inadequate for this. Of course, the monopolistic possession of the secret of the atomic bomb creates a threat, but opposed to this exist at least two means: (a) The monopolistic possession of the atomic bomb cannot long continue; (b) The use of the atomic bomb will be forbidden."

(President of the United Press) asked Stalin specifically how the Soviet Union envisaged the control of atomic energy. Stalin replied laconically: "It is necessary to have a strict international control of atomic energy." [49]

[49] *Pravda*, October 30, 1946. An English text of the interview is in the October 29 issue of the *New York Times*.

3: UNITY AND DISUNITY IN THE UNITED
NATIONS: DECEMBER 1946-MARCH 1947

LATE IN OCTOBER, 1946, THE GENERAL ASSEMBLY MOVED TO NEW York City to begin the second part of its first session. The Atomic Energy Commission's Committee Two was then in the midst of its informal conversations on safeguards for a system of atomic energy control. By then the Soviet Government was fully aware of its inability to achieve any of its main objectives in the Atomic Energy Commission. Principally these objectives were a prohibition of the manufacture and use of atomic weapons and revelation by the United States of the secrets of atomic production. It was equally clear that the majority powers under the leadership of the United States were determined to press toward a majority agreement on a control plan which the Soviet Government could not accept. Nor were the Soviet delegates scoring any great successes in the field of propaganda. To be sure, the Commission floor was as equally accessible to the Soviet as well as the Western governments. However, increasingly the Soviet representatives found themselves in the unpopular position of always rejecting proposals. Under the able leadership of delegates like A. G. L. McNaughton, H. V. Evatt, Alexandre Parodi, Sir Alexander Cadogan and Bernard Baruch, the Western powers had succeeded in keeping the Soviet representatives continually on the defensive. Temporarily, at least, the Soviet Union was stalemated.

THE "DISARMAMENT ASSEMBLY"

The New York session of the General Assembly provided the Soviet Union with the opportunity to break out of the Atomic Energy Commission deadlock and take the initiative. In a letter dated October 29 the Soviet delegation submitted a "Proposal Concerning the General Reduction of Armaments" for inclusion in the Assembly agenda. Several sections of the proposal related to the prohibition and control of atomic energy.

Consistent with the basic Soviet interpretation of atomic weapons, no distinction was made between atomic and non-atomic weapons as the subject of General Assembly action on disarmament. When the Charter was drafted in San Francisco in 1945, the existence of atomic weapons was known only to the highest classified circles within the American, British and Canadian Governments. The Charter specified only that "the General Assembly may consider . . . the principle governing disarmament and the regulation of armaments . . ." without specifying any types of weapons. As has already been observed during the first part of its first session, the General Assembly took action to regulate atomic weapons, but nothing was done to promote disarmament, or the regulation of armaments, generally.

In introducing his resolution, Foreign Minister Molotov made one of the most blistering attacks against the United States that had yet been heard in the United Nations. He singled out for criticism the United States plan of atomic energy and the motivation behind it.

The . . . so-called 'Baruch plan' unfortunately suffers from a certain amount of egoism. It proceeds from the desire to secure for the United States of America the monopolistic possession of the atomic bomb. At the same time, it calls for the earliest possible establishment of control over the production of atomic energy in all countries, giving to this control an international character in outward appearance, but in fact attempting to protect, in a veiled form, the monopolistic position of the United States in this field. It is obvious that projects of this kind are unacceptable, since they are based on a narrow conception of the interest of one country

and on the inadmissible negation of the equal rights of States and
of their legitimate interests . . .

If . . . there are plans to use atomic bombs against the civilian
population of towns and, moreover, to use them on a large scale, as
certain newspapers babble, one should not foster any illusions with
regard to the international effect which would result from the carrying out of atrocious plans of this kind. Justified indignation would
sweep over honest people in all countries, and the sanguine hopes
regarding the decisive importance of the atomic bomb in a future
war may lead to political consequences which will mean the greatest
disillusionment, above all for the authors of these plans.[1]

This speech was not what was expected for the general debate
that opened a General Assembly session. Many delegates reacted
with stunned bewilderment. There was a funereal atmosphere in
the hall when the English and French translations were finished.

Soviet Russia's disarmament resolution called for a general
armaments reduction which "should include as the primary object the prohibition . . . of atomic energy for military purposes." A vaguely worded paragraph of the resolution proposed
the establishment of international control of atomic energy
within the framework of the Security Council.

The phrase "within the framework of the Security Council"
is a legal-diplomatic euphemism for the veto. Inasmuch as the
Security Council's procedures under Article 27 provide for
unanimity of the permanent members in voting on questions of
substance, any organ operating within that framework would
include the veto. To supervise the disarmament provisions the
resolution proposed the creation of two commissions. One
commission would supervise conventional disarmament and the
other would supervise the prohibition of atomic weapons. Both
these commissions were to be "special organs of inspection."
In addition, the Soviet Union called upon the United Nations
members to submit information regarding "all their armed
forces and armaments."[2]

[1] UN, *ORGA, First Session, Part II. Plenary Meeting. Verbatim Record 23
October-16 December 1946*, pp. 842-43.
[2] UN, Department of Public Information (New York, 1947). *Yearbook of
the United Nations 1946-47*, p. 139. This resolution was the combined proposal of the one Molotov made before the General Assembly on October 29

During debate in the First Committee meetings on November 28, 29, 30 and December 2 the Russian draft proposal was subjected to a barrage of criticism. The United States objected to the section of the resolution calling upon all states to submit information regarding all armed forces and armaments to the Security Council. In itself this section was not objectionable; but as part of a resolution dealing with atomic energy it was absolutely unacceptable. If adopted, it would have given the Soviet Union a good claim to demand that the United States reveal not only the size of its atomic stockpile, but perhaps even the secrets of atomic weapons production. The objectionable feature of this resolution was the inclusion within one resolution of subject matter which, to the United States, legitimately should have been separated in two resolutions: one on disarmament and one on atomic energy. All the Western powers found other objectionable features in the Molotov resolution: its ambiguity, its insistence on prohibition before control, retention of the veto and bypassing the Atomic Energy Commission. Sir Hartley Shawcross, one of the West's most vehement spokesmen, complained that the Soviet resolution "was so ambiguous that he could not be sure that its adoption would not fetter the Member States with a 'veto.' " [3] Andrei Vyshinsky in reply asserted, "If renunciation of the 'veto' were regarded as a basis for acceptance of the proposal for reduction of armaments, it would be a bad sign and perhaps the Committee members had been overhasty in thinking unanimity possible." On the question of prohibition Molotov adamantly withstood the Western assault. "Without the prohibition of the manufacture and use of such weapons as the atomic bomb, which hang like the sword of Damocles by a thin thread, there could be no collective security." [4] Even the Soviet lack of confidence in the Atomic Energy

---

and a supplement submitted on November 26, *i.e.*, two days before the General Assembly First Committee began its debate. For the original proposal see UN, *ORGA, First Session, Part II. Verbatim Record 23 October-16 December 1946*, p. 847; A/Bur/42.

[3] UN, *ORGA, First Session, Part II. First Committee . . . Summary Records of Meetings 2 November-13 December, 1946*, p. 198.

[4] *Ibid.*, pp. 198-99 and 196.

Commission was acknowledged openly. No great results had been obtained by the Atomic Energy Commission, asserted the Czechoslovakian representative, so its work should be brought within the framework of a larger organ—the Security Council—and should be considered as part of the larger problem of general disarmament. This condemnation of the Atomic Energy Commission even in the midst of its work and before its final report had been made was particularly discouraging to those who were looking toward the Atomic Energy Commission for positive results. By the end of November optimism in the First Committee was at a low ebb.

The general process of negotiation within the United Nations is initiated when one nation submits a draft proposal. A submitted resolution may either be formally or informally accepted by the majority as a basis for further discussion. If one of the important negotiators refuses to accept a resolution as a basis for further discussion, then variant resolutions are submitted until there is established an agreement "in principle." Without such an agreement in principle, either avowed or tacit, discussion may continue but it is usually nearer to wrangling than negotiation. Following agreement "in principle" further refinements are made by amendment to the original draft proposal until a consensus is reached.

Between East and West there was not the slightest agreement in principle on Molotov's disarmament resolution. Australia and Canada both submitted variant resolutions which the Soviet delegation found unacceptable. On December 2 the United States delegation offered a resolution in hopes of establishing a basis for negotiation. Its major difference from the Soviet draft was in urging the Security Council to give first consideration to the pending Atomic Energy Commission report rather than suggesting any new approach to the problem of control.[5]

At the thirty-eighth meeting of the First Committee on December 4 the Soviet delegation had a complete change of heart. For the first time since he introduced his resolution on

[5] The text of the United States resolution is in UN, *ORGA, First Session, Part II. First Committee, Summary Records of Meetings 2 November-13 December, 1946,* p. 343.

October 29 Molotov revealed a sincere desire to reach agreement. In spite of the suddenness of this change his action was clearly not whimsical. It was part of a calculated and broader change on the part of the Soviet Union toward the Western powers. Simultaneous with his concession in the United Nations, Foreign Minister Molotov equally suddenly changed his mind in the Council of Foreign Ministers sessions, where the European peace treaties had been under discussion. When the Council of Foreign Ministers opened its meeting in New York on November 4, 1946, Molotov had voiced objections to virtually all the recommendations of the Paris Peace Conference. Following an abrupt change in early December he approved of seventy-one out of ninety-four of the recommendations. The result was final agreement on peace treaties for Italy, Bulgaria, Finland, Rumania and Hungary.[6] Apparently, in both the United Nations and Council of Foreign Ministers the Soviet Government had decided against assuming the onus in world opinion for total deadlock; and by early December it felt that it had achieved as much in the way of concessions as could possibly be obtained at that time.

At the thirty-eighth First Committee meeting Molotov announced his willingness to accept the United States draft resolution as a basis for further discussion. The all important first step —agreement "in principle"—had been made. Thereafter Molotov ceased to press for adoption of his own resolution and offered instead several amendments to the United States proposal. By his amendments Molotov sought to retain at least three elements of his original proposal: (1), consideration of a draft convention for the prohibition of atomic weapons; (2), maintenance of the control agency within the framework of the Security Council; (3), establishment of two commissions for control of disarmament and atomic energy respectively.[7]

[6] Byrnes, op. cit., pp. 153-54. Byrnes' comment on this sudden change in Soviet policy was, "When Mr. Molotov decides the time has come to agree, he does it in a big way," ibid., p. 154.

[7] UN, ORGA, First Session, Part II. First Committee, Summary of Meetings 2 November-13 December 1946, pp. 255-57. The texts of the Soviet amendments are in A/C.1/113.

In spite of his insistence on keeping the control agency "within the framework of the Security Council," Molotov made an important concession on the problem of the veto. He said: "The rule of unanimity in the Security Council had nothing to do with the work of the control commissions. Therefore, it was incorrect to say that a permanent member with its 'veto' could prevent the implementation of a control system. Any attempt to prevent an inspection would constitute a violation of the Security Council's decision." [8] Obviously this line of policy on the veto problem involved no change where questions of sanctions were concerned. And sanctions were what was uppermost in Mr. Baruch's mind. But in conceding that in its day-to-day operations the control agency would not be frustrated by the vote of the permanent member, the Soviet Union had made its first substantial concession toward majority rule in the control agency. This concession was repeated shortly in the Atomic Energy Commission. Even inflexible Sir Hartley Shawcross declared his belief that Molotov's speech "indicated important concessions from his originally rigid view."

Agreement on a resolution was now just a question of time. Each side had shown its willingness to make concessions. A subcommittee of twenty nations was appointed to draft a resolution reconciling the yet conflicting points of view. In four meetings a resolution was drafted and brought before the First Committee, where it was adopted "unanimously and by acclamation." In the speeches of approval, emphasis was made of the co-operative spirit displayed in the debate on the disarmament resolution and even V. M. Molotov was included in the accolade. On December 14 the General Assembly, in plenary session, adopted its resolution on "Principles Governing the General Regulation and Reduction of Armaments."

The General Assembly proclaimed, in this resolution, a comprehensive set of principles and procedures for action governing several different aspects of disarmament. Some of the resolution's sections dealt exclusively with atomic energy and some exclusively with conventional armaments.

[8] *Ibid.*, p. 257.

Concerning atomic energy the most important of the General Assembly's recommendations was,

that the Security Council expedite consideration of the reports which the Atomic Energy Commission will make to the Security Council and that it facilitate the work of that Commission, and also that the Security Council expedite consideration of a draft convention or conventions for the creation of an international system of control and inspection, these conventions to include the prohibition of atomic and all other major weapons adaptable now and in the future to mass destruction and the control of atomic energy to the extent necessary to ensure its use only for peaceful purposes.

Prohibition of atomic weapons was declared to be an "urgent objective." By implication, however, the attainment of this objective was conditional upon the establishment of an international control system. The control system was to be established "within the framework of the Security Council." It was to operate through "special organs" which would derive their powers from a special convention or series of conventions.[9]

Compared to both the original Soviet and American proposals, the final resolution was a middle path—though not evenly down the middle. It was not so much a synthesis as a blending. For its part, the West conceded that the international system of control would operate within the framework of the Security Council. That meant that, unless otherwise specified, no sanctions could be imposed by the Security Council without agreement by all the permanent members of the Council. However, since the "powers and status" of the control organ would derive from the conventions creating it, the West mantained its claim to majority rule on questions not involving sanctions. Another concession by the West was its recognition of the urgency of a draft convention prohibiting the military use of atomic weapons. Prohibition would be included in the convention establishing the control and inspection system.

Of the remaining parts of dispute between the Soviet Union and the majority, the Russians conceded. They agreed that the

[9] General Assembly Resolution 41 (I). UN, Department of Public Information (New York, 1947), *Yearbook of the United Nations 1946-47*, pp. 142-43 (doc A/267).

Security Council should expedite the work of the Atomic Energy Commission; control would be established by a treaty or convention, not the Security Council; no priority of prohibition over control was stated or implied; control would not necessarily be limited to inspection; and lastly, the request for information on armaments and armed forces was embodied in a separate resolution.[10]

To what extent was the disarmament resolution a viable agreement? Each side had compromised some of its views but nothing new was created in the resolution. The resolution was a projection of two disparate lines of policy. There was little in the agreement that represented a real harmonizing of views. Agreement was wanted both for its own sake and for propaganda value, and agreement was obtained. One positive, though fleeting, result was a breathing of new life into the spirit of the General Assembly. The disarmament resolution was generally looked upon as the most notable achievement of the United Nations since its inauguration. As the first session of the General Assembly ended on December 15, many delegates looked with pride on this great accomplishment of "the disarmament assembly."

ACTION BEFORE THE SECURITY COUNCIL

At the beginning of 1947 the question of disarmament and atomic energy control came before the Security Council under three different headings: (1), the First Report of the Atomic Energy Commission; (2), the General Assembly Resolution on "Principles Governing the General Regulation and Reduction

[10] At the same session in which the Disarmament Resolution was passed the General Assembly adopted the following resolution on "Information on Armed Forces of the United Nations":

The General Assembly,

"Desirous of implementing, as soon as possible, the resolution of 14 December 1946 on the principles governing the regulation and reduction of armaments, "Calls upon the Security Council to determine, as soon as possible, the information which the States Members should be called upon to furnish, in order to give effect to this resolution." UN *Security Council Official Records* (hereinafter abbreviated to *SCOR*) *Second Year Supplement No. 2,* Annex 4, p. 30 (doc S/230).

of Armaments"; and (3), the General Assembly Resolution on "Information on Armed Forces of the United Nations." Implementation of all three of those actions required the approval of the highest political organ of the United Nations.

Having successfully taken the initiative on the disarmament resolution before the General Assembly, the Soviet Government was prepared to do the same before the Security Council. Less than a fortnight after passage of the General Assembly's disarmament resolution the Soviet representative asked the Security Council to establish a disarmament commission and charge it with preparing a set of proposals within a period of one to two, or a maximum of three, months.[11] It became quickly apparent that the Soviet Union was again seeking to submerge the work of the Atomic Energy Commission in disarmament negotiations generally. Even before the Atomic Energy Report had been adopted, the Soviet Union was seeking to bypass it. The General Assembly, in its December 14 resolution, had urged the Security Council to expedite consideration of the Atomic Energy Commission report and also called for the regulation and reduction of armaments and armed forces. No priority was explicitly stated; but as soon as the Security Council convened on December 31, 1946, the Russian delegate sought to establish a priority for the latter. For the next six weeks discussions in the Security Council centered around the Soviet-inspired proposal to establish a new commission for disarmament. During this period Soviet negotiators tenaciously pursued two objectives: (1), to minimize the importance and delay consideration of the Report of the Atomic Energy Commission to the Security Council; (2), to integrate discussion of atomic and conventional weapons control.

Discussion of the Soviet proposal began on January 9 at the ninetieth meeting of the Security Council. Throughout six Security Council meetings extending to January 20 the central question under debate was whether or not the First Report of the Atomic Energy Commission should be given priority over the implementations of the General Assembly's December 14 reso-

[11] UN, SCOR, Second Year, Supplement No. 2, p. 29.

lution. Sharply disagreeing with the Soviet proposal to proceed immediately to a discussion of an armaments commission, the United States delegation proposed that the Security Council give "first priority" to the establishment of international control over atomic energy by considering the Atomic Energy Commission's report as soon as it was received. In defense of the United States proposal, Herschel V. Johnson, the United States representative on the Security Council, maintained that the problem of atomic energy control was fundamental to the whole problem of arms regulation and thus must be considered first. He found it difficult to imagine that success in the general field of arms regulation could be established without a prior agreement in the crucial field of international control of atomic energy.[12]

Andrei Gromyko for the Soviet Union and Oscar Lange for Poland strongly attacked the United States position on the question of priority. Both representatives based their objection to the United States resolution on its alleged incompatibility with the General Assembly disarmament resolution. As they saw it, the Assembly resolution failed to give priority to either problem, whereas the United States proposal explicitly put atomic energy control first. "If we accept the proposal by one of the delegations [the United States]," warned Mr. Lange, ". . . we may run into a very substantial delay . . ."[13]

One of the advantages of the Soviet initiative in the Security Council was the opportunity to exploit the general feeling for rapid action. Whereas, within the Atomic Energy Commission the Soviet delegates had been subject to charges of stalling and delaying tactics, now before the Security Council they became insistent advocates for immediate action. Essentially they were seeking to forestall action on the Atomic Energy Commission report; but inasmuch as their tactic took the form of promoting another objective, they were able to reap the benefit of assuming a positive position. When on January 15 Ambassador Warren R. Austin assumed his new duties as United States representative on the Security Council, he requested a postponement of debate for

---

[12] UN, *SCOR Second Year No. 2, 90 Meeting 9 January 1947*, p. 32.
[13] UN, *SCOR Second Year No. 4, 92 and 93 Meeting 15 January 1947*, p. 8.

three weeks (until February 4) on the plea that he needed time for examining the resolutions before the Security Council. Both Gromyko and Lange objected to the delay. Austin was compelled to put his request to a formal resolution for postponement, which was passed by a nine to two vote.[14]

When the Security Council convened on February 4, a new and more acrimonious phase in the disarmament negotiations began. Mr. Austin presented to the Council a new United States resolution which included acceptance of the Russian demand for a new commission to study conventional armaments. For the next eight days, the subject of United States-Soviet debate now became the terms of reference of the new commission. Mr. Gromyko staunchly defended the argument that the new commission should consider both atomic and nonatomic weapons. Mr. Austin even more steadfastly insisted that the proposed commission be excluded from considering proposals for atomic energy control. At the suggestion of Mr. Hasluck, the Australian delegate, the Security Council agreed that the authors of the various draft resolutions should meet unofficially with the President of the Council (Mr. F. Van Langehove of Belgium) to work out a common text upon which unanimous agreement of the Council could be obtained. Whereupon the representatives of Belgium, Australia, France, Colombia, the United States and Soviet Union adjourned to the sixty-third floor of the Empire State Building.

Three days of secret negotiations failed to resolve the deadlock on the jurisdiction of the proposed commission. The debate centered around a paragraph of the United States proposal which stated: "Those matters which fall within the competence of the Atomic Energy Commission as determined by the General Assembly resolutions of 24 January 1946 and 14 December 1946, shall be excluded from the jurisdiction of the commission hereby established." [15] On February 11 the Security Council again resumed its debate: the Soviet and American delegates stood

---

[14] UN, *SCOR Second Year No. 6, 95 Meeting 20 January 1947*, p. 123.
[15] UN, *SCOR Second Year No. 11, 102 Meeting 11 February 1947*, p. 194 (doc S/268).

squarely against each other on this issue. Mr. Austin emphatically stated the United States position:

. . . The United States insists that it [the Security Council] must not delegate to the proposed commission any authority in the field which has been set aside for the jurisdiction of the Atomic Energy Commission. We insist that this is essential.

I think it is clear from the discussions we have had up to date that the Soviet Union is not willing that the new commission should be expressly barred from considering matters which have been assigned to the Atomic Energy Commission. I make no attempt to give any reason for that refusal, but it is clear that one reason might well be an intention on the part of the Government of the USSR to introduce proposals into this new commission which appropriately fall within the terms of reference of the Atomic Energy Commission.[16]

In reply Mr. Gromyko returned to the basic Soviet argument that there was no qualitative difference between atomic and non-atomic weapons. For confirmation of his thesis he referred his listeners to the General Assembly December 14 resolution which, he declared:

. . . does not differentiate atomic weapons from conventional weapons. For the purpose of solving the problems confronting the Security Council and the United Nations, the resolution, while mentioning atomic weapons, does not make the distinction contained in the United States proposals between atomic weapons and other types of weapons. The thesis that atomic weapons should be considered separately from conventional weapons is contained only in the United States proposals.[17]

Throughout meetings 102, 103 and 104 of the Security Council, the debate continued. All arguments having been exhausted by February 12 the issue was put to a vote after seven hours of almost continuous debate. By 8:15 P.M. the delegates were not only tired and hungry, but in a semifrozen state because someone had mysteriously turned off the heat during the debate. However heated the arguments, their caloric content was insufficient to warm the body. In the final vote the United States proposal was accepted ten to nothing with the Soviet Union

[16] *Ibid.*, p. 196.
[17] *Ibid.*, p. 206.

abstaining. The newly established commission, designated the Commission for Conventional Armaments, was forbidden from concerning itself with the problem of control of atomic energy.[18]

Following his nocturnal victory, Warren Austin offered his hand to the "dark-visaged" Soviet representative. Gromyko shook it without any outward sign of resentment. It is improbable that the Russian diplomat expected to succeed in side-tracking the Atomic Energy Commission altogether. His extended efforts, however, gave his government some margin of victory. In all, discussion of the Atomic Energy Commission's first report had been pushed back over six weeks. The sense of urgency which had propelled so much of the Atomic Energy Commission negotiations in 1946 had been dulled by six weeks of digression. Time, the Russians felt, was on their side, and they were willing to trade rejected resolutions for it.

With the establishment of the Commission for Conventional Armaments the stage was set for the showdown on the Atomic Energy Commission's Report before the Security Council. Through seven meetings, beginning February 14 and ending March 10, the First Report of the Atomic Energy Commission stood before the highest political body of the United Nations. Gromyko's first words opening the Security Council debate set the tone for the position adopted by the Soviet delegates during the ensuing three weeks. That his speech was a carefully prepared statement of Soviet Russian policy was indicated by his slow and deliberate reading of it in English. Unlike the usual Russian procedure, Gromyko made copies of his speech available to the press as soon as he started speaking. He began: "The past work of the Atomic Energy Commission has been useful in the sense that it has made it possible to clarify the attitude of individual States on this question. Unfortunately, however, it

[18] That part of the Security Council resolution which pertained to the Atomic Energy Commission provided: "Those matters which fall within the competence of the Atomic Energy Commission as determined by the General Assembly Resolution of 24 January and 14 December 1946 shall be excluded from the jurisdiction of the Commission hereby established." The complete text can be found in the UN, Department of Public Information, *Yearbook of the United Nations 1946-47* (New York, 1947), pp. 380-81.

must be stated that the Commission has not been able, so far, to reach an agreement on recommendations concerning atomic energy control . . ."

While soundly rejecting the First Report as it stood, Gromyko let it be known that his government would still consider it as a basis for further negotiation. In principle he even supported the United States position that atomic violators must be punished ". . . even involving the applications of sanctions." However, the most important part of Gromyko's speech was his declared willingness to consider the report "item by item" and his announcement that he was prepared to meet the "serious defects" of the report with appropriate amendments and counter-proposals.[19]

The amendments mentioned by Gromyko on February 14 were presented at the 108th session of the Security Council four days later. Twelve in number, they pertained only to that part of the report under the heading of "General Findings" and "Recommendations." Some of the amendments would have made only minor linguistic changes in the report; others struck at the most fundamental Soviet objections to the work of the Atomic Energy Commission. Taken as a whole these amendments constituted the most important official statement of Soviet atomic energy policy since Gromyko's proposals of the previous June. They can be summed up under the following six points:[20]

(1) The only real concession among the amendments was Soviet agreement in principle that the control organ would have the powers of "inspection, supervision and management." (This concession was shortly to be revoked.)[21] Some doubts as to

[19] UN, SCOR Second Year No. 14, 106 Meeting 14 February 1947, pp. 279-80 and 286-87.

[20] The text of the original amendments is contained in UN, SCOR Second Year Supplement No. 7, Annex 16. During the Atomic Energy Commission committee discussions of these amendments the Soviet delegation made some modifications from the original text. For a list of the revised text alongside the relevant sections of the First Report to which each amendment refers see Part III of UN, AECOR Second Year Special Supplement, Second Report to the Security Council, 11 September 1947 (hereinafter referred to as the AEC Second Report), pp. 74-88.

[21] On March 25, 1947, Gromyko deleted the words "inspection, supervision and management" and replaced them with "control and inspection."

its seriousness were inferred from the Russian demand that such control should be applied "in regard to all existing plants . . . *immediately*." This would have put all United States fissionable fuel production plants under international control without the system of stages which United States Congressional and executive officials felt to be necessary.

(2) Four of the amendments referred to the veto. They deleted sections of the report which denied to the members of the control agency the right of veto; instead the amendments specifically provided that the control agency should operate "within the framework of the Security Council." The Soviets did agree that the control agency should adopt some of its decisions by majority vote.

(3) One of the Soviet amendments deleted a paragraph of the report which asserted that a convention outlawing atomic weapons without a comprehensive system of control would be inadequate to meet the problem. Another amendment called upon the Security Council to recognize the urgency of prohibiting atomic weapons.

(4) Several amendments reworded the report to have the control system established by a "convention" rather than by a "treaty." Compared to the majority of Soviet changes this was relatively minor.

(5) In place of the report's recommendation that the control agency have positive research and development responsibilities including the exclusive right to carry on atomic research for destructive purposes, the Russians proposed merely that the agency assist in promoting the exchange of scientific information for peaceful purposes. This same amendment deleted a section of the report authorizing the control agency to govern the operations of national atomic energy agencies.

(6) Where the Commission's report proposed "the disposal of existing stocks of atomic weapons and for the proper use of nuclear fuel adaptable for use in weapons," the Soviets proposed simply the destruction of all finished and unfinished atomic weapons.

The majority reaction to Soviet Russia's amendments was

mixed. Warren Austin, while welcoming constructive suggestions, denied that the Soviet Union, by its amendments, had
offered anything constructive: "They provide for a system
which at least would give no security, and at worst would be
a constant incentive to distrust and war." [22] He particularly objected to any attempts by the Council to amend the majority report. Other members took the more optimistic view that the
Soviet amendments made future agreement more possible. Sir
Alexander Cadogan (United Kingdom) expressed the view that
the amendments "indicate that there is a large field on which we
now seem to be agreed." He suggested that only a few amendments represented fundamental differences of view.[23]

In truth, the Russian amendments contained both the germs of
agreement and deadlock. In them the Soviet Government for
the first time offered a systematic critique of the majority plan
along with definite proposals to ameliorate the report's "defects."
One could assume that the Soviet Union agreed to those portions
of the report which they did not seek to amend. This assumption was not made explicit by Gromyko, however. On this assumption, it would seem that the Soviet Union did agree that
international control of atomic energy was technically and
practically feasible; that it approved of methods of accounting,
inspection, supervision, management and licensing as safeguards
against diversion, clandestine production and seizure; that a
single unified system of international control of atomic energy
was necessary; that the development and use of atomic energy
were not essentially matters of domestic concern; that the duly
accredited representatives of the control agency should have
unimpeded rights of ingress, egress, and access for purposes of
inspection; and that the control system should be put into effect
by stages.

On the other hand, Gromyko refused agreement on several
points of such magnitude, that, whatever concessions the Russians might have offered, no final agreement was likely. These

[22] UN, SCOR Second Year No. 24, 117 Meeting 10 March 1947, pp. 492-93.
[23] UN, SCOR Second Year No. 19, 112 Meeting 25 February 1947, pp. 355-56.

included the problem of the veto, the research authority of the agency and the question of the priority between control and outlawing of atomic weapons. In the same meeting that Gromyko offered his amendments, Mr. Michalowski, the Polish representative, made a lengthy speech devoted primarily to the argument that outlawry of atomic weapons must precede any control system. He said:

We have often heard the argument that the outlawing of atomic weapons must be preceded by the formation of a system of control and inspection. May I draw the attention of this Council to the fact that nowhere in the world has the prosecution of crime and punishment ever preceded the formation of principles of human conduct. The commandment 'thou shalt not kill' existed long before the first court came into being and the first policeman was appointed. Thus, before we can form a system of control and inspection, we must outlaw the production and possession of atomic weapons and all other weapons of mass destruction.

We have heard the reasoning that the problem is that of giving away the secret of this dangerous weapon. But actually it is not. The peace-loving nations are not interested in the manufacture of the atomic bomb.[24]

Michalowski went on to warn that any solution to the problem of control must be unanimously reached.

Although the full extent of Soviet willingness to negotiate further agreement remained in doubt, it was clear that further agreement in the Security Council was unlikely. The United States, therefore, on February 25 proposed transmission of the record of Security Council consideration back to the Atomic Energy Commission for further consideration. It asked that the Security Council recognize "that any agreement expressed by the members of the Council to the separate portions of the report is preliminary, since final acceptance of any part by any nation is conditional upon its acceptance of all parts of the control plan in its final form." [25] Before Mr. Austin's resolution

[24] UN, *SCOR Second Year No. 15, 107 and 108 Meeting 18 February 1947*, p. 310.
[25] UN, *SCOR Second Year No. 19, 112 Meeting 25 February 1947*, pp. 400-401.

came to a vote, Mr. Gromyko announced that he had "some particular remarks which I should like to make" and asked that any decision be postponed until the next meeting of the Security Council.

Originally scheduled for Friday, February 28, the next Council meeting devoted to atomic energy control was postponed because instructions from Moscow to the Soviet delegation were delayed. When Gromyko addressed the Security Council Wednesday, March 5, he spoke for an hour and eighteen minutes, occupying the full time of the Council's session. He announced to the delegates in Russian that he was going "to deal with a number of important questions of substance" and then went on to speak in English.[26] Whatever hopes for a reconciliation between the Soviet and majority views may have existed before Gromyko's March 5 speech, they were thoroughly destroyed after it. Gromyko's address revealed an unbridgeable chasm between the Soviet and non-Soviet approaches.

Fundamentally, the non-Soviet majority looked upon the management and licensing features of their control plan as the main guarantee of security against diversion and clandestine manufacture of nuclear fuel. Gromyko drew attention to the report's definition of management as "the direct power and authority to take day-by-day decisions governing operations as well as responsibility for planning." This idea he characterized as "thoroughly vicious and unacceptable."

One cannot imagine [said Gromyko] a situation in which a control organ would possess establishments in different countries, decide whether or not to allow the creation of such establishments on the territories of these or other countries, and have the exclusive right to carry on scientific research in the field of the production and use of atomic energy. It is impossible to imagine such a situation. Only people who have lost the sense of reality can seriously believe in the possibility of creating such arrangements.[27]

[26] One indication of the importance of this speech is the fact that mimeographed copies of it were made available immediately after Gromyko spoke. This was generally rarely done.

[27] The quotations from this speech are taken from UN, *SCOR Second Year No. 22, 5 March 1947*, pp. 443-61. They are not necessarily quoted in the order in which he spoke them; in some cases the order of his paragraphs are juxtaposed to present an orderly arrangement of his ideas.

Then Gromyko went on to explain why the Soviet Government would never accept this control: it constituted interference in the internal affairs and internal life of a nation. "I deem it necessary to emphasize that the granting of broad rights and powers of such a kind of control organ is incompatible with State sovereignty." As far as the Soviet Union was concerned, there were no limits to the authority given the proposed control agency and, "Unlimited control would mean an unlimited interference . . . in the economic life of the countries on whose territories this control would be carried out . . ."

The Soviet delegate became even more direct.

It is easy to understand [said Gromyko] that the granting of such rights to control organs would mean a complete arbitrariness of these organs and, first of all, of those who would be in a position to command a majority in these organs.

.   .   .

The Soviet Union is aware that there will be a majority in the control organ which may take one-side decisions, a majority on whose benevolent attitude the Soviet Union the Soviet people cannot count [sic]. Therefore, the Soviet Union, and probably not only the Soviet Union, cannot allow that the fate of its national economy be handed over to this organ.

Gromyko, however, did not rest his criticism with an attack on the potentially hostile motives of an amorphous "majority." Behind the machinations of the majority delegates he saw the wily hand of the United States. In his attack on the motives of the United States Gromyko for the first time made official the propaganda charges in the Soviet press, journals and radio that the Baruch Plan represented an attempt on the part of the United States to create an American dominated world atomic supertrust.

In reality, to grant to the control organ unlimited rights and possession and management of the atomic establishments cannot be looked upon as anything but an attempt by the United States to secure for itself world monopoly in the field of atomic energy.

.   .   .

The United States proposals on control proceed from the erroneous premise that the interests of other States should be relegated to the background during the exercise by the control organ of its functions of control and inspection. Only by proceeding from such fundamentally vicious premises was it possible to come to the conclusion, contained in the proposals submitted to the Atomic Energy Commission by the United States representative, on the necessity of transferring atomic enterprises to the possession and ownership of the international organ which is to be responsible for the realization of control. A proposal of this sort shows that the authors of the so-called Baruch plan completely ignore the national interests of other countries and proceed from the necessity of subordinating the interests of these countries to the interests actually of one country— that is, the United States of America.

This speech, the bitterest yet made exclusively on the subject of atomic energy, ended one phase in the long struggle for an international control system. After three quarters of a year of study, planning and negotiations, the Soviet Union and Western powers found themselves in total disagreement. Throughout innumerable drafting sessions and planning conferences the majority delegates had hammered out a well thought-out, positive plan of control which the Soviet Union found "unacceptable and unjustifiable." No comparable alternative was proposed in its place. The deadlock as of March, 1947, was particularly ominous, not because of specific Soviet objections to the majority plan, but because Soviet criticism was made a part of its ideological conflict with the West. As long as any strong control agency was looked upon as part of the basic struggle between capitalism and socialism, accommodation with the West by the Soviet Government would be impossible.[28] Gromyko, in his March 5 speech, came nearer to making that identification than had any Soviet spokesman previously.

At its 117th meeting on March 10 the Security Council voted unanimously to refer the discussions back to the Atomic Energy Commission. It requested a second report before the next regular session of the General Assembly.

[28] This idea will be developed further in chap. IX. Eugene Rabinowitch, one of the editors of the *Bulletin of Atomic Scientists*, suggests, without citing any sources, that the State Department probably ceased to consider an atomic control agreement with the Soviet Union likely after March, 1947. Rabinowitch, *op. cit.*, p. 70.

As the first period of the struggle to obtain international control of atomic energy ended in March, 1947, three major political events transpired which opened a new phase in East-West relations: The Truman Doctrine was announced (March 12); the Moscow Foreign Ministers Conference opened (March 14); and the Brussels Pact was signed (March 17). The cloud hovering over the Atomic Energy Commission negotiators as they began their second round was several shades darker than before.

4: THE SOVIET PLAN vs.

THE MAJORITY PLAN

As the second round of atomic energy negotiations began in the spring of 1947, feelings were mixed about the seriousness of Soviet intentions to negotiate. According to a close observer of the Atomic Energy Commission, the majority of delegates were more pessimistic than at any time since the Commission began its work.[1] Frederick Osborn, Deputy United States Representative on the Commission, believed, however, that at this juncture the Russians still desired to continue the negotiations.[2] For one thing, Andrei Gromyko on February 14 had told the Security Council that the Soviet Government had its own set of counterproposals to the United Nations Plan. As yet they had not been presented. Even Premier Stalin, whose few comments on atomic energy control were always vague and enigmatic, on April 9, 1947, predicted success in establishing international control of atomic energy. "Things are leading up to it," he said.[3]

[1] See the article by Thomas J. Hamilton in the *New York Times,* April 13, 1947.

[2] Osborn, *loc. cit.,* p. 220. Frederick Osborn was appointed United States Deputy Representative to the Atomic Energy Commission and served in that capacity until the end of 1950. He conducted the bulk of the negotiations for the United States during this period.

[3] Interview with Harold Stassen on April 9, 1947. Stalin gave as the reason for his feeling, his belief that "the desire and conscience of the peoples of the world demanded that the use of atomic energy for warlike purposes be prohibited." *Izvestia,* May 8, 1947.

When the Commission reconvened in March, 1947, it had before it two orders of business: formal consideration of the twelve Soviet amendments and an elaboration of the functions and powers of the International Control Agency proposed in the First Report. It was unanimously agreed to consider the two separately, the former in the Working Committee (the previous Commitee One) and the latter in Committee Two. The negotiations in both committees were to be carried out concurrently. Inasmuch as the membership of the Working Committee and Committee Two was the same, it was found most convenient to hold meetings on alternate dates.

DEBATE ON THE SOVIET AMENDMENTS

The Working Committee began debate on the first Soviet amendment on April 8, 1947. By July 23, all twelve amendments had been discussed and, in effect, rejected. In its Second Report to the Security Council the Atomic Energy Commission concluded: "The discussion of the USSR amendments . . . has not led the Commission to revise the general findings and recommendations of the first report." [4] During the course of the debate, successive chairmen of the Commission ruled that the first report could not be amended literally. It was agreed that any of the Soviet modifications would be reflected in the Commission's second report. Inasmuch as a formal adoption of their position was closed to them, the Soviets bent their efforts in the Working Committee toward securing agreement on a series of propositions which they might later use to support and justify their general position before the United Nations. Soviet and Western delegates became involved in a subtle and complex propaganda duel, with the Soviet team on the offensive. Mr. Gromyko and his assistants were eager for discussion of the amendments. Frederick Osborn, the American negotiator, describing the debates in the Working Committee, later observed that in great contrast to its position on the proposals discussed in Committee

[4] *AEC Second Report*, Introduction, p. 1.

Two, the Soviet position on these amendments "was always clear and unswerving."[5]

Although twelve in number the amendments brought under purview only four problems. They were the question of the veto, the adoption of control and prohibition by one or two conventions, the priority of prohibition over control, and the problem of disposing of or destroying atomic bombs. In each of these four questions Gromyko pressed for recognition of a particular point which would complement the general Soviet position.

The Soviet amendments sought to save the veto in two ways, one direct and one indirect. The indirect way was to replace the expression "within the framework of the United Nations" with "within the framework of the Security Council" in those parts of the report that referred to the control agency. Gromyko's defense of this change was the legally sound one that the latter phrase had been incorporated in the compromise Assembly disarmament resolution of December 14, 1946. As used in the General Assembly resolution the expression was a general one applicable for all control agencies concerned with disarmament. A compromise was finally worked out by which the Working Committee reaffirmed that portion of the General Assembly resolution that:

> There shall be established, within the framework of the Security Council, which bears the primary responsibility for the maintenance of international peace and security, an international system . . . operating through special organs, which organs shall derive their powers and status from the convention or conventions under which they are established.[6]

Australia, Belgium, Brazil, Canada, France, the United Kingdom, and the United States, in voting for this compromise, gave notice that they did not consider in any way modified those parts of the First Report which made special provision for elimination of the veto in questions of sanctions against atomic control violators.

[5] Osborn, *loc. cit.*, p. 218.
[6] *AEC Second Report,* Part III, pp. 77-78.

Two Soviet amendments directly sought to preserve the veto by proposing to eliminate those paragraphs in the First Report which expressly condemned the veto. Here Gromyko met with considerably less success. It was generally agreed that there were two distinct areas where the veto could be applied: in the day-to-day activities of the control agency and in questions of sanctions. Gromyko emphasized this distinction. He hoped to persuade the committee to accept removal of the veto in the former area and by implication accept the veto in question of sanctions. The phraseology by which he proposed to accomplish this objective was a well thought-out formula. He suggested that

> Reference to the question of the 'veto' . . . should be understood in such a way as relating to the day-to-day operations of the international control organ. The questions on which such organs would take decisions by majority vote should be specified and listed in the convention, as well as those questions on which the organ would have power to make recommendations to the Security Council, but not to take decisions.[7]

The Western delegates were neither to be outwitted nor outargued. They were, of course, glad to accept removal of the veto in the day-to-day operations of the agency, but would not condone the implication that in all other situations the veto would be valid. General McNaughton parried the Soviet gesture with an amendment simply stating that ". . . decisions within the competence of the agency would be taken by a majority vote." Gromyko in disgust abstained from voting on the Canadian amendment. It "contained no new ideas," he said, and "settled no disagreements." [8]

Another objective of the Soviet amendments was to have the committee accept the idea that more than one convention should be signed in establishing prohibition and a control system. This was an expression of their general desire to separate prohibition from control. Accordingly, three of the amendments used the plural term "conventions"—the implication being that there

[7] *Ibid.*, Annex 4, p. 173.
[8] *Ibid.*, Annex 4, pp. 178-80.

would be more than one. Western delegates again were aware
of this Russian maneuver and resisted it. Prolonged discussion
failed to resolve the differences, and ultimately no decision was
taken on each of these three amendments.

Coupled with the idea of two treaties was the Soviet insistence
that a treaty prohibiting atomic weapons should go into effect
before a control treaty. This demand was made explicitly in two
amendments. Gromyko did not press strenuously for adoption
of these amendments. Since there was a general reluctance to
reopen debate on the question of priority of either control or
prohibition, discussion was limited and no decisions were taken.

In Amendments One, Eight, and Eleven, Soviet hostility to
Bernard Baruch's plan for stages of control was manifested.
Baruch and his successors, in defense of America's national interest, had repeatedly insisted that the United States could not
afford to abandon its atomic weapons monopoly until a proven
system of control had been established. Such a system, they
felt, would not come about all at once; it would evolve through
stages. In Amendment One the Soviet Government sought the
application of control and inspection "in regard to all existing
plants . . . immediately after an appropriate convention or conventions. . . ." Amendment Eight provided for the "destruction of stocks of manufactured atomic weapons and of unfinished
atomic weapons." No reference to stages was made in the latter
amendment.

Soviet Amendment Eight provoked some of the most heated
and prolonged debates of the entire series. Its wording differed
from the First Report in providing for "destruction" of atomic
weapons instead of the original "disposal." Disposal meant that
the bombs might either be dismantled or placed in the hands
of the United Nations. Destruction had no precise meaning at
all. Did it mean that the nuclear fuel and bomb mechanism and
casing were to be destroyed? Or was only the outer casing and
detonating mechanism to be demolished? These questions were
asked of Gromyko. "Destruction of atomic bombs" was a
meaningless expression, if it meant the latter. The bomb mechanism could be manufactured in a short time, at a relatively small

expense and in secrecy, regardless of how strict the control. On the other hand, actual destruction of nuclear fuel would be extremely wasteful. It was made at tremendous cost and could be used for peaceful purposes—especially for the production of power.

There is little evidence that the Soviet Government seriously believed it could put the United States in a position to "destroy" its atomic stockpile before it felt safe to do so. However, the Soviet Government could make great propaganda use of its insistence on the destruction of atomic bombs. If it could obtain some sort of condemnation of the possession of atomic weapons, the Soviet Government could put the United States in a shady moral position by its very possession of the bomb. In addition to its influence on world public opinion a condemnation of atomic weapons could affect American internal public opinion and impede the will of the government should there be consideration of using the bomb. That the Russian government was making propagandistic use of this argument is evidenced by its use of this theme in the Working Committee and in subsequent debates in the Security Council and General Assembly. From the point of view of propaganda tactics, the Soviet delegation was more successful with Amendment Eight than any other amendment.

Debate on the amendment began July 7, 1947. Coincidentally, on that date the Working Committee decided to open its meetings to the press.[9] In his defense of his amendment Gromyko argued that there was no direct connection between control of nuclear fuel and destruction of atomic weapons. "No matter what system of control were established, the convention should provide for the destruction of atomic weapons."[10] Canada, China, and the United Kingdom preferred the term "disposal" because, their representatives argued, nuclear fuel was too valuable to be destroyed. Gromyko reiterated his demand for the acceptance "in principle" of the destruction of atomic weapons and the ma-

[9] Previously both the Australian and Soviet representatives had suggested that the meetings be made public. *Ibid.*, Annex 4, p. 185.

[10] *Ibid.*, Annex 4, pp. 188-89. See pages 185-96 for a full summary of the important debate on July 7.

jority repeated that they would not approve the destruction of nuclear fuel.

Then Gromyko posed a new proposition to his colleagues on the committee. Would they agree "to stating that all atomic weapons should be destroyed, and that nuclear fuel should be used only for peaceful purposes"? Ostensibly the major Western objection was met. The verbal trap was cleverly laid. Sir George Thomson for the United Kingdom immediately answered "yes." The representatives of Canada, China, Australia, and Brazil followed suit before Mr. Osborn was able to voice his objections. The United States representative immediately objected on the ground that such a decision would prejudice the possibility of the control agency's retaining a supply of atomic weapons—presumably for possible use in sanctions against an aggressor. Gromyko replied that as he saw it the majority were agreed on the principle that atomic weapons should be destroyed. He called for a subcommittee to draft a resolution "embodying the statements of the majority." Suddenly the "majority" had a strangely different spokesman. For the moment Gromyko had succeeded in isolating the United States from its usually consistent supporters.

No verbatim records of the discussions of the subcommittee are available for study; nor are the private conversations of the Working Committee delegates between July 7 and 14 on record. It can be assumed that Mr. Osborn exerted considerable effort to rectify the breach among the majority delegates. The subcommittee finally limited itself to reporting a deadlock between the Soviet demand for immediate destruction of atomic weapons and the majority preference for bomb destruction in conjunction with the implementation of control by stages. In vain did Gromyko atempt to force the committee to adopt a resolution formally expressing the agreement that had been stated. In vain did he try to have the committee approve the destruction of atomic weapons, even with the proviso on the peaceful uses of nuclear fuel. Beginning at the twenty-sixth meeting on July 18 those representatives who had answered "yes" to Gromyko's question on July 7 started their retractions one by one. Colonel

Hodgson for Australia was the first; then Canada, and finally the Brazilian representative who, in restating his position, did so on the grounds that "there was apparently a misunderstanding." [11]

Formally, Gromyko had failed. He did not even bother to press his amendment to a vote. For propaganda purposes, however, he had scored an important victory. The record of the July 7 discussions was referred to repeatedly in later Soviet speeches before larger forums of United Nations delegates.[12] These references usually contained statements like ". . . with the exception of the representative of the United States, no one objected to the destruction of atomic weapons." Gromyko delivered a series of bitter speeches before the Working Committee accusing the United States of refusing to destroy its bombs and of having made a hypocritical offer which was unmasked.

The debate from April through July on the Soviet amendments fared poorly in bridging Soviet and non-Soviet points of view. Western representatives on the committee found that they were no more sure of Russian intentions in July than they had been in March. If anything, they were further from agreement. On one essential point Gromyko had actually backtracked from an earlier concession. In presenting his First Amendment on March 25, Gromyko offered a revised version from that of February 18. The earlier version of Amendment One began, "Inspection supervision and management on the part of an international organ should be applied in regard to all

[11] *Ibid.*, Annex 4, pp. 204-210. Not all the retractions were as frank as that of the Brazilian representative, Capt. Alvaro Alberto. The French representative considered Gromyko's resolution "valueless" and the Colombian and British representatives agreed.

[12] See, for example, the debates in the Working Committee on March 29, 1948, *AEC/C.1/SR42*, and *UN, AECOR, Third Year No. 2, 16 Meeting 17 May 1948;* UN, SCOR, *Third Year No. 85, 321 Meeting 16 June 1948;* UN, *ORGA, Third Session. First Committee . . . Summary Records of Meetings 21 September-8 December 1948,* 145th meeting, p. 30, and 162nd meeting, p. 177. UN, *AECOR, Fourth Year No. 3, 19 Meeting 15 March, 1949,* p. 14; UN, *ORGA, Fourth Session. Ad Hoc Political Committee, Summary Records of Meetings 27 September-7 December 1949,* 35th meeting, p. 10; UN, *ORGA, Sixth Session. First Committee, Summary Records of Meetings 7 November 1951-2 February 1952,* 453rd meeting, p. 24.

existing plants . . ." This version was changed to read "Control
and inspection on the part of an international organ . . ." A
similar change in Amendment Three was made on June 3,
when the original wording, "including supervision and inspection," was changed to read "including inspection." When originally presented, these two amendments offered some hope of
Russian acquiescence in the principle of managerial and super-
visory control by the international agency. That hope was
dashed in March and June.

What was revealed during the course of the Working Committee's discussion was an intensification of a trend in atomic
energy negotiations. That trend was a hardening of the Soviet
position and an emphasis on the use of these negotiations for
propaganda purposes. Many of Gromyko's colleagues felt that
he was acting under explicit instructions from Moscow as to
the very smallest details of his proposals. Frederick Osborn, the
United States representative, was convinced that several of the
Soviet speeches were written in Moscow and sent with instructions that they be delivered without change. As a result of the
discussions in the Working Committee, he believed, the majority
delegates developed "some very definite impressions which undoubtedly colored their attitude during the balance of the negotiations . . . After three months of such experiences, the other
delegates came to look on any new Soviet proposals with grave
suspicions." [13]

THE SOVIET JUNE 11 PROPOSALS

Ever since the original Baruch and Gromyko proposals of
June, 1946, the Soviet Government had been criticized and
chided for failing to accept the Western plan for atomic control or provide a viable alternative. Frederick Osborn reflected

[13] Osborn, *loc. cit.*, pp. 222-23. Osborn added: "To a very real extent they
became hardened to Soviet name-calling, and learned that it was often
wiser to reply briefly, or even not to reply at all, than to become involved
in arguments which seemed to have no purpose except delay or the attempt
to catch up on some poor use of words," p. 233. It must be remembered that
this testimony is from one of the victims of Gromyko's "name-calling."

a lighthearted aspect of American feeling in April when he said: "The fact is that the seed was planted in the womb of the Soviet administration nine months ago, the proper period of gestation. The idea should have born fruition and if it does not we are forced to conclude the Soviet is incapable of a live birth." [14] Mr. Gromyko wryly called this a "half-joke." The half of Osborn's statement that was not a joke to Gromyko was the serious handicap which belabored Soviet propagandistic labors in United Nations discussions: they had always to be on the defensive, always in a position of rejecting proposals.

Suddenly, in early June, Andrei Gromyko announced that his government had a new series of important proposals to make. Here at last was the Soviet plan for control. Both the Working Committee and Committee Two interrupted their labors to receive the Soviet proposals. A special meeting of the full Atomic Energy Commission was called for June 11. Gromyko's opening remarks virtually dismissed the accomplishments of the Commission to date. "Almost a year and a half has passed since the adoption . . . of the resolution on the establishment of the Atomic Energy Commission," he noted. "Meanwhile, one must say frankly that the Atomic Energy Commission has not made due progress in its work." Gromyko then offered a set of proposals which, he said, constituted the Soviet Union's contribution toward "practical action." Because these proposals of June 11 are the most comprehensive and definitive statement of Soviet policy toward international control of atomic energy, they deserve quotation in full. They provided:

(1) For ensuring the use of atomic energy only for peaceful purposes, in accordance with the international convention on the prohibition of atomic and other major weapons of mass destruction and also with the purpose of preventing violations of the convention on the prohibition of atomic weapons and for the protection of complying States against hazards of violations and evasions, there shall be established strict international control simultaneously over all facilities engaged in mining of atomic raw materials and in production of atomic materials and atomic energy.

[14] Osborn's comment was made before the Control Committee. This quote was taken from the *New York Times*, April 18, 1947.

(2) For carrying out measures of control of atomic energy facilities, there shall be established, within the framework of the Security Council, an international commission for atomic energy control, to be called the International Control Commission.

(3) The International Control Commission shall have its own inspectorial apparatus.

(4) Terms and organizational principles of international control of atomic energy, and also composition, rights and obligations of the International Control Commission, as well as provisions on the basis of which it shall carry out its activities, shall be determined by a special international convention on atomic energy control, which is to be concluded in accordance with the convention on the prohibition of atomic weapons.

(5) With the purpose of ensuring the effectiveness of international control of atomic energy, the convention on the control of atomic energy shall be based on the following fundamental provisions:

a) The International Control Commission shall be composed of the Representatives of States Members of the Atomic Energy Commission established by the General Assembly decision of 24 January 1946, and may create such subsidiary organs which it finds necessary for the fulfillment of its functions.

b) The International Control Commission shall establish its own rules of procedure.

c) The personnel of the International Control Commission shall be selected on an international basis.

d) The International Control Commission shall periodically carry out inspection of facilities for mining of atomic raw materials and for the production of atomic materials and atomic energy.

(6) While carrying out inspection of atomic energy facilities, the International Control Commission shall undertake the following actions:

a) Investigate the activities of facilities for mining atomic raw materials, for the production of atomic materials and atomic energy as well as verify their accounting.

b) Check existing stocks of atomic raw materials, atomic materials, and unfinished products.

c) Study production operations to the extent necessary for the control of the use of atomic materials and atomic energy.

d) Observe the fulfillment of the rules of technical exploitation of the facilities described by the convention on control as well as work out and prescribe the rules of technological control of such facilities.

e) Collect and analyze data on the mining of atomic raw materials and on the production of atomic materials and atomic
energy.

f) Carry on special investigations in cases when suspicion of
violations of the convention on the prohibition of atomic
weapons arises.

g) Make recommendations to Governments on the questions relating to production, stockpiling and use of atomic materials
and atomic energy.

h) Make recommendations to the Security Council on measures
for prevention and suppression in respect to violators of the
conventions on the prohibition of atomic weapons and on the
control of atomic energy.

(7) For the fulfillment of the tasks of control and inspection
entrusted to the International Control Commission, the latter shall
have the right of:

a) Access to any facilities for mining, production, and stockpiling
of atomic raw materials and atomic materials, as well as to the
facilities for the exploitation of atomic energy.

b) Acquaintance with the production operations of the atomic
energy facilities, to the extent necessary for the control of
use of atomic materials and atomic energy.

c) The carrying out of weighing, measurements, and various
analyses of atomic raw materials, atomic materials, and unfinished products.

d) Requesting from the Government of any nation, and checking
of, various data and reports on the activities of atomic energy
facilities.

e) Requesting of various explanations of the questions relating
to the activities of atomic energy facilities.

f) Making recommendations and presentations to Governments
on the matters of the production and use of atomic energy.

g) Submitting recommendations for the consideration of the
Security Council on measures in regard to violators of the
conventions on the prohibition of atomic weapons and on the
control of atomic energy.

(8) In accordance with the tasks of international control of
atomic energy, scientific research activities in the field of atomic
energy shall be based on the following provisions:

a) Scientific research activities in the field of atomic energy
must comply with the necessity of carrying on the convention
on the prohibition of atomic weapons and with the necessity
of preventing its use for military purposes.

b) Signatory States to the convention on the prohibition of atomic weapons must have a right to carry on unrestricted scientific research activities in the field of atomic energy, directed toward discovery of methods, of its use for peaceful purposes.

c) In the interests of an effective fulfillment of its control and inspectorial functions, the International Control Commission must have a possibility to carry out scientific research activities in the field of discovery of methods of the use of atomic energy for peaceful purposes. The carrying out of such activities will enable the Commission to keep itself informed on the latest achievements in this field and to have its own skilled international personnel, which is required by the Commission for practical carrying out of the measures of control and inspection.

d) In conducting scientific research in the field of atomic energy, one of the most important tasks of the International Control Commission should be to ensure a wide exchange of information among nations in this field and to render necessary assistance, through advice, to the countries parties to the convention, which may request such assistance.

e) The International Control Commission must have at its disposal material facilities including research laboratories and experimental installations necessary for the proper organization of the research activities to be conducted by it.[15]

For a few observers these proposals did rekindle the diminishing hope that the Soviet Union might be observing the problem in the same light as the majority.[16] However, this child of over twelve-months gestation died stillborn. There was little in the content of the proposals that was new. They did put the Soviet Union on record as desiring "strict international control"; but the sum of the June 11 proposals amounted to continual national control over atomic energy production. International jurisdiction was limited to the type of inspection-police action condemned in the Acheson-Lilienthal Report and by the majority of delegates during the previous twelve months. The proposals

[15] UN, *AECOR Second Year No. 2, 12 Meeting 11 June 1947*, pp. 20 and 21-24. Also Document AEC/24.

[16] See editorial by Eugene Rabinowitch in the *Bulletin of Atomic Scientists*, III, No. 8 (August, 1947), p. 202.

provided only for "periodic" inspection which the First Report had condemned as inadequate by itself. Where suspicion of violation would arise, the International Control Commission was empowered to carry on "special investigations." No hint was given, however, as to how the Control Commission would learn to uncover illicit activities or how its suspicion might be stimulated. Accounting verification, inventory checking, production studies, data collection, and general investigation were felt by the majority to be inadequate to guarantee security. Mr. Harry of Australia expressed the general consensus when he said, "A year ago these same proposals might have been regarded as useful and hopeful." [17] After more than a year's study and rejection of most of the ideas contained in the June 11 proposals, the Atomic Energy Commission found it difficult to accept Russia's demand that everything be scrapped and all discussion begun anew.

Far from beginning discussion anew, the Commission temporarily shelved consideration of the new proposals. The Commission after lengthy discussion agreed that Committee Two would consider the Soviet proposals, but only *after* it had completed its elaboration of the powers and functions of the International Control Agency. When, in August, Committee Two finally got around to the proposals it devoted only four days for formal consideration of them.

Every member of the committee, with the exception of Professor Zlotowski of Poland, rejected the Soviet June 11 proposals as inadequate. For Poland the proposals constituted "an excellent basis for discussion." Professor Zlotowski strongly urged the Western powers to use the Soviet proposals as a basis for bridging the differences between East and West. He said, ". . . even if we cannot agree at the moment, and even if we feel that there are certain fundamental discrepancies between certain points of view, it is our duty to try right to the very last moment to reach an agreement. Even if we cannot agree, we should first of all try to do our best to understand each

[17] *AEC Second Report,* Annex 5, Appendix 2, p. 219.

other." [18] Mr. Gromyko was much more blunt. "It is obvious," he warned, "that I should not be frank if I did not say that if the USSR proposals were not accepted, and if some of the representatives continue to state that those proposals do not constitute a basis for agreement on the question of establishing control over atomic energy, then we shall find ourselves in a more difficult position." [19]

By August 11, it was fully apparent that rejection of the Russian proposals was imminent. Gromyko argued desperately for a point-by-point consideration of them. He wanted the committee to record formally whatever area of agreement there was between the two plans. For the Soviet Union such a procedure would have placed the West—and particularly the United States—in the position of rejecting Soviet principles. In rejecting the Soviet proposals point by point, the Western representatives would be not always intending disagreement with the proposals *per se* so much as criticizing the inadequacy of the Russian proposals. However, in view of the Soviet past performance, there is no doubt that Soviet propaganda would have construed such opposition before world opinion as opposition to prohibition and control of atomic weapons *per se*. This opportunity was denied them, when on August 15, by a vote of ten to two, Committee Two adopted a Canadian proposal resolving that the Russian proposals "as they now stand and the explanations given thereon do not provide an adequate basis for the development by the Committee of specific proposals for an effective system of international control of atomic energy." [20]

The reference to "explanation given thereon" might have been made partly with tongue in cheek. One of the major criticisms of the Soviet presentation was its failure to explain points which appeared vague to the majority delegates. For example,

[18] *Ibid.*, Annex 5, Appendix 5. Professor Zlotowski, a physicist, had extensive contacts with the West. From 1940-1947 he had taught at the University of Minnesota, Ohio State University and Vassar College.

[19] *Ibid.*, Annex 5, Appendix 1, p. 241.

[20] *Ibid.*, Part IV, pp. 95-96.

Frederick Osborn asked Gromyko, "What is this strict international control? Is it inspection?" Gromyko replied:

To the question, "What is strict international control?" I answer: The proposals submitted by the USSR delegation. They relate to the principal questions and not to all of them. If adopted, these proposals would constitute a basis for the establishment of complete international control.[21]

It was this circular type of argument which so exasperated and frustrated the non-Soviet representatives. Realizing Gromyko's inability to go beyond the explicit instructions set by the Soviet Government, Sir Alexander Cadogan compiled a list of the most pertinent questions which he submitted in writing to the Soviet delegation on August 11. He asked that these questions be submitted to the Soviet Government. Gromyko agreed to do so. Soviet Russia's answers were received September 5, too late for discussion before the Atomic Energy Commission's second report was due. The text of "Cadogan's questionnaire" and the Soviet answers were merely included without comment in the body of the report.[22] These questions and answers added nothing in the way of reconciliation of the points of contention. They, however, mark the last official clarification of its position which the Soviet Government would make in the next two and one-half years.

COMMITTEE TWO AND THE SECOND ATOMIC ENERGY COMMISSION REPORT

While the Working Committee was engaged in examining the Soviet February 18 amendments, Committee Two was concurrently seeking to develop the "specific proposals," for a concrete plan for international control of atomic energy. Committee Two's function during the summer of 1947 was to study in detail the questions left unanswered by the Atomic Energy

[21] *Ibid.*, Annex 5, Appendix 4, p. 261.
[22] The text of the "Cadogan Questionnaire" is in *ibid.*, Part IV, p. 92. The answers given by the Soviet Government are in *ibid.*, Part IV, pp. 93-95.

Commission in its First Report. These questions included: the detailed powers, characteristics and functions of the international control agency; means of organizing, financing, and staffing the agency; the relationship between the agency, United Nations, and participating States; powers of the agency in matters of research, development and planning; and the stages of transition to full international control of atomic energy. All of these questions had been considered in a general way in the First Report. Committee Two was to examine these subjects in detail and, if possible, make the specific recommendations to be embodied in a treaty.

With or without Soviet support the Western delegates were determined to forge ahead with a complete plan. Soviet intransigence posed a particularly difficult problem. The Western representatives were concerned lest the propaganda tactics of the Soviet delegates stalemate the progress of the Commission. Even before Committee Two's first session April 10, the Western delegates met privately and discussed among themselves the advisability of holding informal rather than formal committee sessions. The French, British, Canadian, and Belgian delegates felt that relatively informal meetings where the Russians could not air their views in public and would feel no need to make a record for themselves with their superiors in Moscow would facilitate progress. It was accordingly agreed among the majority delegates that they would propose a series of informal meetings to be held in a small office in New York City, at which there would be no regular interpreter and no record other than a brief summary of actions taken.

In order further to expedite the committee's work Frederick Osborn early in May proposed the use of small working groups, each studying one specific problem. Each group would receive working papers submitted by individual national delegations and then draft a paper embodying the consensus of the whole group. Osborn's plan was adopted along with the use of informal committee meetings. In accepting this plan the members of the committee acted on the understanding that their statements in the working groups were made in an individual capacity. It was understood that until the discussion reached the full committee stage no government was committed by any statement of its delegate.

From the point of view of those who sought expeditious committee action the plan offered the advantage of permitting greater flexibility in negotiation. Each delegate in the privacy of his working group could freely express the maximum limit beyond which his government was prepared to go on any issue; where grounds for compromise existed, he could compromise with a minimum loss of prestige. Propagandistic utterances, having no wide audiences, would be kept to a minimum; the smallness of the groups would permit greater participation by all delegates who had something to contribute; and it further permitted greater concentration of specialists within each group.

In accordance with this plan the committee established seven Working Groups. Six of the seven groups were made responsible for studying one part of the committee's work, and the seventh was to be a co-ordinating group. The seven Working Groups and the titles of the reports they were asked to prepare were as follows:

Working Group A. "Functions of the International Agency in Relation to Research and Development."
Working Group B. "Functions of the International Agency in Relation to Location and Mining of Ores."
Working Group C. "Functions of the International Agency in Relation to Processing and Purification of Source Material."
Working Groups D-E-F. "Functions of the International Agency in Relation to Stockpiling, Production, and Distribution of Nuclear Fuels and the Design, Construction, and Operation of Isotope Separation Plants and of Nuclear Reactors."
Working Group G. "Rights and Limitations of the International Agency in Relation to Inspections, Surveys, and Explorations."
Co-ordinating Group A-G. "Operational and Developmental Functions of the International Agency and Its Relation to Planning, Co-ordination and Direction of Atomic Activities." [23]

[23] Working Group A's paper was prepared by Sir Charles Darwin (United Kingdom), Professor Zlotowski (Poland), and Mr. Arneson (United States). See Second Report, Part I, pp. 9-10.
Working Group B's paper was prepared by General McNaughton (Canada),

Working Group A-3. "Organization and Administration of the International Agency." [24]

Throughout May and part of June these working groups carried on the bulk of the Atomic Energy Commission's work. They met in groups of three to eight in the offices of the various delegates in New York City. Over a period of several weeks a uniform procedure of operation developed. Before the basic paper on each topic was drafted by the group a preliminary discussion of the topic took place in an informal conversation of Committee Two. Another informal session followed completion of the paper after which revisions would be made to reflect the discussion in the informal conversations. During these informal sessions scientific advisers participated and proffered scientific and technical advice. Periodically the group leaders would meet to co-ordinate their reports and remove ambiguities, contradictions, and duplication in the papers. Finally each paper was considered formally in Committee Two and the full Commission. Ultimately the reports of these groups became the Second Report to the Security Council.

The Soviet delegates contributed even less to the Second Report than they had to the First Report. For the Russian delega-

---

Professor Errera (Belgium), Captain Alvaro Alberto (Brazil), Dr. Goldschmidt (France), and Dr. Vance (United States).

Working Group C's paper was prepared by Dr. Wei (China), Mr. el-Kourdajy (Syria), Dr. Fine (United States), and Mr. Harry (Australia). Professor D. V. Skobeltzyn (USSR) was asked to participate in the work of this group, but he declined.

Working Group D-E-F's paper was prepared by Col. Nichols (United States), Captain Alvaro Alberto, Sir Charles Darwin, Mr. Harry, General McNaughton and Mr. de Rose (France).

Working Group G's paper was prepared by Mr. de Rose, General McNaughton, Sir George Thomson (United Kingdom), Professor Zlotowski, Dr. Briggs (Australia), Dr. de Holte-Castello (Colombia) and Mr. Arneson.

Co-ordinating Group A-G's paper was prepared by Mr. de Rose, Sir George Thomson, General McNaughton, Dr. Wei and Dr. Vance.

[24] The seventh Working Group (Working Group A-3) which was concerned with "Organization and Administration of the International Agency" never completed its report. Committee Two came to the conclusion March 30, 1948, that, until there was agreement on the powers and functions of an international control agency, it was useless to discuss the organization of such an agency.

tion the Working Committee's study of the Russian proposals had a higher priority than the concurrent deliberations within Committee Two and its working groups. Repeatedly the Russian and Polish delegates had stressed the necessity of a plan based upon "unanimous agreement"—by that they meant one acceptable to both the Soviet Union and the United States. To A. A. Gromyko and D. V. Skobeltzyn the work of a committee bent upon filling in the details of the plan outlined in the First Report could offer no advantage for the Soviet Government. Early in May, when the plan to break up into working groups was adopted, Professor D. V. Skobeltzyn was asked to participate in the group studying "Functions of the International Agency in Relation to Processing and Purification of Source Material." Skobeltzyn declared that, though he considered Committee Two's working plan attractive in many ways, inasmuch as the plan was based upon the framework of the First Report which the Soviet Government had not accepted, he could not be a part of the group. He asked that his name be deleted from Working Group C. The Soviet representative did agree to attend the informal conversations of Committee Two as an observer.[25]

No less than their objection to Committee Two's objective the Soviets condemned its procedure. They charged that "red tape" and "procedural delays" resulted from the tactics of United States representatives who "in general preferred informal conferences of experts to official discussion in the Commission."[26] In vain did the Soviet delegates press for formal meetings when in early June the working documents came up for consideration by Committee Two in plenary session.

Dr. Skobeltzyn, who represented his government as an "observer" during Committee Two's informal sessions commanded considerable respect among the Western delegates as a scientist. Some, however, felt that his activity in the informal sessions was deliberately obstructionist. They attributed this to orders from his superiors. Frederick Osborn felt that Skobeltzyn was

[25] *AEC Second Report*, Annex 3, p. 120.
[26] Modest Rubenstein, "Once More on the Atomic Energy Commission," *New Times*, September 3, 1947.

particularly afraid of Gromyko.[27] He and other delegates believed that Skobeltzyn had to be careful to avoid giving the impression that the Soviet delegates were not forcefully presenting the position of their government. Frequently as each of the various working papers were presented in draft form before informal sessions, Skobeltzyn would ask for the floor and launch an attack on the honesty, fairness and legality of the procedure under which the paper had been produced. These attacks were often on the motives and personalities of the delegates and had little reference to the actual content of the paper. It was noted that before speaking Skobeltzyn made certain that a stenographic record of the proceedings was kept even though the records were released only to the delegates for the use of their governments.[28]

[27] Osborn, *loc. cit.*, p. 230.
[28] Frederick H. Osborn, "The Search for Atomic Control," *The Atlantic*, April, 1948, pp. 49-50. The American delegate has recorded a vivid description of Skobeltzyn's behavior before one of the committee sessions. Osborn does not give the date of the particular incident except that it occurred during the end of May.
    "At an informal meeting held in New York a number of these papers [the reports of the subgroups] were presented in fairly complete form and for the first time it was evident that the Commission was going to be in a position to put out a Second Report which would contain sound and carefully written specific proposals. Dr. Skobeltzyn was sitting in, in his position as observer, flanked by the two younger members of the Soviet staff who usually accompanied him wherever he went. As the discussion developed, one of these young men handed Dr. Skobeltzyn a paper. When he opened and read it, he became highly excited and interrupted with the demand that he be given the floor at once. The Chairman suggested that the delegate then speaking might complete his remarks, but Dr. Skobeltzyn insisted he be given the floor. The other delegate withdrew and Dr. Skobeltzyn then spoke quite excitedly. He demanded, first, that a verbatim record be made of what he was about to say. When this was arranged (fortunately a stenographer-interpreter was present, although no record was being made of any other talks) Dr. Skobeltzyn launched into an extraordinarily bitter attack on the meetings and the people taking part in them. He said that the meetings were illegal, conducted according to unauthorized procedures, and represented a treacherous attempt of the tools of the ruling clique to develop their sinister purposes, secretly and without participation of the Soviet Union, and that he, for one, repudiated any part of the proceedings; all of this delivered with much vehemence. When he was through he handed to the men sitting behind him the paper they had given him. None of the other delegates who were present at this outburst made any reply." Osborn, "Negotiating on Atomic Energy, 1946-47," *loc. cit.*, p. 225.

The six working groups and two committees of the Atomic Energy Commission worked diligently throughout August in order to complete the Second Report before the September session of the General Assembly. The detailed plan which emerged was primarily the product of Committee Two's six working groups. Essentially this Second Report was an amplification of the First Report. But it was more than that, too. It advanced several ideas not contained in the First Report. These deserve particular attention before going on to an over-all review of the contents of the Second Report. There were three important new features in the Commission's Second Report. They were (1), the plan to curtail the peaceful development of atomic energy by individual nations in order to safeguard the over-all security of international control; (2), the ownership powers of the contemplated control agency were considerably expanded; and (3), restraints were placed upon the production policy of the control agency by the use of a quota system.

International control of atomic energy posed a problem for the proponents of the national development of atomic energy for peaceful purposes. It was obvious that as more and more atomic installations were demanded to supply fissionable fuel for power, the greater would be the difficulty of an international agency to assure that none of the fuel escaped into weapons production.

The First Report suggested, but did not reconcile, the problem of conflict between security and national development of atomic energy for peaceful uses. In its Second Report the Atomic Energy Commission resolved the conflict by establishing security as "the paramount requirement to be fulfilled." [29] National control of atomic energy for peaceful purposes was, in the opinion of the Commission, incompatible with the requirements of international security. But this was not all. Even with international control, atomic energy production for peaceful purposes would have to be kept to a minimum. The report dampened considerably the hopes of any who saw in atomic energy a quick substitute for conventional fuels. It noted that:

[29] *AEC Second Report*, Part II, chap. I, p. 13.

In considering what the initial mandate to be given to the agency should be, recognition was given to the conflict between the requirements of security and those of preparing for large-scale application of peaceful developments. It is recommended, therefore, that the disposition to be included initially in the treaty or convention should make it mandatory for the agency to keep the production of nuclear fuel, in a form suitable for ready conversion to use in atomic weapons, *at the minimum required for efficient operating procedure necessitated by actual beneficial uses,* including research and development.[30]

In itself this passage demarcates one of the principal distinctions between the two Atomic Energy Commission reports. In general the emphasis of the First Report followed that of the Acheson-Lilienthal Plan in encouraging the positive development of nuclear fuel production. Here was no such encouragement. While not positively discouraging nuclear production for peaceful purposes, the report would have nuclear fuel production limited to the minimum required for actual beneficial uses as of the date of the signing of a control agreement. Insofar as the peaceful uses of nuclear fuel in 1947 were very limited, it is difficult to imagine much of an expansion in the future had an agreement with the Soviet Union been consummated during 1947.

A second important modification of the majority plan concerned the agency's powers of ownership. Going beyond the recommendations of the First Report, the second one called for international ownership of mined uranium and thorium ore, all facilities for producing dangerous nuclear fuels, and all nuclear fuel. No nation or person could lawfully possess or dispose of any source material after it had been mined or any nuclear fuel after it had been refined. Ownership by the agency of source materials and fuels was defined as including the exclusive right to move or lease the materials, the right to use and produce energy from them and the same rights with regard to all products formed from them. It was clearly specified, however, that the materials and facilities held by the agency would be held "in trust" for the signatory states to the treaty. As trustee for

[30] *Ibid.,* Part II, chap. I, p. 16. Italics added.

the signatory states the agency would be bound by the provisions of the treaty or convention in regard to their disposition.

The third new element of the majority plan added an important limitation to the authority of the control agency. With regard to the authority of the agency to make substantive decisions on the mining, refinement and use of nuclear ores and fuels the report stated:

> . . . it is recommended that the agency should not be authorized to define the policy to be pursued in the production and use of atomic energy, but that the principles governing this policy should be established by international agreement, and that it should be the duty and responsibility of the agency to implement such an agreement. It was decided that the agency should not be given the right to decide this policy, because the signatory nations would rightly require that policies which substantially effect world security should be defined in the treaty or convention. Perhaps the most striking example is provided by the production of nuclear fuel. If the agency were free to decide the rate of production of nuclear fuel and were to embark upon a policy of production exceeding recognized or actual beneficial uses . . . the conditions of world security would be greatly affected. Moreover, the possible exercise of these powers might cause serious conflicts within the agency, since the establishment of quotas for distribution constitutes a most difficult task. The treaty or convention establishing the agency should lay down fairly strictly the general principles to be followed in deciding such questions and should even go so far, in certain cases, as to prescribe a numerical quota. Any modification of these principles should be subject to a revision procedure, the rule of which should be laid down in the treaty or convention . . .[31]

The creation of a quota system in the treaty itself went further than any proposal hitherto made to meet the Soviet objection to an all-powerful "supertrust" which would infringe upon Russian national sovereignty. Quotas were contemplated for the mining of ores, the distribution of refinement facilities throughout the world and the disposition of the end product, highly dangerous nuclear fuel. As a suggestion for a quota principle for mining ores, the report recommended that comparable national deposits throughout the world be depleted proportion-

---

[31] *Ibid.*, Part II, chap. I, pp. 15-16.

ately. Producing plants (for example, refineries) could be located wherever each nation concerned wanted them, with agency agreement. But the number and type of such plants would be established by a prior quota or other agreed-upon system. Power would be made available "on a fair and equitable basis to any nation that may require it." [32] As will be noted below, the system of quotas established by treaty was one of the few features of the report acceptable to the Soviet Union.

Other than these three features the Second Report essentially was an amplification of the First. Its provisions can best be summarized by a review of the reports of the six working groups, five of which became chapters in the final report. The group reporting on "Functions of the International Agency in Relation to Research and Development" added nothing substantially new. It reaffirmed and amplified several proposals which had already met with strong Soviet objections. Chief among these were the affirmation of extensive freedom of research for the control agency and limitation of that freedom for nations to "nondangerous" activity (as defined by the agency).

Working Group B reported on "Functions of the International Agency in Relation to the Location and Mining of Ores." Mention has been made above of its proposal for international ownership of all ore once separated from its natural deposits. Equitable compensation would be paid for all uranium and thorium ores acquired. Mines, mills and dumps which are used in extracting ore might be owned either by the international agency or nations or individual persons. Before any control could be exercised over ore, however, the agency would have to know in detail the location and size of all natural ore deposits throughout the world. For this purpose it must be endowed with "unequivocal powers of survey." This included the right to inspect, survey and explore all sources of raw materials reported by any nation. Every nation would be obligated to furnish the agency with reports describing the location, amount, character, concentration and mode of occurrence of source material known to be present in deposits, mines or dumps,

[32] *Ibid.*, Part II, chap. I, p. 16.

or elsewhere within its territory. On the basis of these reports, routine inspections and surveys would be conducted. Where the agency had reason to believe that a nation was not revealing all its sources of material, it would be empowered to conduct special investigations. For both routine and special investigations the agency would have unimpeded freedom of movement in a nation.

The provisions mentioned above, establishing national quotas for atomic energy production, would apply also to the mining of ores. The agency itself would be empowered to establish annual quotas to determine how much raw material each nation would be permitted to mine. It was felt that the treaty, rather than providing for specific mining quotas, should establish the principle which should guide the agency in making specific national quotas. The report established as the basis of a nation's mining quota the following principle: ". . . the ratio of the quota of a nation to its currently exploitable reserves shall be approximately the same as the ratio of the annual world needs to the total currently exploitable world reserves." [33] Thus, for example, if the agency determined that only 10 per cent of the world's exploitable resources were needed to fulfill the "world's needs," each nation would be obligated to contribute approximately 10 per cent of its exploitable reserves of uranium and thorium ores.

Working Group C reported on "Functions of the International Agency in Relation to Processing and Purification of Source Material." Processing and purification involve intermediate steps between the mining of ores and the production of fissionable nuclear fuel. There are two types of facilities which purify source materials: refineries and chemical and metallurgical plants. Refineries are closely associated with mills; materials treated in refineries are not at such an advanced stage in the process of producing atomic energy as the products from chemical and metallurgical plants.

In the case of refineries the international agency was given the authority to determine whether it or a nation or person could

[33] *Ibid.*, Part II, chap. III, p. 38.

own, operate and manage a particular refinery. However, no nation or person could own, operate or manage a refinery without a license from the control agency. Provision was made for each license to provide the agency such extensive powers of inspection and control [34] that at all times the agency would be sure each refinery fully complied with its policy. In addition to its specified authority granted by the license, the agency reserved the power to modify the provisions of the license to revoke the license, taking over the ownership and management of the refinery, with due compensation to the owner. '

In the case of chemical and metallurgical plants the agency assumed outright ownership and management. Nations and persons were categorically prohibited from ownership, possessing, operating or managing any chemical or metallurgical plants which treated key substances.

The most dangerous phase of atomic energy production, the direct production of fissionable nuclear fuel by isotope separation plants and nuclear reactors was covered by the report on "Functions of the International Agency in Relation to Stockpiling, Production and Distribution of Nuclear Fuels and the Design, Construction and Operation of Isotope Separation Plants and of Nuclear Reactors" (Working Groups D-E-F). The Second Report repeated the demand of its predecessor calling for international ownership of all nuclear fuel and "dangerous facilities" capable of producing or utilizing it.

Working Group G's report, "Rights and Limitations of the International Agency in Relation to Inspections. Surveys and Explorations," was the last and lengthiest of the chapters on control. It sought to draw a line between the agency's powers of investigation, which would necessarily be wide to be effective, and the limitations on the agency's powers required to avoid undue interference with activities unrelated to atomic energy.

[34] *Ibid.*, Part II, chap. IV, pp. 42, 43, 45. In general there was no presumption of ownership of refineries by nations or the agency. However, the report did stipulate that "Refineries customarily engaged in the processing of source material for the purposes of extracting other important constituents will normally be owned, operated and managed by nations or persons, and, in that event, shall be granted licenses by the agency for this purpose." *Ibid.*, Part II, chap. IV, p. 43.

Among the many powers assigned to the international agency, none were more pervasive than its powers of inspection. All duly accredited inspectors were to be accorded special rights and privileges of entry into, movement within and egress from the territory of all participating nations. Where inspectors were engaged in geological and mineralogical ground surveys they had to be admitted to private as well as public lands including military or other restricted areas.[35]

No nation, least of all the Soviet Union, could be expected to consent to such infringements upon its territorial sovereignty without the erection of a system of guarantees to prevent abuses of these powers by the agency. It was the guarantee provisions of this report that marked the most significant advance of the Second Report from the First on the subject of inspections. Four general limitations were made applicable to all inspections:

(1) Inspections, surveys or explorations shall be conducted by the agency only for purposes related to atomic energy. Inspections, surveys or explorations which, although properly commenced, are found by the agency during their course to be serving no such authorized purpose shall be discontinued as soon as such fact becomes apparent to it.

(2) In conducting inspections, surveys and explorations, the agency and its personnel shall have regard to domestic laws and customs relating to rights of personal privacy and private property to the fullest extent consistent with the effective discharge of their duties under the terms of the treaty or convention.

(3) Neither the agency nor its personnel shall disclose confidential or private information unrelated to atomic energy which is acquired in the course of inspections, surveys or explorations. The agency shall take special precautions to prevent such disclosures by its personnel.

(4) The agency shall be liable to give just compensation for damages caused by its personnel in the course of inspections, surveys or explorations.[36]

Advance notice to the nation concerned had to be given by the agency for every geological survey or exploration. If it desired, the nation under survey could send a liaison representative to

[35] *Ibid.*, Part II, chap. VI, pp. 59 and 63.
[36] *Ibid.*, Part II, chap. VI, p. 64.

accompany the inspectors. This proposal did not, however, require the agency at all times to give a nation advance notice of inspection. Any activity which was managed, licensed or leased by the agency or generally open to the public was exempt from the obligation to give advance notice.

Special consideration was given to inspections for suspected illegal, clandestine activities. Here, of course, no advance notice would be given. The working group recognized that inspections of this sort could be abused and, if abused, would lead not only to irritation but serious friction. For one thing, not only were the powers of inspection very broad, but in so investigating the agency would be questioning the good faith of a government. In order to minimize possible friction, the report proposed a system of warrants for inspections for illegal activity. Inspectors for clandestine activities had to receive a special warrant from any one of three sources: (1), by a domestic body or officer of competent jurisdiction upon a showing of "probable or reasonable cause"; (2), by warrant or other authorization issued by an international court or body of competent jurisdiction, also upon a showing of "probable or reasonable cause"; (3), by special consent of the nation or lawful consent of a responsible official. Normally, but not necessarily, recourse would first be made to domestic courts or officials; and for this purpose participating nations were called upon to adopt legislation creating local courts and officials with authority to issue such warrants. But neither a national denial nor undue delay by a domestic court would preclude the agency from receiving the necessary warrant from an international court. Whether issued domestically or internationally, the warrants were to describe the premises or areas authorized to be entered and the facilities or other property authorized to be inspected or the areas to be surveyed. Military facilities or reservations were not exempt.[37]

Lastly, the report proposed that the treaty authorize the agency to conduct spot aerial surveys every two years over areas not exceeding 5 per cent of a nation's territory or two thousand miles, whichever was the larger. The location of the areas

[37] *Ibid.*, Part II, chap. VI, p. 65.

for these routine aerial surveys would be determined by the agency. Every nation so checked by air would receive advance notice and would examine the aircraft used by the agency and send at least one observer on each spot flight. Similar provision was made for routine and exploratory aerial surveys over areas known to contain uranium and thorium ores. As in the case of ground inspections to verify reports of clandestine activities or to clear up suspicion, aerial inspections for this purpose would require the consent of the inspected nation or authorization by warrant. Military facilities and reservations were not exempt from observation by aerial flights, whatever the purpose of the survey or inspection.[38]

Soviet opposition to the Second Report was a foregone conclusion. The refusal of the Soviet delegation to so much as take part in the discussions of the working groups presaged their opposition. The majority had a good preview of coming attractions when Committee Two formally reviewed Working Group A's report on research and development in mid-July of 1947. At that time Andrei Gromyko and Professor Zlotowski vigorously attacked those recommendations which limited national freedom to engage in atomic research and which invested ownership rights over plants and raw materials in the control agency.

The Soviet critique in July offered one ray of hope: they did endorse the proposals on quotas. When the proposal that quotas for the peaceful use of atomic energy be fixed in the treaty was originally introduced by the French, Gromyko displayed considerable interest and said it was something the Russians would like to discuss. He informed Committee Two that the Soviet Union considered a quota system as the best method of protecting the interests of all nations which had atomic industries. By incorporating a system of quotas in the treaty creating atomic control, it would be possible for every nation to develop its "proper, fair and just place" in the field of atomic development. Gromyko suggested that here was a subject upon which

[38] *Ibid.*, Part II, chap. VI, pp. 66-68.

the Atomic Energy Commission could reach a greater degree of agreement than had existed in the past. He called for the establishment of a special convention "in which all countries would assume specific obligations." [39] This acceptance by the Soviet Government constituted the most significant Soviet concurrence with the West since Molotov had agreed in the fall of 1946 to inspection and elimination of the veto in the day-to-day activities of the control agency. The prospects of it being used as a peg for a larger working agreement were marred by the over-all lack of agreement on other aspects of control.

It is even questionable that the Russian leaders entertained much expectation of results from agreement on the subject of quotas. In its accounts of what was going on in the Atomic Energy Commission negotiations, the Soviet press hardly mentioned the subject of quotas. *Pravda* and *Izvestia* continued to speak of the majority proposals as an attempt by Western monopolists to exploit all atomic industries throughout the world. *Pravda* on August 22 published a lengthy account of the work of the Commission. In it the proposed control organ was referred to as "the sovereign master of the sources of atomic energy in all countries of the world." "To it," continued the article, "would belong the rights of property, directing production and research everywhere it thinks worthwhile. The national sovereignty of other governments is thrown off as an 'historical remnant.' " [40] No mention was made of quotas as a check on the authority of the control agency, even though Gromyko had spoken a month previously of the possibility of East-West agreement on use of a quota system to guide the decision-making power of an international agency.

Committee Two reserved late August and early September for final over-all review of the Commission's Second Report. September 16 was the date of the second General Assembly's convocation and hence the deadline for the Commission's report. Russian and Polish opposition to the heart of the report—

[39] *Ibid.*, Annex 3, p. 106.
[40] M. Marinin, "Pochemu do sikh por net kontrolya nad atomny energiei?" (Why is there no control of atomic energy to this time?), *Pravda*, August 22, 1947.

the proposals of the six working groups—was emphatic. Andrei Gromyko delivered his government's judgment in a long speech August 29. "These proposals," he said, "are vicious in their foundation and . . . cannot constitute a basis for agreement on the establishment of international control of atomic energy." [41] His criticism of them involved a reiteration of several old themes: they relegated prohibition of atomic weapons to a secondary position; they were an attempt to secure the monopolistic interests of the United States; they failed to establish a date for the commencement of controls; and they violated the principles of the United Nations. In all, the Soviet Government found them to be so worthless that it declined even to submit any ameliorative amendments.

Following this speech the non-Soviet delegates abandoned any hope of reaching unanimous agreement by September 15. In the final vote before sending the completed report to the full Commission, five of the working paper documents were approved by a ten to two vote, with Poland and the Soviet Union voting negatively. On the paper, "Rights and Limitations of the International Agency in Relation to Inspections, Surveys and Explorations," the vote was ten to one with Poland abstaining. [42]

The Russian delegation continued its opposition to the Second Report when it received final consideration before the full Atomic Energy Commission on September 10 and 11. Almost an entire session of the Commission was occupied by a blistering attack on the motives and accomplishments of the majority delegates and the United States in particular. Even for so caustic a speaker as Andrei Gromyko, his attack was felt by many observers to be the tartest ever delivered by him. [43] Realizing that the sentiment for approval by the Commission was unstoppable, Gromyko could do no more than point to the fate of the First Report which also contained "a number of completely unacceptable provisions." His statement of unacceptable provisions

[41] *AEC Second Report,* Annex 3, Appendix 1, p. 134.
[42] *AEC/C.2/115,* pp. 3-6.
[43] See the article by A. M. Rosenthal in the *New York Times,* September 11, 1947.

was a summary of objections and criticisms made many times previously. Most objectionable to the Soviet Union was the proposal to grant to the international agency ownership rights over plants producing atomic energy and over raw materials. Aside from being contrary to national sovereignty, ownership was "radically unsound."

> Ownership is not control [said Gromyko], unless we are to reduce the idea of control to an absurdity, or to imply a kind of control of the organ by the organ. The very idea of international control precludes any possibility whatsoever of monopolistic ownership of atomic plants, even though such ownership were vested in an international organ. International control of atomic energy means a system of international measures based on the existence of plants for the production of atomic energy held by the States participating in such a system.[44]

What Gromyko said of control, he applied to the management of plants and the right of the agency to grant licenses for the construction and operation of state factories producing atomic energy. In conclusion, he called for the complete rejection of the report.

On September 11 the Second Report was approved by a ten to one vote. Australia, Belgium, Brazil, Canada, China, Colombia, France, Syria, the United Kingdom and the United States, voted in favor; the Soviet Union voted against, and Poland abstained.

[44] UN, *AECOR Second Year No. 3, 13 Meeting 10 September 1947*, p. 44.

5: TOTAL DEADLOCK:

SEPTEMBER 1947-JUNE 1948

THE ADOPTION OF ITS SECOND REPORT IN SEPTEMBER, 1947, marked a climax in the life of the Atomic Energy Commission. Together with the First Report it clearly established the scientific assumptions upon which a control system could be built; it described the kind of organization necessary to guarantee national and international security; and it prescribed in detail the powers and rules of operation to make it effective. This Second Report, although built upon the foundation of the First Report, differed in two important and diverse ways. On the one hand it increased the power of the control organization by providing for even more strict regulation of atomic fuel production, including outright ownership of uranium and thorium once removed from the mines. On the other hand it limited the authority of the control agency by erecting safeguards against its abuse. Most important in this connection were the provisions for production quotas which would be written into the treaty itself and would prescribe exactly how much fissionable fuel each nation could produce. As a further check on agency powers of inspection and exploration the report established a system of search warrants.

Technically, the Commission had fulfilled its mandate under the General Assembly resolution of January, 1946. Politically, the Commission had failed. It had failed to reconcile the Soviet and Western positions on any of the major points of dispute. Repeatedly the Soviet representatives condemned the work of the majority which failed to adjust to the minority positions. When in early September the Second Report was nearing final approval in committee, Professor Skobeltzyn chided the committee for being more concerned with deadlines than agreement with the Soviet Union.[1] To a large extent his criticism was valid.

Behind this kind of Soviet criticism lay a conception of the Atomic Energy Commission markedly at variance with the majority point of view. To the latter the Commission was primarily a technical—not a political—body. It was created to determine the terms of an international treaty to control atomic energy. The majority looked upon the political differences which made agreement on atomic energy between East and West impossible as outside the sphere of its authority. To the Russians, atomic energy negotiations in the United Nations could not be divorced from the political events outside the United Nations. They could not understand the Anglo-American insistence that the technology of atomic production circumscribed the types of control plans that could insure international security. Andrei Gromyko insisted before one of the working groups that:

The problem of international control over atomic energy is, first of all, a political problem . . .

. . . the tendency to which I have referred to subordinate the political tasks of control to considerations of technical detail threatens the whole establishment of international control over atomic energy.

I have pointed to this circumstance because the majority in the Atomic Energy Commission still holds the point of view that it is necessary to conduct negotiations using as a starting point only matters of technology and production. This point of view had already done much harm to our negotiations, and those who share it are responsible to a great extent for the impasse which the work of the Atomic Energy Commission has now reached.[2]

The Soviet representatives acted as though operating on the assumption that before any agreement on atomic energy was

[1] AEC/C.1/75.
[2] AEC/C.1/PV. 42.

possible, either an over-all political settlement had to be made, or at the least, that the atomic agreement must be part of such a settlement.

At the same time no one was more aware than the Russians of the unlikelihood of a political settlement during 1947-1948. Two meetings of the ex-Allied foreign ministers, one in Moscow during the spring and the other in London during the winter of 1947, failed to resolve the problem of German unification. East-West relations deteriorated rapidly following these abortive conferences. They reached a postwar nadir with the communist coup d'état in Czechoslovakia in February, 1948, and the Berlin blockade in June.

The Kremlin interpreted the American responses to the challenge of Soviet expansion in Europe as proof that Western capitalism was seeking to build up an anti-Soviet coalition in Europe. This was particularly true of the Truman Doctrine and the Marshall Plan. Undoubtedly the gravest threat to Soviet political objectives in Europe during this period was the American program of aid for European economic recovery. From its first comment on June 16, 1947, in *Pravda*, the Soviet Government continued to attack the Marshall Plan and its later derivatives as a veiled attempt by the United States to secure control of the "Marshallized" nations of Europe. From the Soviet point of view the infringement on national sovereignty in Europe caused by American economic aid was in substance no different from what the United States was trying to do on a world scale with its atomic energy proposals. During the summer of 1947 the Soviet press made frequent equations between the Baruch Plan and the Marshall Plan as twin instruments of American expansion.[3]

[3] For example, *Pravda*, on August 22, 1947, made the following attack on American policy:
"Of course American pretension to world supremacy cannot be reconciled with the preservation by other governments of their national sovereignty. The liquidation, or in all events, the infringement upon, and the restriction of their national sovereignty appears not only the purpose, but the conditions of the realization of the policy of expansion of the United States of America, to the service of which have been placed the political, military and economic levers. In this sense, atomic diplomacy unites the 'Baruch Plan' with the 'Marshall Plan,' and brings down the free and independent governments to the role of offices without rights of the all mighty American

DEADLOCK IN THE COMMITTEES

During the winter and spring of 1948 a final effort was made in committee to come to some sort of an agreement with the Soviet Union. The Security Council did not in this period examine the Second Report because of other urgent political questions on its agenda. The Commission decided to utilize both the Working Committee and Committee Two in order to expedite negotiations. It was agreed that Committee Two would work on the organizational and administrative aspects of the control agency and that the Working Committee would reopen the study of the Russian proposals. The two committees met concurrently in parallel sessions.

Committee Two met only five times in 1948, four times formally and once informally. Whereas the Soviet Government refused to permit its representatives to take part in the work of this committee during 1947, it now reversed itself and assigned Messrs. Gromyko and Skobeltzyn to take part in the discussions. Neither Gromyko nor Skobeltzyn had changed in their position of hostility to the majority plan. Gromyko had, however, stated earlier his willingness to take part in any study of the composition of the international control agency.

Taking Gromyko at his word, Mr. François de Rose (France) proposed at the first 1948 meeting on January 19 that Committee Two limit itself to "Organizational Structure" so as to encourage Soviet participation. Organizational structure concerned the composition of the agency's board of directors. There had been very little consideration of this matter earlier because there were so many prior subjects which required agreement before the agency's composition need be discussed. The only known Soviet policy toward the composition of the agency's control board had been the fifth of their June 11 proposals which provided that the control commission would be composed of the representatives of states-members of the Atomic Energy Commission and

---

atomic concern. It is a fact that the businessmen of atomic diplomacy would want to place a lock on the individual existence of sovereign governments."

that the personnel of the commission should be selected "on an international basis."

The Russian delegation had consistently taken the position that discussion of the agency's composition was generally meaningless until agreement on the broader principles of control had been established. This attitude was one of the primary causes of the committee's inconclusive accomplishments throughout the early months of 1948. After the committee agreed to limit its discussion to organizational structure, Gromyko reversed his previous intimations of co-operation and stated that as far as he was concerned the committee was wasting its time "studying details." For its part, he said, the Soviet delegation would limit its activity to stating its opposition to the program of work.[4]

Committee Two held its last meeting March 30. By then the general consensus was that further discussion offered little profit. Even at this meeting negotiations by both sides had degenerated into quibbling as to who was responsible for the committee's deadlock. Skobeltzyn complained bitterly that as soon as the Soviet delegation joined the committee it ceased to function. Mr. Miles (the United Kingdom) pointed out that the majority realized that any discussion of the agency's organization would be somewhat hypothetical until more was known of the nature of the organization. Deciding upon the organization, he said, would be like frosting a cake; but the committee had not yet agreed on how to bake the cake. Skobeltzyn could not refrain from a parting jibe. Referring to Mr. Miles' culinary analogy, he insisted that the bakers had baked a large and heavy cake (the majority proposals). He, Skobeltzyn, preferred an architectural metaphor: in his eyes the majority had created a huge building, on a foundation gravely weakened by disagreement, and then found it impossible to put on a roof. Without taking a decision the committee adjourned *sine die*.

The debate in the Working Committee was more prolonged and vigorous but equally as repetitious as that of Committee

[4] *AEC/C.2/SR.42*, p. 2.

Two. Beginning January 16, 1948, the Working Committee devoted seven meetings to a detailed consideration of the Soviet June 11 proposals one by one. Three additional meetings were then devoted to a review of the proposals as a whole. The Russians again sought to have the committee formally record some majority agreement with the Soviet proposals. They had nothing new to offer and there was no indication that the Soviet Government intended any concessions whatsoever for purposes of negotiations. On March 9, shortly before discussions were terminated, Gromyko admitted that "we do not have any intention of giving a new interpretation to our old proposals."[5]

To the majority delegates the discussions had merit only to the extent that the Soviet Union might offer clarifications to their original proposals—clarifications which might reveal some common ground. They, therefore, engaged the Soviet delegates in a series of questions. Throughout most of the debate Mr. Osborn, the American delegate, remained silent while the representatives from China, Canada, France and the United Kingdom did most of the questioning. Two aspects of the Soviet position were particularly disturbing to the majority: (1), Soviet insistence upon a convention on prohibition before control was established; and (2), the Soviet refusal to endow the control agency with adequate investigatory powers.

If there had been any doubts as to Soviet firmness on the prerequisite of a convention on prohibition before a convention on control was signed, Gromyko removed them. In response to a question by Mr. John Babbitt (Canada) whether the Soviet Union might agree that a convention on prohibition be made conditional to the satisfactory implementation of a control convention Gromyko replied:

We consider that the convention on the prohibition of atomic weapons must be not only signed but also put into force before the other convention is concluded. Otherwise, the signing of the first convention would not make sense. We should sign it and then leave it as a piece of paper. In saying that the first convention

[5] *AEC/C.1/PV.40.*

must be concluded we mean that it must be signed, ratified and put into force.[6]

Dr. Wei (China) then asked what assurance the majority would have that once the first convention was signed a second convention would be concluded. There was no lack of frankness in Gromyko's answer:

It is difficult for me to understand what the Chinese Representative has in mind. He speaks about guarantees. I think he understands very well that it is impossible to speak in such terms in connection with the second convention, on which agreement has not yet been reached. I may ask the same question: whether the other members will guarantee that they will agree with our point of view on this subject. The second convention—the establishment of a system of control and inspection—and any other convention should be formulated as a result of negotiations. It would be wrong to speak in terms of guarantees given in advance of the negotiations. I think this point is so simple to understand that it is not desirable to dwell on it at length.

The second convention should come about as the result of our negotiations in the Atomic Energy Commission and in the Security Council, under which the Atomic Energy Commission carries out its work. If we reach an agreement as a result of such negotiations, then the Convention will be concluded. If there is found to be no basis for agreement, then naturally the convention cannot be concluded, whether it be the second convention or any other convention.[7]

[6] *AEC/C.1/PV 36.*
[7] *AEC/C.1/SR. 36,* p. 5. On February 5 Mr. Miles (United Kingdom) asked Gromyko: "If we were to make the important concession of agreeing that there should be two separate conventions, and if, furthermore, we were to agree to the preparation of the convention on prohibition now, would the representative of the Soviet Union meet us by agreeing that implementation could be postponed until we had also agreed on the terms of the second convention on enforcement?" This suggestion closely resembles the idea of simultaneous conclusion of two conventions which the Soviet Union itself proposed almost a year later. Gromyko in response to this question answered evasively and then himself asked Mr. Miles if his question was based upon "curiosity" or the possibility of concluding a convention on prohibition. *AEC/C.1/SR. 37,* pp. 2-3.
It is possible that at this time the majority and minority positions on the question of priorities might have been bridged, but none of the major Western powers followed up on Gromyko's counterquestion. Thus when the Soviet proposal for a simultaneous conclusion of two conventions (see page

Furthermore, when asked point blank whether the convention on prohibition implied the destruction of existing atomic bombs, Gromyko replied, point blank, "yes . . ." This was in effect a direct challenge to the United States that it must destroy its atomic bombs before the Soviet Union would agree to a control plan.

Another series of questions directed to Gromyko related to the agency's powers of inspection under the Soviet plan. Mr. de Rose (France) asked for clarification of the Soviet Union's stand on the investigation of clandestine operations. In answering this and similar requests which bordered on those parts of the Soviet position which were either negative or considerably less positive than the majority proposals, Gromyko was very evasive. He replied to Mr. de Rose's request, "I should only like to say that our position is to be found in our statements concerning this, as well as other questions and, therefore, I believe there is no necessity for repetition." [8]

This type of answer discouraged the majority, but they persisted. The fifth of the Soviet June 11 proposals had provided for "periodic" inspection and this was particularly incompatible with the majority plan. Gromyko was pressed to amplify the meaning of "periodic." He defined "periodically" in his proposals to mean that inspection would not be a continuous process but would be carried out at definite intervals which could be varied by the Commission. Inspection, he said, should be a permanent and continuous operation for the control commission, but not for a given enterprise or facility. Permanent inspection over all plants and facilities, he insisted, would cease to be inspection and would become supervision or management. In response to a question from the French delegate whether states which were parties to the control convention could deny entrance to the inspectors, Gromyko replied that every govern-

---

140 in chapter VI) was made in 1948 the East-West position had so hardened that one concession more or less was meaningless. Actually there is little doubt but that even early in 1948 a major Soviet concession on the question of priorities would not have produced an over-all agreement.
[8] *AEC/C.1/PV 39.*

ment must retain the right to prohibit inspectors in individual cases upon personal grounds.[9]

Almost without exception none of the debate in the Working Committee involved real negotiations. There was no give and take. Gromyko repeated the same proposals and when asked for clarification either repeated the same formula or referred his questioners to previous statements. By March it was becoming fully apparent that the questioning technique was futile. The major cause of this futility was the Soviet resistance to probing by the majority delegates. Following a series of questions on the technical problems of control and inspection asked by Mr. de Rose and Mr. Wei, Gromyko erupted:

> It seems to me that, in substance, there are no unanswered questions in so far as questions which merit the attention of the Committee or questions which follow directly from the discussion are concerned. I believe that these questions have received their appropriate answer. But I should like to draw the attention of the Committee to the fact that one may ask questions indefinitely; one might think of tens of hundreds of questions, and devote as many meetings to these questions and to the answers which have to be given to them.[10]

One serious attempt was made to circumvent the sterility of the debates. Frederick Osborn suggested February 16 that the delegations might be better informed on each other's position if some informal conversations were held in advance of Committee Two's formal sessions. This suggestion did not meet with Gromyko's approval. Gromyko explained that he would have some difficulty in reporting to his government under such a procedure because he would not know whether the opinions expressed by other delegates would be personal or official government policy. Such a procedure he felt made negotiations difficult.[11]

---

[9] *AEC/C.1/SR. 37*, p. 6 and *AEC/C.1/SR. 38*, p. 3.
[10] *AEC/C.1/PV. 38.*
[11] Gromyko did offer a suggestion for a modification of Osborn's proposal. Nothing, he said, prevented the various delegations from meeting and conversing informally without any chairman or permanent record. Any delegation could take the initiative and invite the others to an informal meeting to ascertain their opinion. However, in such a case, Gromyko insisted, each delegation must be free to decide whether or not to take part, and such

Further discussion appeared senseless. The Working Committee was as inexorably drawn to a recognition of total impasse as Committee Two had been earlier in March. A formal statement of this recognition was made by the delegations of Canada, China, France and the United Kingdom on March 29. They cited three basic considerations which compelled the four governments to reject completely the Soviet proposals:

(1) The powers provided for the international control commission by the Soviet Union proposals, confined as they are to *periodic inspection* and *special investigations*, are insufficient to guarantee against the diversion of dangerous materials from known atomic facilities, and do not provide the means to detect secret activities.

(2) Except by recommendations to the Security Council of the United Nations, the international control commission has no powers to enforce either its own decisions or the terms of the convention or conventions on control.

(3) The Soviet Union government insists that the convention establishing a system of control, even so limited as that contained in the Soviet Union proposals, can be concluded only after a convention providing for the prohibition of atomic weapons and the destruction of existing atomic weapons has been 'signed, ratified and put into effect.' [12]

Accordingly the four powers proposed that the Working Committee formally resolve that "no useful purpose can be served by further discussion of [the Soviet] proposals in the Working Committee." The United States delegation immediately endorsed the statement in its entirety, and the remaining delegations with the exception of the Ukrainian representative followed suit. Gromyko attacked it in violent terms. He condemned the "militaristic circles" of the United States for causing the deadlock. The United States representatives, he said, met the Soviet proposals "with bayonets." Were it not for the intransigence of the

---

meetings must not be regarded as "committee" meetings. *AEC/C.1/SR. 38*, pp. 8-9. There is no record of anyone having followed through on Gromyko's suggested alternative.

[12] "Report and Resolution on the Union of Soviet Socialist Republics Proposals of 11 June 1947," *AEC Third Report*, Annex 4, p. 32. This report and resolution is the most authoritative and concise critique of the Soviet proposals that has been written. The italics are in the report.

United States and the hold which America exercised over the majority delegations, a greater degree of agreement would have been forthcoming. He appeared convinced that the Four Power statement had been planned "a long time ago" and confessed the belief that nothing he could say could convince its authors.[13] On the latter point he was correct. Just before the close of its April 5 meeting the Working Committee adopted the Four Power resolution by a nine to two vote. It too then adjourned *sine die.*

THE THIRD REPORT TO THE SECURITY COUNCIL

The paralysis of the Commission's two branches meant in effect the death of the full body. Further negotiation was obviously impossible. For the Western powers the only remaining question was whether it was more advisable to maintain the form of a negotiating body or to recognize publicly the impasse. It was clear that further discussions would have value only as a means of influencing world public opinion. Insofar as the Soviet Union opposed terminating discussion, it could be assumed that they calculated some further propaganda advantage in continuing negotiations. It is more plausible to assume, however, that the Russians too were glad to cease discussions, principally on the grounds that over the twenty-one month period since negotiations began they had been bested in the propaganda duel. If they had genuinely wanted to continue negotiations— even solely for propaganda value—they would have offered some form of concession to raise the hopes of the majority that agreement was in the realm of possibility. Instead the speeches of Gromyko and Tarasenko (Ukraine) during the waning days of the Commission's committees bristled with vitriolic accusations and name-calling. More likely, the Soviet objection to discontinuing the debate was part of their over-all propaganda technique of placing the blame for the Atomic Energy Commission's failure on the Western powers.

A third and final report was prepared by the French, British

[13] *AEC/C.1/SR. 42*, pp. 20-28 and *AEC/C.1/SR. 43*, pp. 7-8.

and American delegations and proposed May 7 before the Commission. It began: "The Atomic Energy Commission reports that it has reached an impasse." It concluded with the recommendation that further negotiations be suspended and that this report along with its two predecessors be transmitted to the General Assembly "as a matter of special concern." [14] The report was approved ten days later by a nine to two vote. For the first time since its inception the Atomic Energy Commission had ceased working and offered no hope of future progress.

Andrei Gromyko, in opposing the Commission's Third Report warned that discussion in any other organ of the United Nations would lead to little results because "the Governments . . . will continue to maintain the same standpoint they maintained during the negotiations in the Commission." [15] In his final speech before the Commission he sought to blame the United States for the deadlock. His constant reference to the majority proposals as American proposals underlined the fact that the Soviet Union looked upon the Commission's debates primarily as a struggle between the two superpowers in the cold war. Even the Polish delegate, Professor Zlotowski, just before he sailed for Europe in April, stressed the political conflict between the two powers as the source of the Commission's difficulties. "The underlying difficulty that must be eliminated," said Zlotowski, "is the basic mistrust and mutual fear of Russia and the United States." [16]

As Gromyko had forewarned before the Atomic Energy Commission, when the issue came before any other organs of the United Nations, the governments involved would not change their views and the deadlock would be perpetuated. Thus when the Security Council took up the issue June 11, 1948, the charges had a familiar ring. The whole tenor of the Security Council debate on June 11, 16 and 22 was one of maneuvering

[14] Draft Report of the United Nations Atomic Energy Commission, UN, *AECOR Third Year No. 1, 15 Meeting 7 May 1948*, pp. 2 and 7.
[15] UN, *AECOR Third Year No. 2, 16 Meeting 17 May 1948*, pp. 16-17.
[16] *New York Times*, April 20, 1948.

for an advantageous propaganda position when eventually the issue would come before the General Assembly.

Philip Jessup for the United States submitted the first and only substantive proposal to the Security Council on the subject of international control of atomic energy. It called upon the Council to approve the findings and recommendations of all three reports. If adopted, this proposal would have done three things: (1), made official the majority plan of control; (2), by implication condemned the Soviet Union for its unwillingness to agree with the majority; and (3), terminated discussions in the Atomic Energy Commission. Gromyko's veto, however, prevented its adoption. None of the Western delegates had any illusions about the proposal being adopted. For them the principal value of the proposal was that it put the Soviet Government in the position of rejecting the majority's work of several years; it put the Soviet Union in a negative position before world opinion.[17]

Gromyko's speech June 16, 1948, before the Security Council, was a furious tirade against the United States. He accused American leaders of fostering a "war psychosis" and using the atomic bomb as a means of political pressure. American talk of the necessity of establishing international control, he said, was done

. . . in order to hoodwink public opinion, to confuse the whole question of control, to drag out the discussion for years in the United Nations, and to endeavour to shift the blame from the guilty to the innocent by making out that it is not the USA but the USSR which is hindering the establishment of control . . .

The United States . . . wishes to convert the international control agency, which is to carry out the day-to-day functions of control and inspection, not only into a kind of trust controlling all the atomic facilities of the world, but into something like a

[17] Gromyko was aware of the position in which he and his compatriots had been placed so often. At the 321st meeting of the Security Council (June 16) he said of Philip Jessup's proposal: "The submission of such a resolution [the American one asking Security Council approval of the three reports] is utterly senseless in view of the serious divergencies between the positions of the USSR and the United States. It is apparently dictated only by the desire to elicit a USSR veto. It cannot be explained in any other way." UN, *SCOR Third Year No. 85, 321 Meeting 16 June 1948*, p. 19.

police organization. The final touch would be to place at the head of that organization some retired American general.

Again he revealed the depths of Soviet distrust of the power of a strong control agency and his country's determination to resist encroachment on national sovereignty:

> The USSR Government has no intention of permitting a situation, whereby the national economy of the Soviet Union or particular branches of that economy would be placed under foreign control. The Governments of some other countries may look at this question in a different light; that is their affair . . .
>
> The meaning of the United States proposals [on the veto] is not hard to grasp. Their acceptance would mean that decisions on sanctions would be adopted by a simple majority at the dictation of the United States representatives. If we recall what happened to a good many decisions taken in the General Assembly, the Economic and Social Council and other organs of the United Nations, it is easy to realize what this would lead to in practice. To hope that the USSR would accept such proposals is indeed to lose all sense of reality.[18]

Following defeat of the United States resolution the Canadian representative introduced a procedural resolution to transmit the three reports to the General Asesmbly. It was adopted by a vote of nine to two (Soviet Union and Ukraine). Technically, since the recommendation of the Third Report had not been formally approved, the Atomic Energy Commission was not suspended. In fact, however, a full cycle had passed since the June days of 1946. Both the Soviet Union and United States had made their proposals, compared them, amplified them and found each other's wanting. By June, 1948, each nation's atomic control policies had hardened into total deadlock. In the fall of 1948 the General Assembly would take up the problem. In so doing, it would be starting from where it began—but with these differences: two years' negotiations had revealed two entirely different conceptions of the nature of the problem; the Soviet Union looked upon control as essentially a political problem; the majority found it to be a scientific and technical problem. By the fall of 1948 the United States had already built

[18] *Ibid.,* pp. 3-19.

up a stockpile of atomic bombs and the Soviet Union was within one year of exploding its own bomb. And lastly, in the interim the cold war had reached a new peak of intensity. Only two days after the Security Council took leave of the question, the Berlin Blockade began. At no time in either nation's history had the possibility of a state of war between them been so imminent.[19] Gromyko's parting words before the Security Council were prophetic: "There is . . . no sense in referring the matter back from the Security Council to the General Assembly. It is obvious to all that this can lead nowhere, that nothing positive or useful can come of it." [20]

[19] Walter Millis, editor of the *Forrestal Diaries*, notes that the Berlin Blockade compelled a "serious reappraisal" of the role of the atomic bomb in American policy and strategy. During September and October, 1948, Secretary of Defense Forrestal systematically queried men on both sides of the Atlantic as to public reaction to be expected should the United States use the atomic bomb against the Russians. See Forrestal, *op. cit.*, p. 488.

[20] UN, *SCOR Third Year No. 88, 325 Meeting 22 June 1948*, p. 14.

6: THE STRUGGLE TO INFLUENCE

WORLD PUBLIC OPINION: 1948-1952

A THIRD AND FINAL PHASE IN THE NEGOTIATIONS FOR INTERNA-
tional control of atomic energy began in September, 1948, when
the General Assembly took up where the Atomic Energy Commission and the Security Council had failed. The first phase,
covering the period from June, 1946, to March, 1947, included
the development of the basic principles of the majority plan and
their rejection by the Soviet Union. During the second phase
from March, 1947, to June, 1948, the majority erected a comprehensive plan based upon the principles established earlier and
prodded the Soviets either to accept it or to propose a viable
alternative. In both the earlier phases an element of genuine
negotiations in the traditional sense of the word existed, though
month by month it became increasingly apparent that the Soviet
representatives were using the discussions more as a forum for
propaganda than negotiations. In the third phase the issue became
almost entirely a propaganda football.

This third round of atomic energy debate began during a
period of increased tension between the Soviet Union and the
Western world. The Communist coup d'état in Czechoslovakia
(February), followed four months later by the Berlin Blockade,
alerted the United Kingdom and continental Western Europe to
the possibility of a Russian military assault. United States intelligence agencies in 1948 reported that a Soviet attack against

138

Western Europe was a real possibility.[1] Fear of both Russian military power and of communist uprisings, particularly in France and Italy, resulted in the Brussels Pact in March, 1948, a fifty-year treaty of economic, social, and cultural collaboration and of collective defense among the nations of Western Europe. In June the United States Senate passed Senator Vandenberg's resolution expressing American support for a regional pact militarily uniting Western Europe and the United States. With this Congressional support President Truman, in July, authorized exploratory talks between the United States and the members of the Brussels Pact and Canada for a regional defense pact to protect the North Atlantic Area. NATO was in the making.

Soviet Russian reaction to these turns of events was immediate and strong. Beginning in 1948 military appropriations claimed an increasingly larger share of the budget. This rise in allocation to the Russian defense ministries, claimed the Soviets, was necessitated by the military conversations in Washington in the summer of 1948.[2] As a countermove against American reconstruction of Western Germany, the Soviet Union in June, 1948, called a foreign ministers' conference for the states of Eastern Europe in order to undertake closer collaboration with Moscow. At the same time, the Russian government asked the speedy organization of a Peoples' Police in the East Zone of Germany. These anti-Western foreign policy moves were paralleled within the Soviet Union by an intensification of Andrei Zhdanov's condemnation of all Western (bourgeois) influence in Soviet cultural and intellectual life.

ACTION AT THE THIRD GENERAL ASSEMBLY

The growing East-West chasm killed any possibility for the third General Assembly meeting in Paris in the fall of 1948 to resolve the differences between the two plans. Nevertheless international control of atomic energy was very much in the

[1] William Reitzel, Morton A. Kaplan and Constance G. Coblenz, *United States Foreign Policy 1945-1955* (Washington, D.C., 1956), p. 125.
[2] Georg von Rauch, *A History of Soviet Russia* (New York, 1957), p. 407.

fore of public discussion and it was placed on the Assembly's agenda. The stage was set for a large-scale propaganda battle.

Soviet efforts to seize the propaganda initiative were manifested by two new dramatic proposals. As the Assembly began its general debate, Andrei Vyshinsky proposed that the permanent members of the Security Council reduce by one third all current land, naval and air forces; that atomic weapons be prohibited; and that an international control body be established within the framework of the Security Council to supervise both these measures.[3]

During debate on this proposal the Soviet representative insisted that it was useless to talk of reducing conventional armaments without any provisions for prohibiting atomic weapons. In the Soviet view the two problems were closely interrelated and required concerted action. Western spokesmen did not deny an interrelation, but they criticized the Soviet proposal as unrealistic and illogical by assuming that conventional disarmament was possible without a prior agreement on atomic energy control. Eventually the Assembly referred Vyshinsky's proposed one-third arms cut to the Commission on Conventional Armaments where it was divorced from atomic energy.

Andrei Vyshinsky's second new proposal was more directly related to the problem of agreement on a control plan. Addressing the Assembly's First Committee October 2, Vyshinsky offered a resolution calling upon the Atomic Energy Commission to prepare two conventions, one prohibiting atomic weapons and the other establishing a control system, "both conventions to be signed and brought into operation simultaneously."[4] For the first time since negotiations began, the Soviet demand that prohibition precede control had been abandoned. The wording of the Soviet proposal suggested a compromise with the majority provisions that control precede prohibition. Whether in fact the two would begin simultaneously would depend upon the

[3] UN, *ORGA, Third Session, Part I. Plenary Meetings . . . Summary Records of Meetings 21 September-12 December, 1948,* 143rd meeting, p. 135. Draft Resolution A/658.
[4] *A/C.1/310.*

practical meaning given to the words "signed and brought into operation." If prohibition were to go into effect as the control system began to function and before it had proved itself, then the Soviet compromise was a compromise in words only. If, on the other hand, "brought into operation" meant that prohibition would take effect when control proved itself to be operating effectively, the guarantee sought by the majority would be met. By failing to specify what kind of a control system would be established simultaneously with a prohibition agreement, the Russians implied their old plan of limited inspection which the majority had already rejected as inadequate.

The representatives of Great Britain, France and the United States saw no real compromise in this new proposal. They found it difficult to accept Soviet sincerity when only the day before both Vyshinsky and Mr. Katz-Suchy, the Polish representative, had reiterated the need to prohibit atomic weapons before establishing control. Western suspicion of a propaganda maneuver was confirmed by the subsequent speeches of Vyshinsky attacking the United States in the harshest terms possible. The Russian delegate made no disguise of his efforts to appeal to world public opinion when he said:

The minority was systematically over-ridden by a closely-knit majority which ignored, not only the views of the minority, but also of that immense majority throughout the world which stood behind the minority in the United Nations. The minority in the United Nations represented, in fact, the majority of the public opinion; the majority of the peoples who wanted peace at all costs, who were against warmongers, and who demanded measures to ensure peace throughout the world. In the United Nations, however, there existed a majority which ignored the views of the minority. It was the latter's duty, therefore, to state its case so that the peoples outside the precincts of the General Assembly hall should hear the voice of truth.[5]

The immediate Russian objective of preventing disruption of the Atomic Energy Commission discussions received some sup-

[5] UN, *ORGA, Third Session, Part I. Plenary Meetings . . . Summary Records of Meetings 21 September-12 December, 1948,* 156th meeting, p. 405.

port from the smaller nations which wanted the Atomic Energy Commission to continue its work. India and the Philippines, among others, were convinced that Vyshinsky's new proposal created a new and more promising situation for continued negotiations. The representative of New Zealand proposed that the six permanent members of the Atomic Energy Commission consult in private together to determine when a basis for agreement existed and then reconvene the Atomic Energy Commission.

Most of the spokesmen for the majority plan were under no illusions about the nature of the propaganda duel which confronted them. Warren Austin, speaking before the First Committee, made clear the determination of the major Western powers to resist the Soviet effort. "The impasse in the Atomic Energy Commission," he said, "could only be broken if an overwhelming majority in the General Assembly supported the majority plan and thus aroused world opinion. If the members of the First Committee were divided in their views, or if any significant member abstained from participating in the judgment, there would be little hope of breaking the impasse." [6] Support by the United Nations for the majority plan as outlined in the first two reports was proposed in a Canadian resolution introduced September 30.

The debate on the Soviet, New Zealand and Canadian resolutions was among the bitterest endured at the United Nations to that date. In order to examine the proposals more closely, the First Committee created a subcommittee to come up with a unified resolution. Jacob Malik for the Soviet Union opposed the creation of a "numerically limited subcommittee," arguing that since the six permanent members of the Atomic Energy Commission had made no progress in three years, there was no reason to limit membership in a subcommittee studying the problem. [7]

[6] UN, *ORGA, Third Session, Part I. First Committee, Summary Record of Meetings 21 September-8 December 1948*, 144th meeting, pp. 20-21.

[7] UN, *ORGA, Third Session, Part I. First Committee, Summary Record of Meetings 21 September-8 December 1948*, 152nd meeting, p. 89. The subcommittee was composed of representatives from Brazil, Canada, China, Equador, France, India, Sweden, Ukrainian SSR, the Soviet Union, the United States and the United Kingdom. For the debate of the subcommittee see *A/C.1/A III/SR. 1-7*.

He apparently felt that the Soviet view would receive a wider hearing in more open sessions. Consistent with this Soviet approach Malik and Manuilsky (the Ukrainian representative) attempted to have the subcommittee, contrary to usual procedure, keep a verbatim record of the debate.[8]

When the subcommittee reported back to the First Committee, it recorded its rejection of the Soviet proposal and acceptance of a revised Canadian resolution. The revision was an amendment incorporating New Zealand's proposal for a six-power consultation to determine whether a basis existed for agreement on control and a request that the Atomic Energy Commission resume its sessions. Undaunted by his defeat in the subcommittee, the Soviet delegate reintroduced his proposal before the First Committee and again before the full Assembly where it was voted down a third time. On November 4, 1948, the Assembly responded to the Western appeal for world-wide support of the majority plan with a vote of forty in favor, six against and four abstentions for the Canadian resolution. Thus for the first time since negotiations began, the majority plan became officially the United Nations Plan. Passage of this resolution marked the most serious diplomatic defeat for the Soviet representatives since the inauguration of atomic energy negotiations.

Salim Sarper (Turkey), *rapporteur* for the First Committee, when presenting the committee's report to the Assembly described its debates as "heated and sometimes acrimonious." It was an understatement. Andrei Vyshinsky gave a display of polemical fireworks that went a long way toward establishing his reputation in the United Nations as a fiery orator. One correspondent reported that he was red-faced with anger as he told the United Nations that the Soviet Union would "never, never" accept its control plan. "Our chest," he said, "is a strong one. Your knee cannot crush it . . . Our neck is not the neck of a chicken." Twice during a speech October 1, Vyshinsky was interrupted by a breakdown in the simultaneous communi-

---

[8] *A/C.1/A III/SR.1*, p. 2. The effort was in vain.

cation system. Exasperated, Vyshinsky insisted that he would continue talking even if no one listened.[9]

The violence of the Soviet charge that the United States wanted adoption of the majority plan to subjugate the Soviet Union was not at all a reflection of Vyshinsky's histrionic qualities as a speaker. A similar tone echoed throughout other Russian official and unofficial channels of communication. *Pravda* compared the majority proposals to the approach of a robber: "Your purse or your life." It described the great excitement generated by Vyshinsky's appearance before the General Assembly and the trepidation of the Anglo-American bloc as he exposed them. Vyshinsky's speeches, it reported, "made a big impression not only within the General Assembly but beyond its confines." [10]

The Assembly resolution calling for a resumption of Atomic Energy Commission discussions and consultation among the Big Six powers to determine the existence of a basis for agreement was in part a compromise between the Anglo-American desire to end negotiations and the demand of several smaller nations that negotiations not be terminated. Vyshinsky repeatedly contrasted the positive desire of the Soviet Union to continue negotiations with what he called the negativeness of the Anglo-American approach. Six-power consultation, to Vyshinsky, hardly qualified as continued negotiations. In his view, any expectations of results from such talks were merely "wishful thinking." Nor was he satisfied with the limited scope of work which the General Assembly called upon the Atomic Energy Commission to undertake. The Atomic Energy Commission, he said, was called upon to deal "with trash." [11]

In accordance with the General Assembly's wish, the Atomic Energy Commission reconvened February 18, 1949. No one ex-

[9] *New York Times,* October 22, 1948.
[10] *Pravda,* October 2, 3 and 4, 1948. Unlike its coverage of much of the United Nations discussions of atomic energy *Pravda* devoted considerable coverage to the debates at the third General Assembly session in Paris. Cf. *Pravda* October 1, 2, 3, 4, 5, 8, 10 and 12, 1948.
[11] UN, *ORGA, Third Session, Part I. Plenary Meetings . . . Summary Records of Meetings 21 September-12 December 1948,* 156th meeting, p. 407.

pected much in the way of agreement between the communist and noncommunist groups. But neither did the Commission members anticipate the almost complete breakdown of communication that ensued. From February to the end of July the Commission's discussions degenerated into interminable haggling over procedural matters, name-calling episodes, long repetitive speeches, and tactical maneuvers whose sole objective was to discredit the opposition and influence world opinion. Even the traditional practices of diplomatic courtesy were abandoned in several instances.[12] Much of the debate had a mechanical quality about it. Soviet speeches made ostensibly in answer to questions from other delegates often had no relation to the questions asked. They consisted chiefly of lengthy statements repeated in earlier sessions or even the same sessions. Irritated and bored by these harangues, Western delegates frequently sought to dispense with the translation of Russian speeches into French—a violation of the usual procedure.[13]

The Soviet spokesmen totally discarded any efforts to influence their listeners. Their audience was world public opinion and the Kremlin. Malik's, Tsarapkin's, Manuilsky's and Tarasenko's speeches bristled with repeated references to "the ruling clique in the United States," the "United Kingdom-United States bloc," "the sadly notorious Baruch Plan" and the like. No adjective or accusation was too strong to express Soviet indignation toward the majority plan. "World public opinion," said Malik, "cannot allow those who base their bloodthirsty and

[12] Typical of several instances of such discourtesy was the refusal on February 25 of Jacob Malik, then Commission Chairman, to permit Mr. Osborn to introduce a resolution until he (Malik) had given a prepared speech. Mr. Osborn was denied his request after he had already been given the floor. When Osborn objected, Malik retorted curtly, "I shall finish my speech and then I shall call upon the representative of the United States of America." UN, *AECOR, Fourth Year No. 2, 18 Meeting 25 February 1949*, pp. 2-3.

[13] Jacob Malik complained before the Commission in March that the question of dispensing with the interpretation of speeches into French was never raised except after statements of the Soviet Union and Ukrainian representatives. "I do not understand it," he said, "and consider it an abnormal situation." Mr. de Rose promptly accused Malik of talking too much. UN, *AECOR, Fourth Year No. 4, 20 Meeting 22 March 1949*, pp. 10-11 and 15.

hateful plans on the atomic weapons against humanity . . . against open cities and against millions of children, women and old people." [14] This behavior provoked continuous objections from the majority. One of its most vigorous spokesmen, Mr. de Rose (France) resorted to an unusual procedure to demonstrate his feeling. On March 25 he stated to the Commission:

> He [Malik] has . . . ridiculed or interpreted in the most tendentious way—the entire responsibility for which I place on him—our efforts to understand him better and our appeals for an attitude more constructive than that so far adopted by the representatives of his country on the question now before us.
>
> Since the representative of the USSR seems impervious to our points of view when stated according to the intellectual processes familiar to Latin or Anglo-Saxon minds, I should like for a few minutes to address him in a manner which he must understand, since it is the one he adopts toward us.

Mr. de Rose then proceeded to repeat parts of a speech which Malik had given ten days previously, substituting the USSR for the majority countries and vice versa.[15]

The smaller nations of the Atomic Energy Commission, caught in the fury of accusations and counteraccusations, attempted occasionally to moderate the asperity of the debate. Mr. Arce (Argentina) noted that: ". . . if we make an arithmetical calculation of the contents of the speeches made in this gathering, we shall find that 99.99 per cent of the references made, aim at disproving and discrediting the views of the members of the Commission and only a tiny 0.01 per cent have anything to do with atomic energy." [16] Nothing, however, that he or any of the other representatives of smaller nations said or

[14] UN, *AECOR, Fourth Year No. 3, 19 Meeting 15 March 1949,* pp. 2-3.

[15] UN, *AECOR, Fourth Year No. 5, 21 Meeting 25 March 1949,* pp. 2-3. Malik called de Rose's parody "verbal acrobatics" and added, "And we can only stand amazed that the French representative should have had the courage to mention . . . the special characteristics of thought of the Anglo-Saxons or of the Latins. As, however, he has thus admitted that his argument was illogical, and has thereby refuted it, there is no need for a logical answer, because it is unnecessary to reply with logic arguments bereft of it." UN, *AECOR, Fourth Year No. 6, 22 Meeting 25 May 1949,* p. 4.

[16] *Ibid.,* p. 21.

did could dent the bedrock of disagreement between the principal antagonists.

Mr. Tsarapkin in February resubmitted the proposal for simultaneous conventions on prohibition and control that had been rejected by the third General Assembly. Only now he set a time limit of June 1, 1949, for their completion. No one took the proposal seriously. The French and United States representatives informed Mr. Tsarapkin that his government must offer something new if further debate was to take place. Tsarapkin replied: "I think it is not a question of making new proposals of any kind. What we have to do is something very realistic and concrete." At the same time he announced: "I am expecting . . . new proposals from the representative of the United States . . ." [17]

By June both the Soviet and Western delegates had abandoned all hope of a change in policy from the opposing side. An example of the indifference toward genuine negotiation felt by most delegates was their reaction to a speech made by Jacob Malik in the Working Committee June 3. In summing up the several concessions to the West made by the Soviet Union, Malik made the statement, "We agreed not only to periodic inspection, but to constant inspection." [18]

Here was a new and clear change in Soviet policy. Never before had a Soviet representative agreed to constant inspection. It might have been a slip of the tongue or an attempt to prolong negotiations by intimating a willingness to agree. The fact is that the Russians themselves failed to play up this change, and it was completely ignored by the others. So hardened were both sides and so bent on propagandistic utterances that agreement was not felt to be within the realm of the possible.

On July 29, 1948, the Commission formally rejected the Soviet demand for simultaneous conventions and approved an American resolution which reported:

That the impasse as analysed in the third report of the Atomic Energy Commission still exists; that these differences are irrecon-

[17] AEC/C.1/PV. 45, pp. 23-25, 37.
[18] AEC/C.1/PV. 46, pp. 44-45.

cilable at the Commission level, and that further discussion in the Atomic Energy Commission would tend to harden these differences and would serve no practicable or useful purpose until such time as the Sponsoring Powers have reported that there exists a basis for agreement.[19]

No one knew, but some may have suspected, that when it adjourned at 1:45 P.M. the Atomic Energy Commission had concluded its last session.

Only a formal consideration of the issue by the Security Council remained before it would be again tossed in the lap of the General Assembly. As expected the Council rejected a Soviet move to refer the issue back to the Atomic Energy Commission. Instead on September 16 it approved the majority recommendations that the impasse again be reported to the General Assembly. It called upon the five permanent members of the Council and Canada to consult privately to find a possible basis for agreement. This was the last action taken by the Security Council on the subject of international control of atomic energy.

Private consultation among the major powers never appealed to the Soviet Union. Adamantly opposed to any genuine system of atomic control, the Soviet representatives had little to gain in closed session with the equally stubborn representatives of the Western powers. Andrei Vyshinsky had earlier called any expectations of success in private consultation "wishful thinking." Unpublicized speeches afforded Soviet spokesmen no opportunity to disseminate propaganda. They had voted against both the General Assembly and Atomic Energy Commission resolutions calling for six-power consultations.

To have refused to engage in such negotiations after the collapse of the Atomic Energy Commission talks, however, would have been too great an affront to world public opinion. It would have also undermined the sincerity of their insistence upon the continuation of negotiations. When the first (of fourteen) private meetings convened at Lake Success August 9,

---

[19] See AEC/41 for the full text of the resolution. The final vote was nine to two (Ukrainian SSR and the Soviet Union).

1949, Mr. Tsarapkin suggested that the meetings be open. He deferred, however, to the desire of the majority that the meeting be held in closed session in order to facilitate the exchange of views on a confidential basis.

The views exchanged confidentially differed little from those exchanged publicly. In tone and reasonableness of argument the discussions took on an atmosphere of beginning negotiations. Very quickly, however, the basic disparities asserted themselves; Tsarapkin insisted on prohibition before a control system was established, he rejected international ownership of atomic industries, and condemned the majority plan as an infringement of national sovereignty.

Jacob Malik's replacement of Tsarapkin on October 6 brought a renewal of Soviet invective. Even the five Western powers were convinced of the uselessness of further talks. On October 25, 1949, they issued a report to the General Assembly which was then convened in New York. These consultations, the report concluded,

have not yet succeeded in bringing about agreement between the USSR and the other five Powers, but they have served to clarify some of the points on which there is a fundamental difference not only on methods but also on aims. All of the sponsoring Powers, other than the USSR, put world security first and are prepared to accept innovations in traditional concepts of international co-operation, national sovereignty, and economic organization where these are necessary for security. The Government of the USSR puts its own sovereignty first and is unwilling to accept measures which may impinge upon or interfere with its rigid exercise of unimpeded state sovereignty. If this fundamental difference could be overcome, other differences which have hitherto appeared insurmountable could be seen in true perspective, and reasonable ground might be found for their adjustment.[20]

[20] Document A/1050 in UN, *ORGA, Fourth Session, Supplement No. 15,* p. 35. In this report the five powers reaffirmed the basic ideas of the United Nations plan. The "Statement by Five Powers to the General Assembly" began, "The five powers remain convinced that any system of inspection alone would be inadequate and that in order to provide security the international control agency must itself operate and manage dangerous facilities for making and using dangerous quantities of such materials in trust for Member States." *Ibid.,* p. 34.

The importance in this report of such an abstract concept as "sovereignty" was a measure of the unreality of the discussions toward practical attainment of atomic control. Intellectualization and rationalization had gradually replaced negotiation.

THE RUSSIAN ATOMIC EXPLOSION

Early in September, 1949, a large explosion was reported in the Soviet Union. No announcement had been made by the Russian government that it had successfully achieved nuclear fission. By September 19 the atomic nature of the Soviet explosion had been 95 per cent established by American scientists, and President Truman announced to the world September 23 the news of Soviet Russia's achievement. Two days later the Soviet news agency, *Tass*, confirmed the discovery. The government communiqué read in part:

In the Soviet Union, as is known, building work on a large scale is in progress—the building of hydroelectric stations, mines, canals, roads, which evoke the necessity of large scale blasting work with the use of the latest technical means.

In so far as this blasting work has taken place and is taking place pretty frequently in various parts of the country, it is possible this might draw attention beyond the confines of the Soviet Union.

As for the production of atomic energy, Tass considers it necessary to recall that already on November 6, 1947, Minister of Foreign Affairs of the Union of Soviet Socialist Republics, V. M. Molotov, made a statement concerning the secret of the atomic bomb when he declared that this secret had been non-existent long ago.

Officially this revelation made no change in either side's policy. The *Tass* communiqué concluded:

It should be pointed out that the Soviet Government, despite the existence in its country of an atomic weapon, adopts and intends adopting in the future its former position in favor of the absolute prohibition of the use of the atomic weapons.

Concerning control of the atomic weapon, it has to be said that control will be essential in order to check up on fulfillment of a decision on the prohibition of the production of the atomic weapon.[21]

International control of atomic energy was here clearly subordinated to prohibition. Secretary of State Dean Acheson expressed the official reaction of the United States to the Soviet explosion with the announcement that ". . . this event makes no change in our policy." [22]

Public opinion in many areas of the world was led to expect new developments in atomic energy negotiations as a result of the Soviet explosion. Some of the old sense of urgency that existed in 1945-1946 began to reassert itself. Those who felt that the Russians' intransigence stemmed from their inferior position to the United States believed that now Russia could afford to agree to a control plan. This argument was bolstered by the belief that the United States too would be more willing to make concessions, since the Soviet Union would be abandoning an equivalent source of military power. According to a close observer of the United Nations an overwhelming majority of the delegates agreed with the statement by Brigadier-General Carlos P. Romulo, President of the General Assembly, that the atomic question "must be faced squarely" at the fourth General Assembly session.[23]

Those hopes and arguments were fathered by a wish. They

[21] *Izvestia,* September 25, 1949. English text in *New York Times,* September 25, 1949. It is revealing that this important announcement received no banner headlines in the Soviet press. *Izvestia's* announcement occupied two small columns in the upper left side of the second page. A strong feeling of national pride permeated this announcement—viz., part of the communiqué read:

"Scientific circles of the United States of America took this statement by V. M. Molotov [speech given by Molotov in Bolshoi Theater on November 7, 1947, in which he said that the secret of the atomic bomb 'had long ceased to exist,' *Pravda,* November 7, 1947] for bluff, considering that the Russians could not possess an atomic weapon earlier than the year 1952.

They, however, were mistaken, since the Soviet Union possessed the secret of the atomic weapon already in 1947."

[22] Statement by Dean Acheson on September 23, 1949, *New York Times,* September 24, 1949.

[23] Article by Thomas Hamilton in *ibid.,* October 8, 1949. See also James Reston's column in *ibid.,* October 2, 1949.

ignored the more fundamental objections of the Soviet Union to any form of control.[24] Soviet atomic equality with the United States neither facilitated nor hindered agreement with the West. The Soviet Government remained as inalterably opposed as before. The very freedom from control which enabled it to develop atomic energy was necessary to build an atomic stockpile comparable to that of the United States.

For the Soviet Union 1949 was a crucial year. By the spring of that year the United States had built up a stockpile of atomic weapons.[25] While for the first time benefitting from a powerful atomic stockpile, it was at the same time successfully mobilizing Western Europe to meet a potential Soviet threat with conventional arms. The North Atlantic Treaty was signed April 4, 1949, and ratified by the United States Senate in July. By the end of August ratifications were completed and NATO began to come to life. During the same month that the existence of a Soviet atomic explosion was revealed, the first meeting of the North Atlantic Council was held in Washington. America's determination to rearm was given concrete expression in the following month with the passage of the Mutual Defense Assistance Act, providing the members of NATO with nearly $1.5 billion for the first year of operations.

On the very day that President Truman announced the Soviet explosion to the world Andrei Vyshinsky delivered his government's opening speech in the fourth General Assembly's debate on atomic energy. Two features of his speech revealed the trend of Soviet policy as an atomic power. The first was a withdrawal of even the modicum of agreement that had been established with the majority in the past year. This was on the question of quotas.

[24] These objections will be considered in chap. IX. It should not be assumed that only the Soviet Union was opposed to atomic energy control. A strong argument could be made that the United States itself never seriously wanted control. An even stronger argument can be made that the United States Government never believed control to be possible. For some of the doubts of Baruch and his advisers, Ferdinand Eberstadt and Herbert Bayard Swope, see Margaret L. Coit, *Mr. Baruch* (Boston, 1957), pp. 566-603. However, the focus of this study is on Soviet—not American—policy; and the fact is that without agreement by both sides no control was possible.
[25] Truman, *Memoirs*, II, 304.

At the previous General Assembly session in Paris, agreement on the value of establishing a quota system was one of the few common elements of the majority-minority positions. Addressing the General Assembly November 4, 1948, the same Vyshinsky had said:

One of the most important things is to regulate the production of atomic energy and to distribute atomic minerals among countries. This is a quota system. Thanks to this system, each country will have assigned to it, according to the advice of experts, a certain quota—in its own interests and in the interest of all other countries.[26]

Now, a year later, he soundly rejected the idea of a quota system, linking it to the "aggressive designs" of the United States.

The suggested quotas, too, represent a serious violation of national sovereignty. The second Report of the Atomic Energy Commission states that the international control organ will take and enforce decisions with regard to quota provisions, production, distribution of dangerous facilities. Thus, the right to dispose of atomic energy and the possibility of depriving others of this right, will be vested in the international agency. The idea is to make it possible for monopolists to deal, in accordance with their own interests, with the development of atomic energy in all countries of the world.[27]

Secondly, the propaganda campaign against the United States and Great Britain was intensified. During the general debate Vyshinsky introduced his government's usual proposal for unconditional prohibition of atomic weapons. Coupled with it on September 23 was the bitterest resolution yet made in the course of atomic energy discussions, condemning the United States and United Kingdom for conducting "preparations for a new war." It was a resolution which not only could not be adopted, but which made the adoption of any Soviet resolution unlikely.

Vyshinsky's September 23 speech also inaugurated a new theme in the Soviet propaganda campaign against the United

[26] UN, ORGA, Third Session, Part I. Plenary Meetings . . . Summary Records of Meetings 21 September-12 December 1948, 156th meeting, pp. 404-22.
[27] UN, ORGA, Fourth Session, Plenary Meetings . . . Summary Records of Meetings 20 September-10 December 1949, 253rd meeting, pp. 334-41.

States. Insofar as atomic energy was now the property of a socialist as well as a capitalist nation, the very possession of nuclear plants and stockpiles could no longer be condemned as evidence of aggressive intentions against peaceful states. This line of Soviet propaganda ceased. In its place the Soviet spokesmen developed the picture of the Soviet Union using atomic energy primarily for peaceful purposes in contrast to the disregard in the United States for nonmilitary uses of atomic energy. Vyshinsky informed the General Assembly on November 23 that:

We insist . . . that no one must prevent us from utilizing atomic energy to the maximum extent for peaceful purposes because that is a *sine qua non* for further social construction in our great socialist country.

Of course, matters are different in the United States. The development of atomic energy for peaceful ends is disregarded there in scientific and industrial circles.

The United States plans veer toward the military strategic side of the matter. It provides for distribution of atomic facilities on the basis of geographic considerations, to exclude the possibility that a country can attain military advantage through seizure of existing stockpiles. This attitude disregards the economic needs of various countries.[28]

The earlier *Tass* communiqué fully supported this theme. Soviet Russia's atomic explosion was not announced to the world as a part of weapons' testing or even in connection with experimental work; it was announced almost in an offhand manner as an incidental part of the large construction work taking place in the Soviet Union. Soviet comment on the world-wide press reaction to the *Tass* announcement stressed the fact that the "democratic" (communist) newspapers all agreed that in the Soviet Union atomic energy was used for the construction of canals, railroads, and hydroelectric plants while in the Western imperialist and capitalist nations the primary emphasis was on military weapons.[29] Georgi Malenkov gave official expression

[28] *Ibid.*, 253rd meeting, pp. 334-41.
[29] "Krakh Diplomatii Atomnovo Shantazha" (Bankruptcy of the Diplomacy of Atomic Blackmail), *Bolshevik*, XVII (October, 1949), 53.

of this theme in his Report to the Supreme Soviet on the occasion of the thirty-second anniversary of the Bolshevik Revolution. "In reality," he said, "as is known, the Soviet Government
did not discover the secret [of atomic energy] in order to avail
itself of atomic weapons." Rather,

Soviet science is put to the service of peace and the well-being of
our Homeland. If atomic energy in the hands of the imperialists
appears as a source for the production of lethal weapons, as a means
of intimidation, as a weapon of blackmail and violence; still in the
hands of the Soviet people it can and should serve as a powerful means
of technical progress hitherto unknown, for the further rapid
growth of the productive force of our country.[30]

In his eagerness to impress his listeners with the accomplishments of the Soviet Union in peaceful uses of atomic energy,
Vyshinsky made a sensational speech November 10 which
startled the world. "The Soviet Union," he said, "did not use
atomic energy for the purpose of accumulating stockpiles of
atomic bombs, although it did have as many atomic bombs as it
would need in the unhappy event of war." Instead,

It was using atomic energy for purposes of its own domestic
economy: blowing up mountains, changing the course of rivers,
irrigating deserts, charting new paths of life in regions untrodden by
human foot. It was doing so as master of its own land, according
to its own plans, and in doing so it was not accountable to any
international organ.[31]

This fantastic claim, made in the present tense, suggested accomplishments in harnessing atomic energy far exceeding those of
any Western nation. Much of the effect of this speech was lost
when the Soviet representative, under persistent questioning
proved unable to verify any of his claims. *Pravda*, in printing
Vyshinsky's speech, quoted him as saying the Soviet Union
intended to blow up mountains, change river courses, and irri-
gate deserts.[32]

[30] *Pravda*, November 7, 1949.
[31] UN, *ORGA, Fourth Session . . . Ad Hoc Political Committee. Summary
Records of Meetings 27 September-7 December 1949*, 33rd meeting, p. 189.
[32] *Pravda*, November 17, 1949. Immediately after this speech reporters rushed
to Vyshinsky to inquire where in the Soviet Union atomic energy was being

In spite of the discouraging tenor of the Soviet statements before the United Nations, considerable pressure was exerted by the smaller nations for some form of accommodation. Several representatives expressed the sentiment that it would be ill-advised to draw the conclusion that further consultation among the six Powers would be useless. The representatives from India, Haiti and Argentina all submitted resolutions proposing some form of compromise. Canada and France jointly submitted a proposal calling upon the permanent members of the Atomic Energy Commission to continue their consultations. In addition they recommended that "all nations join in mutual agreement to renounce the individual exercise of such rights of sovereignty in the control of atomic energy as . . . are incompatible with the promotion of world peace and security." [33]

The resolution submitted by Jacob Malik for the Soviet Union contained not the slightest hint of an accommodation with the majority. It placed "the whole responsibility" for the Atomic Energy Commission's failure to agree on control with the United States and the United Kingdom. It criticized the work of the six-power consultation and called upon the Atomic Energy Commission to resume its work. Only the Polish, Czechoslovakian, Byelorussian and Ukrainian representatives supported the Russian proposal.

As the debate in the General Assembly's Policy Committee revealed that some form of the Canadian-French resolution would inevitably be adopted, the Soviet representative sought to amend it along the lines of the original Russian resolution. He proposed the deletion from the Canadian-French resolution of all references to the third General Assembly's resolution endorsing the majority plan, national control of atomic energy and national sovereignty. These amendments were rejected. Vyshin-

---

used to alter the terrain. He replied: "I can't [tell] because I am not informed. I only know about it in a general sense." *New York Times*, November 11, 1949. Western correspondents later succeeded in embarrassing the Soviet representative by pointing out the discrepancy between the texts of his speech in the United Nations records and in *Pravda*. He never explained the discrepancy.

[33] A/AC.31/L. 27 in UN, *ORGA, Fourth Session . . . Ad Hoc Political Committee. Annex to the Summary Records of Meetings,* Vol. I, p. 68.

sky warned his listeners that only national ownership of atomic energy could serve as a basis for a control agreement. The Soviet Union, he said, would never grant proprietary rights within its territory, "since those rights could only belong to the people of the USSR who had given their blood for the right to be masters in their own land." [34]

On November 23 the issue returned to the General Assembly in plenary session for final action. The Eastern bloc continued its opposition to the majority plan and six-power consultations to the bitter end. Vyshinsky denounced in the harshest terms possible the quota provisions and use of stages in the United Nations plan. Anglo-American criticisms of the Soviet plan he denounced as "slanders." Mr. Manuilsky (Ukrainian SSR) tersely described the American plan as follows: "The whole problem could be summed up in very simple terms: 'I want to strangle you, and you must not resist me, because I am doing it for your own good.'" [35] Debate on the issue was brief and completed within the one day. Among Western delegates a feeling of resignation prevailed. Sir Alexander Cadogan exemplified their attitude by remarking in debate, "If the position adopted by the USSR was final and unalterable, that was the end of the matter." [36] The Soviet resolution for continuation of the Atomic Energy Commission discussions looking toward a simultaneous signing of conventions on prohibition and control was again defeated and the revised Canadian-French proposal was adopted. It called upon the six permanent members of the Commission to continue their consultations.

1950: THE DEADLOCK OF SILENCE

Further discussion of atomic energy had little to offer the Soviet Union. The actual attainment of control was considered

---

[34] UN, *ORGA, Fourth Session . . . Ad Hoc Political Committee. Summary Records of Meetings 27 September-7 December 1949*, 35th meeting, p. 208.
[35] UN, *ORGA, Fourth Session, Plenary Meetings . . . Summary Records of Meetings 20 September-10 December 1949*, 254th meeting, p. 356. See also pp. 334-40.
[36] *Ibid.*, p. 349.

a threat to its national existence. Propaganda opportunities in the Commission and private debates had reached a point of diminishing returns. Throughout the world the Soviet Union had succeeded in exerting some influence by its reiteration of the disarmingly simple "ban the bomb" theme. But within the United Nations, where the representatives of governments were frequently exposed to speeches explaining the complexity of the problem, Soviet influence was considerably less effective. This was demonstrated by the overwhelming support given to the majority plan. Continually being outvoted, the Soviet Union found the United Nations a less congenial instrument for carrying out its foreign policy than did the Western nations. During 1950 when relations between the Soviet Union and the non-communist world reached a new low, Soviet Russian participation in the United Nations became minimal.

As a compensation for Russia's declining voice in the United Nations, the leaders of world communism determined in 1949 to embark upon a world-wide propaganda crusade independent of the United Nations. In April, 1949, communist leaders throughout the world met in Paris and Prague to organize the "First World Congress of the Partisans of Peace." In November of the following year a Congress held in Warsaw transformed the committee into a World Peace Council supported by representatives of fifty-eight nations. This World Peace Council drew up a "Peace Appeal" to which over 600 million individuals eventually subscribed. These millions of individuals, not the United Nations delegates, represented world public opinion in communist eyes. *New Times* summed up this view in a review of the first six years of the United Nations. "The Soviet proposals [for control of atomic energy]," it said, "had the wide support of world opinion. Only the United Nations remained deaf to them." [37]

The purpose of the "Peace Appeal" was to link the Russian proposals with popular aspirations throughout the world. In contrast, American proposals were pictured as desperate attempts

[37] A. Yerusalimsky, "The United Nations—6 Years," *New Times*, October 24, 1951, p. 7.

by corporate groups in the United States to maximize their profits through the production of atomic bombs. The basic argument of the appeal was that the use of atomic bombs as weapons of mass destruction was morally wrong; that, therefore, anyone who used or contemplated using these bombs was criminally guilty. The solution of the problem was unconditional prohibition of atomic bombs. Those who signed the appeal pledged "as a solemn oath" to "regard as guilty of war crimes the government that is the first to use the atomic weapon against any country." [38]

Shortly following the breakup of the Atomic Energy Commission in July, 1949, *Pravda* began the first of its series of Peace Appeal articles. They flowed with increasing regularity, particularly during the period of active fighting in Korea. Just six days before the outbreak of the Korean War the Supreme Soviet of the USSR, at a joint meeting of the Council of Union and Council of Nationalities, formally announced its adherence to the appeal of the Stockholm Committees to prohibit atomic weapons, establish strict control over the observance of atomic prohibition, and to declare as criminally guilty that government which first used the atomic weapon. The Supreme Soviet stated its readiness to collaborate with the legislative organs of other states in taking measures to realize these proposals.[39]

During the whole of 1950 East-West negotiators on atomic energy met only once. That was the last meeting of the Big Six consulting group which met as requested by the fourth General Assembly. Already the Soviet Union had decided to cease discussions *in toto*. Jacob Malik informed the group that his government would not continue the talks as long as the Nationalist Chinese delegate, "the representative of the Kuomintang group," took part in the discussions. When Malik's proposal to exclude the Chinese representative was declared out of order he walked out. Malik's walkout from the six-power group was not an isolated action. His was the thirteenth Soviet bloc walkout

[38] "A Warning to the Atom Cannibals," interview with T. D. Lysenko, *ibid.*, March 8, 1950, p. 16.
[39] *Pravda*, June 21, 1950.

of several United Nations organs which started January 10, 1950, with the Russian representative's departure from the Security Council. The six-power committee was the sixth group to be affected; but it was the first to collapse as a result.

Increased international tension accelerated rearmament on a vast scale during 1950. On January 31 President Truman ordered the United States Atomic Energy Commission to go ahead with construction of the hydrogen bomb. In Europe plans were begun for rearming both Germanys and incorporating them into the NATO and Eastern European alliances. In Asia the communist and Western worlds became involved in open military conflict when the North Korean Army attacked South Korea June 25, 1950. During the fall of 1951 both nations engaged in a series of atomic bomb tests. The White House announced the second and third Soviet atomic explosions October 3 and October 22. That same month Premier Stalin acknowledged for the first time that at least one of the atomic explosions described by the United States Government was a bomb test. Furthermore, he gave notice that the Soviet Union would continue to test atomic bombs "of various calibres" in conformity with its defense needs.[40] Concurrent with the Soviet tests the American government was conducting a series of tests in Nevada. This series was the first to test small tactical atomic weapons.

Military rearmament was accompanied by a step-up in political propaganda by both sides. Soviet atomic energy propaganda be-

[40] Statement by J. V. Stalin on October 6, 1951, in answer to questions of a *Pravda* correspondent, *Pravda*, October 6, 1951. See also "J. V. Stalin's Replies to Questions of a 'Pravda' Correspondent Concerning the Atomic Weapons," *New Times*, October 10, 1951; "A Blow at Atomic Diplomacy" (editorial), *ibid.*, October 17, 1951; and "Otvet Tovarishcha I. V. Stalina Korrespondentu 'Pravda' Naschet Atomnovo Orushiya" (Comrade J. V. Stalin's answer to *Pravda* correspondent's questions concerning atomic weapons), *Bolshevik*, XIX (October, 1951). On the subject of atomic energy control Stalin said: "The Soviet Union advocates the prohibition of atomic weapons. The Soviet Union advocates establishment of international control to see to it that a decision on prohibition of atomic weapons, on cessation of production of atomic weapons and on exclusively civilian use of the atom bombs which have already been produced is carried out with all meticulousness and scrupulousness. This is specifically the kind of international control advocated by the Soviet Union." In the United States Stalin's reference to "various calibres" of atomic bombs caused much concern since it indicated that the Russians probably already had more than one type of bomb.

came increasingly strident. Less attention was paid to the merits of the Russian proposals (with the exception of prohibition of the use of atomic bombs) than to the aggressive designs of the Anglo-American plan. President Truman's authorization of the hydrogen bomb construction was looked upon as clearly provocatory. Modest Rubenstein, one of the principal Soviet atomic energy propagandists, wrote that President Truman's decision inaugurated a new "devil's-sabbath of atomic blackmail." [41] Periodic statements by President Truman during the year reaffirmed his support of the Baruch Plan; and articles in *Izvestia* continued to reject the plan.

THE MOVEMENT TOWARD MERGER OF THE ATOMIC ENERGY COMMISSION AND COMMISSION FOR CONVENTIONAL ARMAMENTS

Until the outbreak of the Korean War some sectors of American public opinion expressed concern over the total breakdown of communication on atomic energy negotiations between the Soviet Union and the United States. Senator Brian McMahon, Chairman of the joint House-Senate Committee on Atomic Energy, created a stir in government circles by a speech February 2, 1950, proposing that the United States contribute $50 billion for a "peace crusade" to aid the Soviet Union and other countries in return for an effective plan for international control of atomic energy. His speech initiated a public debate over whether there should be a renewal of negotiations with the Soviet Union. Ilya Ehrenburg, the noted Soviet writer, called McMahon's suggestion an attempt to "buy out" the Soviet Union.[42] Nevertheless, the United States administration was under pressure to do something. President Truman declared February 22 that the United States would confine its diplomacy on atomic energy problems to the United Nations. He rejected bilateral negotiations with the Soviet Union.[43]

[41] Modest Rubenstein, "Proval Atomnoi Diplomatii Amerikanskikh Imperialistov" (Defeat of the Atomic Diplomacy of the American Imperialists), *Bolshevik*, VI (March, 1950).

[42] Ilya Ehrenburg, "My Golosuem" (We Lament), *Pravda*, March 12, 1950.

[43] *New York Times*, February 23, 1950.

At the fifth General Assembly session the United States took steps to reinstate negotiations under the auspices of the United Nations. President Truman addressed the Assembly October 24, 1950, and suggested that the Atomic Energy Commission and Commission for Conventional Armaments be consolidated into a new Disarmament Commission. On December 12 a resolution to this effect was submitted by eight Western powers. It proposed the creation of a Committee of Twelve to consider such a merger. For the United States this suggestion was a direct reversal of its previous policy of keeping the work of the two organs separate. Previously the Soviet Union had taken the position that conventional and atomic disarmament were too interrelated to be discussed separately. On the face of it the proposal was a concession made by the Western powers to the Soviet Union. It was not accepted as such by the Soviet Union.

Debate on the proposed merger was relatively brief, lasting only two days. Andrei Vyshinsky, again the Soviet spokesman, directed his remarks less against the merger than against the general tenor of American foreign policy. A large portion of his lengthy speech before the General Assembly December 12 was devoted to showing the relationship between the Morgan, du Pont, Mellon and Rockefeller "monopolies" and the "Acheson-Baruch-Lilienthal" plan. As for the eight-power proposal to merge the Atomic Energy Commission and the Commission for Conventional Armaments, this was, he said, "an excellent way to pigeon-hole the real problem and remove it from the sphere of practical consideration." To him the true meaning of the Western resolution was clear: "It is to toss the Assembly a bone to gnaw, a bone on which there is not even a shred of meat; when it has gnawed at that bone for a year, they say, we shall see." [44]

For the Soviet Union the "practical solution" remained: "The unconditional prohibition of atomic weapons and other weapons

[44] UN, *ORGA, Fifth Session, Plenary Meetings. Verbatim Records of Meetings, Vol. I*, 321st meeting, pp. 610-13.

for the mass extermination of people, and the institution of control to ensure the observance of that prohibition." To prepare the two conventions the Soviet representative again asked that discussion in the Atomic Energy Commission be resumed. The Soviet resolution was rejected December 13 and the eight-power proposal adopted. As of January 1, 1951, a Committee of Twelve was to consider ways and means of merging the Atomic Energy Commission and the Commission for Conventional Armaments and to report to the sixth session of the General Assembly.

Beginning its work Februray 14, the Committee of Twelve held nine sessions extending through the spring and summer of 1951. Like so much previous Russian atomic energy negotiation, their attendance in the committee was dictated less by their own desire than by Western pressure. Insofar as the plan for a merger of commissions and the Committee of Twelve itself originated with the West, the instinctive Soviet reaction was one of opposition. Their reaction, however, had to be tempered because of their intense propaganda against the United States for discontinuing Atomic Energy Commission discussions. As the Committee of Twelve began its work, Soviet policy toward it was not fully defined.

Initially, the Russian representatives maintained the same attitude they had held before the Fifth General Assembly. Jacob Malik insisted that the representative of the Peoples Republic of China replace the representative of Nationalist China. When his demand was refused, Malik announced that henceforth he would not recognize the vote of the "Kuomintang" representative on any decisions taken. But Malik did not leave the committee. Instead he engaged the committee in a series of discussions solely concerned with procedural questions.

Toward the end of May the United States representative formally presented a proposal for merging the two commissions. One of the provisions in the proposal was recognition of the United Nations Plan as the basis for a control agreement "unless and until a better and no less effective system can be devised."

This provision could only arouse Russian opposition. And it did. But in addition to his criticism of the majority plan *per se*, Tsarapkin rejected the idea of the creation of a new commission.

During the following two months an unusual silence emanated from the Soviet delegate. When on August 23 Tsarapkin broke his silence, he announced a reversal of his previous stand on the proposed new commission. ". . . Since his delegation maintained its view that the question of the reduction of armaments and the question of atomic weapons formed an indivisible problem," he said, "it did not in principle oppose the establishment of a single commission within the framework of the Security Council to deal with both questions . . ." Before he could fully accept the United States proposal, Tsarapkin asked that it be amended to express the need for an arms reduction and prohibition of atomic weapons and to eliminate any mention of the majority plan.[45] These amendments were rejected by the majority; consequently the United States resolution was rejected by the Soviet Union. By voting against the United States resolution (which was adopted eleven to one), the Soviet Union placed itself technically in opposition to the creation of a new commission.

Before the committee's report came before the Sixth General Assembly, France, Great Britain and the United States issued a Tripartite Statement indicating the policy they intended to take at the forthcoming session. It marked a new departure in Western thinking. Part of the statement noted:

In an honest programme for regulation, limitation and balanced reduction of all armed forces and armaments a first and indispensable step is disclosure and verification. The system of disclosure and verification must be on a continuing basis and reveal in successive stages all armed forces—including para-military, security and police forces—and all armaments, including atomic. It must also provide

[45] *A/AC.50/SR.7*, Committee of Twelve, 7th meeting, pp. 3-4. Tsarapkin stated that his government's delegation had confined itself to submitting the absolute minimum in the way of amendments in order to achieve agreement. *A/AC.50/SR.8*, Committee of Twelve, 8th meeting, p. 5. In view of the general reasonableness of tone on the part of the Soviet delegation this may have been a sincere statement. However, whether or not Tsarapkin himself was sincere, his superiors must have recognized the basic incompatibility between the Soviet and non-Soviet views toward control.

for effective international inspection to verify the adequacy and accuracy of this information.[46]

Although the three governments affirmed their support of the United Nations Plan, considerably more emphasis was placed upon "disclosure and verification" as the means of embracing the larger problem of disarmament, including both conventional and atomic arms.

Not since the early days of the Baruch Plan had an American policy placed so little emphasis on the need for control. In this Tripartite Statement the key element of "disclosure and verification" was inspection. Soviet objection to (or rather their limited definition of) control has already been noted. For its part the Kremlin would have been only too glad to forget about control entirely. On August 6, 1951, Nikolai Shvernik, President of the Supreme Soviet, sent a message to President Truman doing just that. As part of his suggestion on means of strengthening peace President Shvernik stated:

The duty of all peaceloving peoples consist in steadfastly carrying on a policy of war prevention and preservation of peace, of not permitting arms races, of attaining limitations of armaments and the prohibition of atomic weapons with the establishment of inspection over the implementation of such a prohibition, and cooperating in the conclusion of a five power pact for the strengthening of peace.[47]

Inspection here completely replaced control. The change in wording from the standard Russian propaganda and diplomatic proposals meant little substantively. But it did symbolize a trend that was beginning to extend beyond the Soviet sphere. Both sides were publicly beginning to recognize the unfeasibility of control as far as atomic energy was concerned.

For over a month beginning November 19, 1951, the Sixth General Assembly in Paris debated merging the two commissions. It was a long and complicated debate because, for the first time,

[46] Tripartite Statement issued by France, the United Kingdom and the United States on November 7, 1951 (A/1943).
[47] The complete text of President Shvernik's message to President Truman is contained in the August 7, 1951, issue of the *New York Times*.

two hitherto separate and individually complex issues (disarmament and international control of atomic energy) were combined. United States Secretary of State Dean Acheson acknowledged that America's policy linking the two was a reversal of its initial position. He cited the Atomic Energy Commission's conclusion that further progress could be made only within a "wider framework" of discussion, as the reason for the changed United States position. By "wider framework" was meant the general state of Russian-Western relations. As long as fighting continued in Korea these relations could not be anything but bad; and consequently the United States and its allies looked upon a cessation of fighting as a *sine qua non* for agreement of any sort.

  In addition to broadening atomic energy negotiations to include conventional disarmament the new Western proposals introduced a second new approach toward securing agreement. They introduced the idea of reaching agreement by stages. Not stages in the 1945-1946 conception of gradually implementing a control system, but stages in the broader area of disarmament negotiations leading up to control. What was needed in Western eyes was agreement on a limited first step which when successfully taken would inspire confidence to go on. As the "first and indispensable step" Great Britain, France and the United States proposed their plan for progressive disclosure and verification of all armed forces and armaments including atomic weapons. In anticipation of Russian objections Secretary of State Acheson offered assurances that:

> The plan could include a provision that progress from one stage to another should not be a matter for further political decision but should take place following the completion of certain stages and be an administrative matter in the control of the commission. There could be a provision that the commission should not be controlled by any nation. Thus the programme could be advanced on the basis of its success in the early stages which would create the background of successful operation needed as guaranty when the stages vitally affecting national security were reached.[48]

[48] UN, *ORGA, Sixth Session. First Committee. Summary Records of Meetings 7 November 1951-2 February 1952*, 447th meeting, p. 8.

In addition to disclosure and verification and merging conventional and atomic disarmament talks, the tripartite proposal included the demand that verification of information disclosed be based upon "effective inspection" and a reaffirmation of the majority plan as the basis for atomic energy control.

Soviet proposals were introduced as amendments to the tripartite resolution. They provided for: (1), the primacy of prohibition over control; (2), an unconditional ban on atomic weapons; (3), establishment of a control organ within the framework of the Security Council to control all arms; (4), immediate inspection of all atomic facilities; (5), a deadline of February 1, 1952, for the Security Council to draw up conventions on prohibition and control; (6), the convocation of a world disarmament conference by not later than June 1, 1952; and (7), the creation of a new commission to replace the Atomic Energy Commission and Commission for Conventional Armaments.[49]

In terms of ultimate objectives there was a considerable amount of agreement between the Soviet and tripartite proposals. Both expressed approval for prohibition of atomic weapons and the use of atomic energy for peaceful purposes. They agreed that a control system must include effective inspection and that there must be disclosure and verification of all arms. Both agreed on creating a new disarmament commission and in time a world disarmament conference.

Their disagreements centered primarily on the sequence in which the various measures would go into effect. The order demanded by the Soviet Union was a declaration of prohibition first by the General Assembly, followed by the submission of information on armed forces by nations individually. Then the General Assembly would create a control system to verify the information and guarantee the observance of the decree on prohibition. The three major Western powers would begin with the disclosure by nations of lesser armaments, leading up to atomic weapons; then agreement on a control plan and finally a declaration of prohibition to go into effect as the control went into effect.

[49] A/C.1/668.

In an effort to break the deadlocked argument on stages, Iraq, Pakistan and Syria jointly proposed that the tripartite proposals and Soviet amendments be reconciled in a special subcommittee of French, English, American and Russian representatives and the President of the General Assembly. Surprisingly the proposal was acceptable to all. Expressing his approval, Philip Jessup (United States) added that Vyshinsky's hitherto intransigent speeches made "it clear that the task of the subcommittee would not be easy." [50]

In the subcommittee the discussions went from bad to worse. Vyshinsky, in effect, withdrew his government's support from its previous willingness to agree on simultaneous conventions for prohibition and control. Vyshinsky phrased his government's change of position by defining the control convention which would be signed simultaneously with a prohibition convention as *an agreement that there should be some sort of control.* When the Soviet Union originally offered its "simultaneous convention" proposal in 1949, the control convention was assumed to be the control plan itself—not just an expressed intention in favor of control. As far as the Western powers were concerned even the original conception of the "simultaneous convention" proposal was inadequate. They had demanded that the control plan be operating effectively before the prohibition agreement went into effect. The Soviet restatement of the proposal before the four-power subcommittee was even less acceptable. Vyshinsky described the problem as follows:

With regard to the relation of prohibition and control, the Soviet Union proposed that the General Assembly should decide upon prohibition and declare the establishment of control. That is, the decisions on the two questions would be simultaneous. Then there would be a brief delay for the preparation of an appropriate convention or conventions. However, the convention should be brief and state merely the nature and composition of the control organ and its functions. There would be no need to go into all details immediately and control could at once be begun with the inspection of all atomic energy enterprises. It would not be necessary to have

[50] UN, *ORGA, Sixth Session. First Committee, Summary Records of Meeting 7 November 1951-2 February 1952,* p. 53.

complex agreements with relation to inspection but merely to provide for verification. All that could be done without losing much time. In other words, they could decide in principle on the question of prohibition which would lead to a cessation of the manufacture of atomic weapons and then begin inspection after the short delay needed to set up the control organ.[51]

What guarantees, asked Jules Moch (France), would the West have in the interval between prohibition and the establishment of control? This in Vyshinsky's estimation "did not present a real problem." He added: "A decision by the General Assembly would impose moral, political and legal obligations not to produce atomic weapons. The immediate result would be an abatement of international tension. What it amounted to was that for about a month the production of atomic bombs would be suspended." [52] Philip Jessup asked whether that meant that, if the General Assembly agreed to prohibition on December 15, would the Soviet Union freely admit international inspections on December 16? Vyshinsky answered evasively. Other than references to the "honor and conscience" of nations the Soviet representative was unable to offer a single guarantee that his nation (or any) would not secretly build atomic bombs after they had promised not to do so. Neither the British, French or American delegates were moved by Vyshinsky's solemn utterance that ". . . any State attempting to evade the decision would . . . be covered with endless shame." To their way of thinking the greater danger was being covered with an endless shower of atomic bombs. Vyshinsky admitted that a "certain lapse of time" was inevitable between the pronouncement of prohibition and the establishment of control. But, he promised, it would be a short time; only an amount necessary "to permit the recruiting of staff and so forth." [53]

Soviet assurances that they would consider themselves bound legally and morally by a declaration of prohibition carried little weight in the atmosphere generated by open fighting in Korea and the covert race between the Soviet Union and the United

[51] *A/C.1/SC 18/SR.1*, 1st meeting, p. 12.
[52] *Ibid.*, pp. 10-11.
[53] *A/C.1/SC 18/SR.2*, 2nd meeting, p. 4.

States to be the first to explode the hydrogen bomb. Jules Moch frankly told the Soviet representative that the very minimum of confidence presumed by the Russians did not exist. Some form of compromise was necessary. Moch suggested as a possibility the immediate proclamation of prohibition in principle with the stated reservation that it not become effective until a control plan was established. Vyshinsky could not agree. In rejecting the majority assertion that only a control system could guarantee prohibition, the Soviet delegate again asserted that "atomic energy bore no relation to atomic weapons." [54]

The four-power subcommittee failed to reconcile the Soviet-Western divergencies. The only immediate proposal mutually acceptable was the creation of a new commission. This the Soviet Union recognized to be inevitable. The Assembly was still faced with the question: what kind of instructions to give the new commission? More specifically, would it be instructed to work within the framework of the United Nations plan or not? Since clearly no instructions proposed by the Soviet bloc would find majority acceptance, the Soviet delegation preferred that no specific instructions be included.

The Soviet bloc representatives fought doggedly but in vain to exclude any terms of reference for the new commission. On January 11, 1952, the Assembly replaced the Atomic Energy Commission and the Commission for Conventional Armaments with a new Disarmament Commission. Among the tasks of this new Commission was the preparation of proposals for the elimination of weapons of mass destruction and for effective international control of atomic energy. The Assembly resolution stipulated five principles which should be included in the Commission's proposals. They provided for : (1), progressive disclosure and verification of all armed forces and armaments, including atomic; (2), effective international inspection to verify information disclosed; (3), reliance upon the United Nations plan for international control of atomic energy "unless a better or no less effective system is devised"; (4), safeguards to detect violations which are adequate yet consistent with a minimum of interfer-

[54] Ibid., pp. 8 and 10.

ence in the internal life of each country; (5), adherence to the treaty open to all states. Implementation of the Commission's proposals would be carried out by a control organ whose powers would be defined by treaty but which would operate within the framework of the Security Council. Disclosure and verification was described as a "first and indispensable step" in carrying out a disarmament program.[55] This particular instruction to the Disarmament Commission and the General Assembly's approval of the United Nations plan for atomic energy control were the two most objectionable features of the resolution to the Soviet Government. Vyshinsky's last words were condemnation of the resolution as "an attempt to divert the United Nations into a path of falsehood, concealed by false and absolutely insincere phrases." [56]

"MEASURES TO COMBAT THE THREAT OF A NEW WORLD WAR . . ."

Soviet propagandistic efforts reached a new peak at the Sixth General Assembly in 1951. The speeches of Messrs. Baranovsky (Ukrainian SSR), Kiselyev (Byelorussian SSR) and particularly Vyshinsky, were filled with such sarcasm and bitterness as to make serious negotiation impossible. Their speeches were so lengthy, repetitious and irritating to the majority of immediate listeners that it is unlikely they were designed to influence any official representatives. Soviet utterances during this period could have meaning only to that part of the world opinion already hostile to the Western world or to those who were already somewhat sympathetic to communist aspirations. In which case the Soviet diatribes served to re-enforce, justify and give vent to beliefs and feelings already in existence. To the Western powers such tactics were exasperating. Mr. Lloyd (United Kingdom) expressed Western feeling when he told Vyshinsky "We

---

[55] General Assembly Resolution 502 (VI). Technically the General Assembly did not dissolve the Commission for Conventional Armaments. It recommended that the Security Council do so.

[56] UN, ORGA, Sixth Session. Plenary Meetings. Verbatim Records of Meetings 6 November 1951-5 February 1952, 358th meeting, p. 299.

must attempt—and I am certain that this is a condition precedent
to substantial progress for the cause of peace—to stop these
propaganda speeches." [57]

When Britain, France and the United States secured approval
in the Committee of Twelve for a new Disarmament Commission there was little doubt that the Commission would be authorized to work on the basis of the majority plan for international
control of atomic energy. Any Soviet proposals for an alternate
authorization were bound to be rejected. In an effort, therefore,
to maximize their propaganda attack against the Western powers,
the Russian delegation in November, 1951, introduced a new
item on the General Assembly's agenda entitled "Measures to
Combat the Threat of a New World War and to Strengthen
Peace and Friendship Among Nations." There were eight points
included among the Soviet "measures," none of which were
new: (1), condemnation of the "aggressive Atlantic bloc"
(NATO); (2), cessation of fighting in Korea and the withdrawal
of "all foreign troops"; (3), conclusion of a peace pact among
the five permanent members of the Security Council; (4), prohibition of atomic weapons; (5), a one-third reduction of armaments and armed forces; (6), the submission of information on
all armed forces; (7), establishment of a control organ with the
powers of "inspection on a continuing basis"; (8), convocation
of a world disarmament conference by July 15, 1952.[58]

That the Soviet Government did not seriously entertain hopes
of adoption of its "measures" is indicated by the contentious
nature of its text. For example, to approve of a five-power peace
pact the Soviet Union asked the United Nations to adopt a text
condemning three of those powers, viz.,

It is essential that the United States of America, Great Britain,
France and China and the Union of Soviet Socialist Republics
should unite their efforts and conclude a peace pact with one

[57] *Ibid.*, p. 302.
[58] Introduced originally on November 8, 1951, as draft resolution A/1944,
the Soviet proposal was clarified by an explanatory memorandum (A/1947)
and presented in revised form on November 16, 1951, as A/1962. In the First
Committee discussions another revision was presented as document *A/C.1/698*.
The discussion here is based upon the final revised text.

another, inviting all peace-loving nations to participate in it. These measures should frustrate the aggressive plans of the ruling circles in the United States, the United Kingdom and some other countries and remove the threat of a new war.[59]

Equally objectionable to the majority was the abusive and caustic manner of their presentation. Referring to a speech by President Truman on the United States proposal for an inventory of armed forces and armaments, Vyshinsky commented: "After reading this speech I could not get to sleep all last night—because I was choking with laughter. I am not by nature given to laughter, but even on this platform—although, as the President will attest, I am refraining from laughter—I am unable to restrain my irony over this sensational peace offensive by which the United States delegation hoped to wrest the initiative from the Soviet Union. I trust they will accept our congratulations."[60] This comment as well as others provoked more anger than laughter.

Shortly after establishing the Disarmament Commission, the Assembly referred all but three of the Soviet proposals to the new commission. The remaining three proposals (condemnation of the Atlantic bloc, immediate cessation of fighting in Korea and the five-power peace pact) were overwhelmingly rejected.

[59] UN, *ORGA, Sixth Session. Annexes 1951-1952.* Agenda items 66 and 16 and agenda item 67. This text was in the Soviet explanatory memorandum of November 9, 1951.

[60] UN, *ORGA, Sixth Session. Plenary Meetings. Verbatim Records of Meetings 6 November 1951-5 February 1952,* 336th meeting, p. 26. Although none of his listeners shared his sense of humor, Vyshinsky made frequent use of the "laughable" nature of the majority proposals. At the 348th meeting of the General Assembly he said of the United Nations plan, "It is enough to make a cat laugh." *Ibid.,* p. 190.

7: THE DISARMAMENT COMMISSION:

OLD WINE IN A NEW FLASK

THE CENTRAL PURPOSE OF MERGING ATOMIC ENERGY AND DIS-
armament negotiations in 1952 was to permit discussions of
related subjects on a wider range. By the early part of 1952 a
limitation of atomic bomb production would have required some
degree of change in conventional armament production for the
United States and the Soviet Union so as to retain the same
ratio of military power in juxtaposition. In the new Disarmament
Commission, control of atomic energy could be discussed within
the broader framework of disarmament. Even the general field
of disarmament was a limited one, however. No one seriously
doubted that the existing Soviet-American arms race was a
manifestation—not a cause—of the political tension between
both nations. The events of the previous year (1951) offered
some indication that a more suitable framework for discussing
atomic energy control would have been the full scope of Soviet-
American relations rather than just disarmament.

As a result of the Korean War American rearmament speeded
up along two lines: (1), a military build-up at home and a
strengthening of NATO; (2), an extension of American defensive alliances. Among the several extensions of the American
strategic system during 1951 the following instances could be
cited. In April the United States increased military aid to
Nationalist China and signed an agreement with Denmark for

the defense of Greenland. American forces landed in Iceland in May, and in the following month the United States signed an agreement with Saudi Arabia for an air base, and announced substantial economic aid to Yugoslavia. In July an agreement was signed with France for five air bases in Morocco; a draft of a Japanese peace treaty was released; and negotiations were begun with Spain for naval and air bases. In August a mutual defense treaty was signed with the Philippines; and in September an agreement was reached with Portugal for bases in the Azores. That same month Greece and Turkey were proposed for membership in NATO; a peace treaty with Japan was signed and was followed immediately by a United States-Japanese security pact; and increased aid to Indochina was promised. In October the United States and France, Great Britain and Turkey proposed to establish a Middle East Command with Egypt; and in November a United States-Yugoslavia military aid agreement was signed. Throughout this year the Soviet Union charged the United States with ringing a steel band of military bases around them.

Perhaps the only—and certainly the major—auspicious event leading up to the first convocation of the Disarmament Commission was the spur given by the Soviet Union in June, 1951, to discussion of a cease-fire in Korea. Optimism faded, however, as the United Nations Command and North Korean leaders became bogged down in armistice negotiations. As the Disarmament Commission began its work in New York in March, 1952, the chairman cautioned that it would be misleading to pretend that the Commission had any reasonable right to expect rapid or spectacular results. Time, patience and intelligence would be required, he warned.[1] This, in effect, was a prophecy of defeat. Patience and intelligence the negotiators had. But, if it had not

---

[1] UN, *Disarmament Commission Official Records* (hereinafter abbreviated to DCOR), Special *Supplement No. 1, Second Report* (hereinafter this report will be identified as *DCOR Second Report*), p. 3.

Representatives of the following nations comprised the Disarmament Commission during 1952: Brazil, Canada, Chile, China, France, Greece, the Netherlands, Pakistan, Turkey, the Soviet Union, the United States and the United Kingdom.

already run out, time was certainly a scarce factor. This last attempt to agree on a plan for international control of atomic energy was a race against time. As soon as the Soviet Union and the United States had built up an extensive stockpile of atomic weapons even the most foolproof plan of control would never provide the security from atomic attack envisioned in the original Acheson-Lilienthal plan. Once built, atomic bombs could be stored indefinitely in places well beyond the reach of any inspecting group. Furthermore, as each nation integrated atomic weapons into its defense establishment it would become even more reluctant to agree to control of atomic weapons. During 1952 and 1953 the Commission was engaged in a race to forestall the conditions which would make the accomplishment of its work absolutely impossible.

THE DISARMAMENT COMMISSION IN NEW YORK

After holding one session at the Palais de Chaillot in Paris the Disarmament Commission moved to New York City, where it remained in session from March through October, 1952. Immediately the Soviet Union and the Western powers became involved in a squabble over the agenda. The United States delegate wanted the Commission to consider low-priority items first and then build up to the more difficult issue of arms limitation and their control. He preferred to begin with a disclosure and verification of information in order to create confidence. A freely given inventory of military forces and armaments (including atomic weapons) would do much to increase—and also to measure—that confidence. Jacob Malik, on the other hand, insisted upon an immediate consideration of a ban on atomic weapons along with a reduction of arms and methods of disclosure. Verification and disclosure, he argued, could only follow the establishment of a control system:

The USSR proposals are diametrically opposed to those of the United States. When information is submitted, we are opposed to dividing armaments into categories, establishing special stages for disclosures on each category, and beginning with the simplest types of armaments . . . We demand that immediately after the decision has been taken to reduce armaments and prohibit the atomic weapons, all States shall submit complete official data on their armaments and armed forces, including data on the atomic weapon and on military bases on foreign territory. We propose that the international control organ shall verify these data.[2]

Against Malik's objections a French compromise work-plan was adopted. Disclosure of information and prohibition of atomic weapons would be considered concurrently. A Committee One was created to study the regulation of all arms and armaments including the prohibition of atomic and other weapons of mass destruction. A Committee Two was to study means to bring about a disclosure and verification of all armed forces and armaments.

As the Commission adjourned in the spring of 1952 to go into committee session, expectations of success were very low. Primarily responsible for the Commission's low morale was the uncompromising attitude of the Soviet Union and its repeated use of the Commission's debates to bring charges against the Western powers and the United States in particular. What destroyed any potential good will more than anything else was the introduction by Malik of the charge that American troops were conducting bacterial warfare in Korea and bringing about the mass annihilation of North Korea and Chinese civilians. Malik asked the Commission to consider without delay a charge, for which he claimed to have proof, that American troops in Korea were engaging in bacterial warfare. Benjamin V. Cohen, for the United States, called Malik's charges an affront to the United States and the United Nations. He emphatically repudiated them and countered the Soviet demand with a demand that the Soviet Union permit the International Red Cross to investigate the charges impartially.

Malik rejected the American suggestion. He called the Red Cross a Swiss national organization and therefore unable to act objectively and without bias. Against the repeated objections of the Commission's membership, Malik insisted on including his charges in every lengthy speech he made. Finally, on March 28,

[2] UN, *DCOR, 6 Meeting*, p. 9.

the United States formally objected to Malik's charges as not within the scope of the Commission's work. By a vote of eleven to one the Commission sustained the chairman's ruling that Malik was out of order. Indignant, Malik called the chairman's ruling "unprecedented . . . in the annals of the United Nations." He added: "Truly, this is unheard of and without precedent. You can take any decisions you like in this Commission as you are in the majority. You are organized into an aggressive bloc. You may silence me or deprive me of the possibility of speaking, but have no right to forbid me to mention facts in support of my position or our plan and the points contained therein." [3]

Equally objectionable were the combative parliamentary tactics used by the Soviet representatives. Malik's speeches were long and repetitious. Often he interrupted a speaker to ask a question and took the occasion to engage the Commission in a long polemic. Wherever possible, the Soviet representative sought to distort a Western representative's remarks to make them appear in a bad light.[4] He repeatedly compared the Western powers to fascists and included in his bacterial warfare charges the claim that the United States was recruiting German and Japanese war criminals to aid its biological warfare campaign. Shortly before the Commission adjourned to go into committee session, Jules Moch commented: "The USSR representative's attitude has made me very sad. I consider it almost a reason to despair of the cause of peace." Sir Gladwyn Jebb (United Kingdom) expressed his feeling somewhat more bitterly. Complaining that his right ear was seriously infected "as a result of

[3] UN, DCOR, 8 Meeting, p. 8. See ibid., 2 Meeting, p. 22 and 3 Meeting, p. 2.

[4] One typical instance of this type of behavior occurred at the ninth meeting of the Commission on April 2, 1952. Sir Gladwyn Jebb (United Kingdom) referred to the reduction of armaments as a subject most important to Malik's heart. Malik snapped up this reference and implied that Jebb had said that the question of prohibition and reduction was important to the Soviet delegation "only." He added, ". . . if this question is not dear to the United Kingdom representative, that is his own affair; but this question is dear, important and vital to the peoples of the entire world." UN, DCOR, 9 Meeting, p. 17.

the perpetual dissemination of verbal bacilli by the representative of the Soviet Union," he suggested that "we should now attempt to struggle out of the stinking morass into which we have been plunged by the representative of the Soviet Union . . ." [5]

COMMITTEES ONE AND TWO

Committees One and Two held a total of twelve meetings during April and May, all of which were open. When the Commission first met in Paris, Jacob Malik suggested that its meetings be open because "the . . . Commission has nothing to hide from world public opinion." The early use of the Disarmament Commission sessions for propaganda and the resulting stagnation of the Commission's work prompted several delegates to suggest a new procedure for the committees. Canada, supported by the United Kingdom, the Netherlands, and Greece, moved that the two committees normally meet in closed session. Immediately Malik objected. He accused the United States of using private meetings so as to be able to leak distorted versions of proceedings to the press. "There can be no doubt," he added, "that opponents of USSR proposals also required closed sessions in order to more easily reject USSR proposals." [6] His contention against the United States proved to be unfounded when the American representative abstained on the vote for closed sessions. With the American abstention the vote was six in favor and six abstaining, resulting in defeat of the Canadian proposal. The American representative abstained on the vote, he said, because it was impossible to force co-operation upon the Soviet Union without its consent.

Committee Two, that concerned with a disclosure and verification of information, had the shorter life span. It met only five times. Just as the United States had taken the initiative in the Atomic Energy Commission's first working committee, so dis-

[5] UN, *DCOR, 8 Meeting*, pp. 11, 15.
[6] UN, *DCOR, 9 Meeting*, pp. 6, 12, 18; *ibid., 1 Meeting*, p. 6.

cussions in this committee centered around a working paper submitted by the American delegate, Benjamin V. Cohen.[7]

The American plan proposed that a disarmament agreement begin with a system of disclosures and verification of all armed forces and armaments, including atomic weapons. It was contemplated that disclosure and verification would proceed from the less secret areas to the more secret areas according to a five-stage plan. A general description of the information to be revealed and verified at each stage was offered as follows:

Stage I. A quantitative count in the nature of a report on existing strength levels of all armed forces and of the location of installations and facilities concerned with armaments of all types including atomic.
Stage II. Detailed disclosure of organization of armed forces and of installations and facilities concerned with the basic materials required for production of all armaments including atomic.
Stage III. Detailed disclosure of armaments (except novel armaments), fissionable material and installations and facilities utilized in their production.
Stage IV. Detailed disclosure of installations and facilities utilized in the production of novel armaments including atomic (armaments not in general use by the end of the Second World War but in volume production today).
Stage V. Detailed disclosure of novel armaments including atomic.

As the information sought was revealed and checked in each stage, the investigation would move on to the next stage. In this way the co-operating states would be assured that they were revealing no more, comparatively, than any other nation and would be willing eventually to disclose in good faith the most highly secret knowledge of their national defense.

Some form of permanent machinery would be necessary to secure and verify the information. In the first stage of disclosure, verification was contemplated by periodic visits of inspection, reference to statistical records and in some cases to "on-the-spot" inspection and aerial reconnaissance. Since the second through fifth stages concerned more secret information, "on-the-spot"

[7] *DC/C.2/1*. The full text is in *DCOR Second Report*, pp. 23-30. The quotations are all taken from this text.

inspections and extensive aerial reconnaissance would be the primary means of verification. In order to meet one of the long-standing Soviet objections to control, the plan stipulated that verification should take place "with the minimum of interference in the internal life of the respective countries." However,

It is essential to an effective system of verification that the international inspectors, in addition to examining declared installations and facilities, be permitted in all stages to have access to the entire national territory in order that the Commission may determine within reasonable limits the accuracy and adequacy of the information disclosed. Accordingly, each State should be required during each stage of the process of disclosure and verification to permit the international inspectors such freedom of movement and to give them access to such installations and facilities, records and data as may reasonably be required, including the right to inspect physical dimensions of all facilities and installations wherever situated.

Inspectors would be authorized to report to the Commission any information indicating a major violation of any provisions of the agreements. In the event of a Commission determination, confirmed by the Security Council by an affirmative vote of any seven members, of a major violation during any stage and the failure of the guilty state to repair the violation within a reasonable specified time, other states would be free to suspend the operations of the system. Disclosure and verification would not move from one stage into another until the Commission had determined that the previous stage had been satisfactorily completed.

With some qualifications the non-Soviet representatives to the Disarmament Commission indicated their acceptance of the United States plan as a basis for further discussion. Jacob Malik's rejection, however, was instantaneous. Even before fully studying the United States plan he condemned it as "the same old story." [8] His colleagues on the Commission found a familiar ring too in Malik's objections to the American plan. They were essentially two: (1), Nowhere in the plan was there provision

[8] UN, DCOR *Committee 2, 1 Meeting*, p. 10. Malik himself admitted that he had not fully studied the proposals before rejecting them.

for prohibition of atomic weapons and; (2), the United States designed its system of stages so that it would receive information on conventional armaments without ever revealing its own atomic secrets. He saw the last stage as some "remote" stage which would never be reached. Malik assured his listeners that after the first stage had been completed the United States and its "allies" through a majority vote in the United Nations would suspend the stages by falsely charging a violation. Far from increasing confidence, this plan, in Malik's eyes, would on the contrary increase international suspicion and distrust.

Anger and disappointment characterized the Anglo-American reaction. "If he [Malik] really believes his argument," commented J. D. Coulson (United Kingdom), "it is only another proof of the almost pathological suspicion which infects the Soviet Union's attitude towards the Western Powers." [9] The American representative asked Malik whether there was any form of international control which would be regarded by the Soviet Union as fair and impartial international control and not American control. Malik could suggest none. He did not even find it worthwhile to suggest any amendments or modifications to the American plan. The disagreement between the USSR and the United States, he felt, was one of principle. Consequently, appeals to the Soviet Union to propose modifications were purely demagogic, since no modification of the American plan could eliminate the divergence of principle.

Again the Soviet Union offered its old formula. Malik called upon the General Assembly to recommend that

forthwith, and in any case not later than one month after the adoption by the General Assembly of the decisions on the prohibition of atomic weapons and the reduction by one third of the armaments and armed forces of the Five Powers, all States should submit complete official data on the situation of their armaments and armed forces, including data on atomic weapons and military bases in foreign countries.[10]

[9] UN, DCOR, Committee 2, 2 Meeting, p. 10.
[10] UN, DCOR, Committee 2, 1 Meeting, p. 13.

A control organ, whose powers were not clearly defined, would serve both the functions of observing the ban on atomic weapons and verification of the information submitted to it. Whereas the Western powers condemned this formula as not only inadequate but repetitive of previously rejected proposals, the Soviet representative saw it as a demonstration of his government's consistency:

> We proposed the prohibition of the atomic bomb when we did not have it, and we continue to propose its prohibition when we do have it . . . We proposed international control over that prohibition. You were against it when you had a monopoly in the field of atomic weapons and you are against it now when we have the atomic bomb. Our policy is consistent in principle . . . We are in favor of prohibiting the atomic bomb; you are against it.[11]

Nothing more remained to be done; each side had stated its position. At its fifth meeting on May 16, no one wishing to speak, Committee Two adjourned *sine die*.

Paralleling Committee Two's labors was the work of Committee One. It met a total of seven times. Inasmuch as both committees had the same membership and for the most part, even met on the same days, the tenor of debate in Committee One closely followed that of Committee Two. The task of Committee One concerned disarmament and international control of atomic energy directly. Jules Moch (France) opened the debate by stressing the importance of agreement on the central issue before the group: the nature of the control system. He reminded his colleagues that they did not have an unlimited amount of time in which to complete their assignment:

> If the present deadlock continues for a long time [said Moch], the day may come for mankind when a system of control sufficiently serious and effective to be generally accepted as a guarantee of disarmament can no longer be initiated. The difficulty of establishing effective control increases in proportion to the amount of fissionable material already produced. As time goes on the danger of con-

[11] UN, *DCOR, Committee 2, 3 Meeting,* p. 24.

cealment . . . becomes terrifyingly greater. Let us therefore act before we reach this point of no return . . .[12]

The process of debate in Committee One during April and May was similar to an earlier period of negotiations in the Atomic Energy Commission. In the winter of 1948 the Commission had reached a comparable deadlock when each side had offered its ultimate proposal and reconciliation was attempted by means of clarification. As in the earlier period the French, British and Canadian delegates attempted to bring out the Soviet representative by a series of questions aimed at the heart of their differences.

Jules Moch, at the first meeting of Committee One, got down to the two principal points disturbing the West. He asked Mr. Malik: (1), "Did the Soviet Union mean prohibition to come into effect on the day a control agreement was signed or the day when the controlling bodies were placed in a position and able to work?" and (2), "What constitutes continuous control and how is it to be limited so as not to interfere in the domestic policy of states?" Jacob Malik's answer to the first question was a redefinition of the standard Soviet line:

We [favor] . . . the following proposal: decide on the prohibition of atomic weapons and establish control over that prohibition, it being understood that both these steps would be taken simultaneously. This means that, after the decision is taken to announce the prohibition of atomic weapons and the establishment of control, a certain period should elapse during which an international control organ would be formed and set up. When that organ is set up and its representatives are ready to undertake immediate practical control, then the prohibition of atomic weapons and the establishment of strict international control over the observance of such prohibition are to go into effect simultaneously.[13]

Over a month later at the seventh meeting Malik reformulated his government's position in such a way as to indicate a potential compromise. He quoted with approval a proposal made by Jules Moch at Paris before a subcommittee of the First Committee. At that time Moch had suggested: "Agreement might be reached

[12] UN, DCOR, *Committee 1, 1 Meeting,* p. 6.
[13] *Ibid.,* pp. 18 and 26.

on two stages: in the first stage the General Assembly would prepare a conditional declaration of prohibition and in the second stage the prohibition would come into force with the establishment of control." [14] The idea of a conditional prohibition had earlier been considered as a possible means of compromise. Here it was entirely ignored. In the context of the general Soviet hostility to the Western proposal, it was not felt as sufficient a compromise to justify further consideration. Weighing even more on the minds of the Western powers was the fear that even a conditional prohibition might take on the moral force of an unconditional prohibition. Mr. Santa Cruz (Chile) noted with regret that "suspicion, doubt and distrust" were the salient characteristics of all Committee One's discussions. [15]

As to Moch's second question, Malik evaded answering what constituted interference in internal affairs except to say that it meant "not having General Eisenhower and their headquarters staff in their national capitals." This answer Moch dismissed "with contempt."

For his part the Soviet representative considered the raising of "identical questions" by the "Atlantic bloc" nations to be evidence of a conspiracy to obscure the issue and avoid discussing prohibition. He insisted that the United States proposal for international ownership of all atomic producing facilities constituted the principal obstacle to agreement. In his condemnation of ownership he offered an explanation of Soviet Russia's objections consistent in spirit and argument with the basic Marxist distrust of capitalism:

The atomic 'business' in the United States [said Malik] is, in fact, valued at from $5,000 million to $6,000 million. I have no information on the value of the atomic plants in the Soviet Union, but obviously they must also represent no insignificant sum. The value of concerns mining atomic raw materials in the Belgian Congo is obviously also substantial; atomic plants and the deposits of raw materials in Canada are also worth something. If, therefore, an international commercial atomic super-trust is to be set up, someone will

[14] UN, DCOR, Committee 1, 7 Meeting, p. 15. Jules Moch's suggested compromise is contained in A/C.1/AC.18/SR.2.
[15] UN, DCOR, Committee 1, 4 Meeting, p. 14.

have to provide the funds to buy out these concerns. Who is in a position to do so? The 'rich American uncle' in the person of the big United States monopolies, and he will naturally control it.

"For what purpose would I operate something?" Malik asked rhetorically. He answered, "I do not operate it in order to lose money . . . but . . . to make a profit." [16]

American patience toward this type of argument was wearing thin. Benjamin Cohen warned his Russian colleague by way of quoting a Russian proverb: "If you tell a man long enough that he is a pig, he will begin to grunt." One by one the remaining members of the committee expressed the view that further discussions were useless. Jacob Malik acknowledged that, "obviously we cannot find a common language—we talk about one thing, while you talk about something else." [17] On May 16, the same date as Committee Two's last session, Committee One ended its labors, no nearer agreement than when it began. That same month the Disarmament Commission adopted its first (interim) report to the Security Council. Its only conclusion was that "The discussions . . . are continuing . . ."

Discussion did continue within the Commission during the months June to August, but added nothing toward resolving or clarifying the problem of international control of atomic energy. A considerable amount of heat was added to the ordinarily hot New York City summer climate. Rancor and hostile remarks were generated by such petty or irrelevant issues as who was entitled to the floor, the interpretation of speeches into official languages, the question of Dr. Tsiang's right to represent China, the placing of bacterial warfare charges on the agenda and whether the secretariat or *rapporteur* would prepare the Commission's reports. The subject matter of nearly all the official Soviet speeches was concerned with two subjects not directly related to control of atomic energy: the Russian bacteria warfare charges against the United States and the question of a balanced reduction of armaments versus the Soviet plan for an across-the-board one-third reduction of armed forces and armaments.

[16] UN, *DCOR, Committee 1, 6 Meeting*, pp. 11 and 22.
[17] *Ibid.*, pp. 20 and 27.

As the member nations gathered in New York for the General Assembly's seventh session, the Commission prepared to assemble its second report. Everyone, including the Soviet representative, agreed that the Commission had accomplished very little. But there agreement ended. Even the procedure connected with drawing up the Commission's report entailed bitter argument. Valerian A. Zorin, the Soviet representative, objected heatedly when the Commission voted to discuss its second report at closed meetings. "There is no doubt," said Zorin, "that an understanding [not to publicize the result of the Commission's work] exists between various delegations." [18] As finally adopted October 9, the second report was a detailed summary record of the debates of the Commission held during 1952. No conclusions, no proposals, no censures were included. The record spoke for itself.

THE SEVENTH AND EIGHTH GENERAL ASSEMBLIES

Great Britain's successful atomic explosion in Australia in October, 1952, made her the third "atomic power." Speculation developed throughout the world as to how soon other nations would enter the ranks of the possessors of atomic weapons. Noticeably lacking, however, was the sense of urgency for atomic energy control which followed explosions of the first American and Russian atomic bombs.[19] After seven and one-half years, atomic explosions were losing their novelty. Coupled with this was the general cynicism and feeling of hopelessness which attended the prolonged Russian-American deadlock. When in October the issue was raised before the United Nations, the General Assembly voted to postpone discussion until the second part of the seventh session. It was not until March, 1953, that the Disarmament Commission's second report was taken up by the General Assembly.

[18] UN, *DCOR, 26 Meeting*, p. 13.
[19] One reason for this lack of a sense of urgency undoubtedly was Winston Churchill's announcement as far back as February that Great Britain had perfected the bomb and intended to test it late in 1952.

Between the sixth General Assembly session in Paris and the seventh in New York, nothing had occurred to change the positions of either the Soviet Union or the Western powers. The Disarmament Commission debates had, if anything, hardened the lines between the two sides. Both the United States and Soviet Union entered the United Nations arena with the intention of justifying their positions, each discrediting the other and seeking approval of its policies before the bar of world opinion. With these intentions the debate was bound to become involved in a series of parliamentary maneuvers and vote-getting tactics.

The clash on disarmament began, as usual, in the First Committee. A fourteen-power joint resolution was introduced which asked the General Assembly (1), to commend the Commission for its efforts and the initiative of those nations (the United States and the United Kingdom) which had submitted constructive proposals; and (2), to reaffirm the Sixth General Assembly's disarmament resolution. By having fourteen nations, located throughout the world, introduce the resolution, the Western powers sought to stress the world-wide support of their position.

Countering this resolution was the Soviet one which asked the General Assembly to condemn the United States, United Kingdom and France for diverting the Commission with proposals for illegally obtaining intelligence reports and asking the Commission to proceed with its work.

Motivating this set of proposals was the desire by each side to seek United Nations approval of its position. This motivation was blatantly expressed in the Anglo-American efforts to seek commendation and in the Soviet efforts toward condemnation. Considerably more significant because its implications were more subtle was the support to be accorded to the Sixth General Assembly's disarmament resolution. This resolution, in addition to creating the Disarmament Commission, gave specific approval of the majority plan for international control of atomic energy as well as the plan for progressive disclosure and verification of armed forces and armaments. Between the two central protagonists, each seeking support for its policies, were a large number of states which were more interested in some form of reconciliation of the two positions than in outright support of either side. Traditionally, this middle force was responsible for watering down the extreme elements of both sides so that some workable compromise could be adopted. Thus efforts to censure or praise individual nations often encountered great difficulty.

Representing this middle force in the First Committee, India called upon the smaller powers to assist in bringing about a "conciliatory spirit" instead of supporting either side. Expressing a similar point of view, Egypt, Syria, Iraq and Yemen jointly introduced an amendment to the fourteen-power proposal removing commendation of individual members of the Commission. So amended, the fourteen-power proposal was adopted in the First Committee.

When the First Committee's report came before the General Assembly Andrei Vyshinsky, the principal Soviet spokesman, abandoned his government's direct challenge of the Western position in favor of a more indirect attack. He now urged an attitude of conciliation and mutual concessions in order to reach agreement. In the interests of adopting a unanimous decision, the Soviet Union announced that it would not press for adoption of its own resolution presented in the First Committee. Rather, Vyshinsky asked of the Assembly only that it delete any commendatory references to the Commission and any reaffirmation of the previous Assembly's disarmament resolution. For a brief period not only were the Russian representative's speeches moderate in tone, but even the Ukrainian and smaller states of Eastern Europe were conciliatory in spirit.

For the sake of a "larger agreement" the British representative was willing to eliminate any reference to commending the Disarmament Commission for its efforts. He refused, however, to approve deleting reaffirmation of the previous disarmament resolution. Ernest Gross (United States) adopted the same attitude. He called attention to the "important guiding principles" established by the resolution and added: "If the Soviet Union amendment were accepted, the Soviet Union, as we believe is its intention, would be in a position, at the very least, to cast doubt upon the General Assembly's support of these principles which have repeatedly been endorsed by the majority of the Members of the United Nations." The USSR amendment would raise the question whether the General Assembly continued to support the United Nations plan for the control of atomic energy.[20] Andrei Vyshinsky replied to Mr. Gross:

> It has rightly been said here that it is not essential to reaffirm any given resolution in every case and in every connection. Mr. Gross, however, considers it necessary to reaffirm any given resolution in every case and in every connection, believing that its authority will otherwise be weakened. I do not consider that argument at all convincing. . . .
> We are discussing the question of requesting the Disarmament Commission to continue its work on the basis of the principles set forth specifically in . . . the draft resolution. Does this mean that none of these principles is subject to amendment or modification or that our views in their regard are already crystallized and rigidly defined to the point where . . . they are not subject to modification in any way? Our delegation takes a different view of the matter. We are considering this question now in order that we should be agreed when we meet in the Disarmament Commission to begin new work, or to continue our old work, inspired by the same intention of reaching agreement and settling problems which are still outstanding . . .[21]

The Soviet representative suggested that the Sixth General Assembly's resolution might not reflect "the wishes of the whole Assembly as at present constituted." There was some basis to this supposition. While sympathy toward the Russian proposals was limited to the Soviet bloc, a large number of nations earnestly wanted the Soviet Union and Western powers to establish some basis for a continuation of discussion in the Commission. In the final vote taken April 8, the Soviet amendment removing commendation of the Commission was overwhelmingly accepted. The Soviet amendment deleting reference to the Sixth General

[20] UN, *ORGA, Seventh Session. Plenary Meetings. Verbatim Records of Meetings 14 October 1952-28 August 1953*, 424th meeting, pp. 683-84.
[21] *Ibid.*, pp. 690-91.

Assembly's resolution was defeated; but the total number of nations who either abstained or voted for the defeated amendment was only ten less than the number voting to reject it. The fourteen-power proposal was then adopted by a vote of fifty-two in favor, five against and three abstaining. It reaffirmed the United Nations plan for control of atomic energy and requested the Disarmament Commission to continue its work.

Though the Seventh General Assembly had reaffirmed its support for the majority plan, it was now clear that the battle for international control of atomic energy had been played out. There was much that the Disarmament Commission could fruitfully study and possibly negotiate, but not international control of atomic energy. By the early 1950s political and technological developments had made the subject obsolete. When the original Baruch Plan was proposed in 1946 neither nation had developed any sizable stockpile of atomic weapons and it was reasonable to assume that if the radical American plan were adopted and fully implemented, every nation in the world would be guaranteed security against a surprise attack with atomic weapons. Furthermore, enough good will still remained of the wartime alliance to create an expectation that each nation might be willing to sacrifice its national sovereignty for the greater benefit of world peace and security.

During the eight years since the first Hiroshima blast, three occurrences served to undermine these assumptions: (1), the development of the cold war destroyed the necessary mutual confidence required to implement the plan; (2), in both the United States and the Soviet Union a gradual stockpile of atomic weapons was created; and (3), American fear of Soviet intentions and the existence of a powerful Russian land army compelled the United States to integrate its atomic weapons with its conventional forces. This last movement was completed approximately by 1953 and in effect sounded the death knell for any plan of international control of atomic energy.

Had the Soviet Union in 1946 considered an agreement on

control possible, it would have been to its advantage to see one implemented as soon as possible. Every delay provided the United States with increased opportunity to build secret stockpiles. By the time of America's first hydrogen bomb explosion in November, 1952, the Soviet Union had every reason to believe that a considerable number of bombs was stockpiled in the United States. The entry of Great Britain to the list of atomic powers a month earlier could only serve to increase the danger to the Soviet Union. This aspect of the problem was never publicly aired by the Soviet Union at all. The Soviet Government's policies of minimizing the destructive power of atomic bombs, of refusing to recognize or acknowledge the interrelation between nuclear fuel for peaceful use and weapons production, and its insistence that a public declaration of prohibition would in itself guarantee security, all prevented it from admitting this elementary, yet crucial aspect of the problem. To have admitted the existence of the problem of hidden atomic stockpiles, the Soviet Union would have had to acknowledge the correctness of the scientific and technological facts upon which the majority plan of control was based. Eventually when the majority ceased to push its plan for control the Soviet Government did acknowledge that undetectable atomic stockpiles would render any control plan meaningless.[22]

Conversely, as the Soviet Union developed its own hidden supply of weapons, the majority plan lost its rationale for the Western powers. Just as for the Soviet Union, the majority plan involved a radical sacrifice of American national sovereignty and a significant interference in its freedom to manage its own internal economy. Such a price could be justified only by the security guaranteed by the plan. After the Soviet atomic explosion in 1949 the price increased annually, relative to the diminished security due to the growing Soviet stockpile. In August, 1953, the Soviet Union exploded its own hydrogen device. Shortly after that *Pravda* gave notice that the Soviet Government intended to keep on producing atomic weapons until

[22] See pp. 202-203 of chap. VIII.

the United States accepted the Soviet proposals.[23] Unlike the Soviet Union the Western powers used the growing atomic stockpiles as an argument for concluding a control agreement with all deliberate haste. The French representative warned the General Assembly at its eighth session that even if a control plan were accepted on the spot it would be difficult to determine how much nuclear fuel for bombs had been produced previously.

If by 1952-1953, technological factors had served to weaken the effectiveness of a control plan, the political-military strategy of the United States during this period destroyed whatever motivation the United States may have had in promoting control. From the latter part of 1951 until the beginning of 1954 a continuous process of integration of atomic and conventional weapons took place within the Armed Forces of the United States. The series of atomic tests in Nevada in October, 1951, proved for the first time that atomic tactical weapons could effectively be used in combat. In January, 1952, President Truman announced a $5-6 billion expansion of atomic energy facilities. It was the largest expansion since the United States Atomic Energy Commission had been created in 1946. This announcement, which was part of his budget proposals for the fiscal year beginning July, 1952, indicated a major breakthrough in the bottlenecks that had stood in the way of a vast expansion program.[24] Gordon Dean, Chairman of the United States Atomic Energy Commission, cited as one of the principal factors in the

[23] *Pravda*, October 29, 1953. In connection with the Soviet hydrogen explosion, it is interesting that unlike its announcement of its atomic explosion the Soviet Government revealed the accomplishment before any Western nation reported it. On August 9, 1953, Premier Georgi Malenkov announced to the Supreme Soviet that "The Government deems it necessary to report to the Supreme Soviet that the United States has no monopoly in the production of the hydrogen bomb," *Pravda*, August 10, 1953. On August 20 the Soviet Government announced the successful testing of a hydrogen bomb. The United States Atomic Energy Commission reported the date of the successful firing as August 12. *New York Times*, August 20, 1953.

[24] Extensive excerpts of the budget are printed in the *New York Times*, January 22, 1952. That part concerned with atomic energy is on p. 22. William L. Lawrence commented: "The decision assumes special significance in view of the fact that it comes shortly after the tests of new, tailor-made, tactical atomic weapons in Nevada in the Autumn of 1951." *New York Times*, January 24, 1952.

decision to expand nuclear production the substantial improvement in the uranium supply available to the United States. In the United States Senate Brian McMahon announced, "There is no limit or limiting factor upon which the number of atomic bombs which the United States can manufacture, given time and given a decision to go all out." He suggested that under an expanded American program atomic bombs "numbering in thousands or tens of thousands" were no longer beyond reach.[25]

America's growing reliance on atomic weapons was not limited to its own continental defense. It was logically extended to the North Atlantic Treaty Organization, then looked upon as the West's principal bulwark against Soviet expansion in Europe. General Dwight Eisenhower, Supreme Allied Commander in Europe, intimated in his first annual report (April, 1952) that NATO forces were being equipped with tactical atomic weapons.

The military forces [reported General Eisenhower] we are building must be continually modified to keep pace with new weapons.

[25] *Ibid.*, January 24, 1952. Gordon Dean, Chairman of the United States Atomic Energy Commission, listed four factors which contributed to America's increased supply of uranium. They were:

1. The discovery of new rich uranium deposits in Canada.
2. The extension, through an extensive exploration program, of the uranium-bearing region of the Colorado Plateau in the United States.
3. The development of improved and more economical methods of extracting uranium from low-grade ore.
4. The conclusion of an agreement whereby the United States and Great Britain have obtained access to the very large stores of uranium that occur as a constituent in the residues of gold production in the Union of South Africa.

New York Times, January 24, 1952. Explaining the continued testing at Nevada in the spring of 1952, Gordon Dean said:
"Today atomic weapons are thought of as tactical as well as strategic weapons —that is, they are thought of as weapons that can be employed by military forces in the field. In other words, they are thought of as weapons which tactical air force and armies and navies—as well as strategic air forces—have a legitimate interest in and legitimate need for.
"This, quite naturally, vastly increases the quantity and variety in which atomic weapons are needed. It means, among other things, that the assumption that there is an early saturation point in the development and manufacture of atomic weapons is no longer valid. This explains why we are undertaking a very large expansion of the national atomic energy program, and why we are holding so many of these weapons' tests." *Ibid.*, April 22, 1952.

. . . We are at the very point, for example, of seeing a whole sequence of fundamental changes made in response to the development of new types of arms. The tendency in recent decades to produce weapons of greater range, penetrating power and destructiveness is accelerating.[26]

Shortly before this report was published, General Alfred M. Gruenther, SHAPE chief of staff, publicly warned the Russians that tactical atomic bombs would be used against any Soviet attack on Western Europe. With the advent of a Republican administration in 1953 this policy was extended. President Eisenhower's budget proposals presented in January, 1954, underscored the increased American reliance on atomic weapons. The policy of "massive retaliation," announced by the American secretary of state, John Foster Dulles, relying as it did on a strategic use of nuclear weapons, was a logical extension of this process.

These events had a profound significance for the course of negotiations in 1953. If before control was not wanted, now it was not possible. For the Soviet Union, this permitted a relaxation from its policy of constant opposition to the Western proposals. The Western proposals became essentially meaningless. Any future plan for some type of control would obviously have to be more limited in scope than the United Nations plan. It would have to be part of a larger agreement on disarmament because of Western dependence on atomic weapons. And it would, therefore, have to be linked to some form of political settlement between the United States and Soviet Union. Such an agreement could only be established through private negotiations. Public sessions in United Nations organs could not, in view of the past record of atomic energy negotiations, provide the necessary flexibility for a comprehensive disarmament plan. The death of Premier Stalin in March, 1953, provided the Kremlin leadership with the opportunity to reformulate its policy on disarmament.

Although asked by the General Assembly to continue its meetings, the Disarmament Commission ceased working entirely between the Seventh and Eighth General Assembly sessions. The

[26] *Ibid.*, April 2, 1952. The text of the report is on pp. 14-15.

changing international situation was the reason. In April, 1953, armistice negotiations were initiated in Korea. An armistice was finally signed in July. On August 20, the Commission met briefly to approve its third report. That report merely noted:

> It is hoped that recent international events will create a more propitious atmosphere for the reconsideration of the disarmament question, whose capital importance in conjunction with other questions affecting the maintenance of peace is recognized by all. The Disarmament Commission therefore expects to continue its work, and suggests that it present a report to the ninth session of the General Assembly and to the Security Council.[27]

On the very day the Commission was holding its lone meeting, the Soviet Government announced a successful test explosion of its hydrogen bomb. This event completely overshadowed the work of the Commission. As the delegates assembled for the Eighth General Assembly session in New York more concern was expressed about what propaganda the Soviet Union would make of its hydrogen bomb than of what constructive proposals would be made toward atomic energy control.

When the General Assembly First Committee took up the issue November 8, 1953, it was again confronted with a fourteen-power proposal requesting the Disarmament Commission to continue its efforts to reach agreement. Unlike many previous General Assembly debates, the contest at the eighth session was not entirely a United States versus Soviet Union fight. Considerable concern was manifest during the debate over the stagnation that had resulted. Numerous amendments and amendments to amendments were proposed, making this one of the most complex of all the debates on disarmament and atomic energy control.

Four amendments to the fourteen-power proposal were proposed by nonsponsors of the original resolution. All were adopted. One gave recognition of a state of urgency caused by the continued development of atomic and hydrogen weapons. Another expressed the sense of danger brought about by the competitive arms race. A third included hydrogen, chemical

[27] DC/32, p. 1 in UN, DCOR, *Supplement for July, August and September 1953.*

and bacterial along with atomic weapons as subjects of control and prohibition. Fourth, and most important, the Disarmament Commission was requested to study the desirability of establishing a subcommittee consisting of representatives of the "powers principally involved" which would seek an acceptable solution "in private." [28]

Initially the Soviets' reaction closely followed their activity in previous sessions. The Russian delegate submitted an amendment proposing several revisions of the fourteen-power proposal. As usual Russia asked for recognition of the primacy of an agreement on arms reduction, prohibition and strict atomic energy control, and recognition that such an agreement would contribute to the settlement of other controversial international problems. In place of his usual proposal for an immediate outright prohibition of atomic weapons the Soviet representative offered a variant proposal. According to it the General Assembly

would recognize that the use of atomic and hydrogen weapons as weapons of aggression and mass destruction was contrary to the conscience and honor of the people and incompatible with membership in the United Nations and declare that the government which was the first to use the atomic, hydrogen or any other instrument of mass destruction against any other country would commit a crime against humanity and would be deemed a war criminal.[29]

Speaking of this last proposal, Andrei Vyshinsky made the rare admission that "it was more difficult to set up control than to adopt a decision." However, he insisted, any "self-respecting State" which entered into an international agreement, would be "morally and politically" bound to comply with such a decision. The Soviet representative announced that if a resolution on prohibition were adopted, his government was prepared to declare not only that no atomic weapons would be produced in the Soviet Union, but that not a "fraction of a ruble" would be used

[28] For a comprehensive description of the complex voting on this issue see UN, Department of Public Information, *Yearbook of the United Nations 1953* (New York, 1954), pp. 262-68.
[29] A/C.1/L.75/Rev.3 in UN, *ORGA, Eighth Session, Annexes.* Agenda item 23.

for such production. He protected the Kremlin with the qualifi-
cation: "Of course, if other representatives suggested that their
countries might continue production, that would be an obstacle
to the adoption of such a resolution." [30] To no one's surprise all
the Soviet amendments were rejected.

When the fourteen-power proposal came to a vote in the
First Committee November 18, the Soviet delegation reversed
almost seven years of traditional behavior by not voting against
the majority resolution. As amended, the resolution reaffirmed
the need for international control of atomic energy and the
prohibition of atomic and hydrogen weapons. However, nothing
was said of the United Nations plan for control of atomic energy.
The resolution requested the Disarmament Commission to continue its efforts to reach agreement and suggested that the Commission establish a subcommittee "of the powers principally involved" which should seek an acceptable solution "in private."

The General Assembly in plenary session adopted this draft
proposal by a vote of fifty-four to none. The Soviet bloc abstained. For the first time since 1946 the Soviet Union had failed
to vote against a majority proposal concerned with atomic
energy. Andrei Vyshinsky explained his vote as follows:

> I am . . . answering the question why the Soviet delegation ab-
> stained in the vote . . . It abstained because the amendments it
> considered essential, and which, if adopted, would have enabled it
> to support the draft resolution, had been rejected. That is why we
> cannot vote for this draft resolution. Then why do we not vote
> against it? Because it contains certain points which bring us closer
> together. We have never taken the fanatical attitude of rejecting
> proposals merely because they did not happen to be ours. Even if
> they are not ours, yet contain a grain of truth which we can accept,
> or at least show some hint of readiness to work out the measures
> which the world so badly needs—the prohibition of atomic, hydro-
> gen and other weapons of mass destruction, and the reduction of
> armaments and armed forces—we abstain even though our wording
> is more radical and the decision we propose is not taken into
> consideration. That is only natural. We are entitled to criticize
> the draft upon which the Assembly is about to vote; we have

[30] UN, *ORGA, Eighth Session. First Committee, Summary Records of
Meetings 16 September-7 December 1953*, 658th meeting, pp. 174-175.

submitted amendments to it, and we cannot support it as it stands, but we find it possible to abstain.[31]

Implied in Vyshinsky's enigmatic reference to "certain parts which bring us closer together" was the virtual demise of any realization of international control of atomic energy. The Eighth General Assembly resolution failed to make any reference to the majority plan. Had any reference to the majority plan been a subject of debate, failure to mention it would have been tantamount to a repudiation. So formally the plan was not repudiated. In effect, however, by not including it in the Disarmament Commission's mandate the plan was unofficially recognized to be outdated. All that the resolution called for was "the effective international control of atomic energy" and this was sufficiently ambiguous to receive a Soviet blessing. No longer was the adjective "effective" a subject of debate. For the Soviet Union as well as the Western Powers the technical and political developments between 1946 and 1953 guaranteed that an "effective" plan would not be along the line of the old Baruch Plan. The events that heralded the end of atomic energy negotiations were not so dramatic as the explosion over Hiroshima in 1945 or so publicized as the First General Assembly resolution creating the Atomic Energy Commission, but they were as fateful.

The year 1953 thus marks the end of a period. Having invented a uniquely murderous weapon of destruction, the West had challenged the Soviet Union to guarantee its nonuse forever by a plan involving a radical infringement of national sovereignty. For over eight years the Soviet Union resisted the challenge. During the eight-year period the plan became obsolete and was abandoned. Talk of international control of atomic energy did extend beyond 1953; but after that date discussions were concerned with a significantly more limited control than envisaged in the Baruch Plan. At the same time the world was denied the hope of the almost absolute security from an atomic attack which animated the Baruch Plan.

[31] UN, *ORGA, Eighth Session, Plenary Meetings. Verbatim Records of Meetings 15 September-9 December 1953*, 460th meeting, p. 327.

In 1953 not only the goals of negotiation changed, but the means too. Eight years of fruitless debate had discredited disarmament negotiations in open meetings. One of the most significant accomplishments of the Eighth General Assembly was to commit disarmament negotiations to private sessions of the four major powers. Even more important for the future use of atomic energy internationally was the proposal made by President Eisenhower December 8, 1953, for an international atomic energy agency to promote the peaceful uses of atomic energy. His proposal envisaged contributions of uranium and fissionable materials to an international agency by the atomic energy-producing nations of the world. An effective control plan would be limited to that material freely given to the international agency. Being so limited, President Eisenhower stated that his proposal

has the great virtue that it can be undertaken without the irritations and mutual suspicions incident to any attempt to set up a completely acceptable system of worldwide inspection and control.

The atomic energy agency could be made responsible for the impounding, storage and protection of the contributed fissionable and other materials. The ingenuity of our scientists will provide special safe conditions under which such a bank of fissionable material can be made essentially immune to surprise seizure.[32]

He called upon the Soviet Union to discuss the details in "private conversations." On December 21 the Soviet Government accepted the American offer to take part in negotiations for an international atomic energy agency.[33]

[32] UN, Department of Public Information, *Yearbook of the United Nations 1953* (New York, 1954), p. 286.
[33] *Tass* communiqué of December 21, 1953, in *Pravda*, December 22, 1953. The complete *Tass* announcement is in the *New York Times*, December 22, 1953. See pp. 222-27 of chap. VIII.

8: FROM BANNING THE BOMB

TO BANNING TESTS

As the world moves into the 1960s the subject of atomic energy control is still high on the agenda of East-West negotiations. But today, fifteen years after the first atomic explosion, the object of these negotiations as far as atomic energy is concerned is considerably reduced from the original goal of internationalizing the entire industry.

While the atomic energy aspect of current negotiations is more limited, their over-all scope since 1953 has widened to include the larger issue of disarmament. Nuclear weapons are today an essential element of the military arsenals of the Soviet Union and the major Western powers. They have figured in one way or another in almost every series of disarmament negotiations. In May and June, 1954, the Disarmament Commission's subcommittee began the first of five intensive sessions (ending in September, 1957) that sought to explore every important phase of disarmament. "Package deals," partial "first steps," comprehensive plans, "phased" stages toward agreement—all were considered. Control of nuclear weapons was linked with nonnuclear problems including manpower reductions, prevention against surprise attack, "open skies," disengagement in Europe, the solution of political issues, the establishment of an international peace force and more. Throughout all these negotiations, though, a thread of constancy in Soviet policy remains. Behind every breakdown of negotiations lay the obstacle of Soviet objections to Western demands for control—objections stemming from their monumental suspicion of Western intentions. The Western powers, for their part, have continued to demand rigorous controls as a part of any agreement, no matter how comprehensive.

By the mid-1950s both sides publicly acknowledged the impossibility of internationalizing the production of all atomic energy. The United States tacitly abandoned the ideas of the Baruch Plan before the Disarmament Subcommittee meeting in London in the spring of 1954. On May 25 the United States proposed the creation of a Disarmament and Atomic Development Authority to control atomic energy *"to the extent necessary to insure effective prohibition of nuclear weapons and the use of nuclear materials for peaceful purposes only."* [1] No longer did the United States insist upon international ownership of fissionable fuel or atomic reactors and refining plants. Whatever powers the Authority needed would be determined by treaty among the nations. The plan did authorize field inspections and aerial survey, but that was a far cry from the all-embracing powers of the majority plan of 1948. Subsequently, even this proposal was disavowed when in September, 1955, Harold E. Stassen, President Eisenhower's special assistant for disarmament, placed a reservation upon all American proposals made prior to the Geneva Conference of July, 1955.

The collective leadership succeeding Stalin and the ending of the Korean War in 1953 produced a temporary relaxation in Soviet-Western relations. This relaxation reached its peak in the spring and summer of 1955. "Peaceful coexistence" became one of the principal themes in Soviet foreign policy pronouncements. Enough good will was engendered to pressure the French, British and American heads of government to meet with Soviet Premier Bulganin at Geneva in July to work out a disarmament settlement. Just prior to the Geneva Conference the Soviet

---

[1] 84th Congress, 2nd sess., U. S. Senate, Subcommittee on Disarmament. *Disarmament and Security: A Collection of Documents, 1919-1955* (hereinafter referred to as *U. S. Documents*), p. 329. Italics added.

Government made a belated recognition that a ban against nuclear weapons could not be controlled. In its May 10 proposals the Soviet Union acknowledged that

It is well known that the production of atomic energy for peaceful purposes can be used for the accumulation of stocks of explosive atomic materials, and moreover, in ever greater quantities. This means that States having establishments for the production of atomic energy can accumulate, in violation of the relevant agreements, large quantities of explosive materials for the production of atomic weapons. The danger of this state of affairs becomes still more understandable if account is taken of the fact that where the corresponding quantities of explosive atomic materials exist production of actual atomic and hydrogen bombs is technically fully feasible and can be effected on a large scale.

Thus, there are possibilities beyond the reach of international control for evading this control and for organizing the clandestine manufacture of atomic and hydrogen weapons, even if there is a formal agreement on international control. In such a situation, the security of the States signatories to the international convention cannot be guaranteed, since the possibility would be open to a potential aggressor to accumulate stocks of atomic and hydrogen weapons for a surprise atomic attack on peace-loving States.[2]

In effect the Soviet Union admitted that a point of no return had been reached, since three major powers had produced a stockpile of atomic bombs both unaccountable for and capable of indefinite storage. Thus any absolute ban of atomic weapons would of necessity have to rest partially upon good faith. The Soviet Government quite frankly stated that "a situation may arise in which the adoption of decisions on international control will in reality be reduced to a mere formality which does not achieve the objective."[3] Any hopes the West may have harbored that this admission would mark the end of Soviet demands for banning the bomb were shattered by the same May 10 proposals. In them the Soviets again called for the complete prohibition of the use and production of atomic weapons; and, ironically enough, they called for the establishment of a control organ to guarantee the effective observance of such a prohibition.

[2] *Ibid.*, p. 389.
[3] *Ibid.*, p. 388.

A complete prohibition of the use and production of atomic weapons has remained the ultimate goal of all Soviet disarmament proposals. Under Western pressure, however, the Kremlin had agreed at various times to negotiate for some lesser goal either in isolation from a larger agreement or presumably as a first step toward a larger agreement. In general the following observation has remained valid: the more isolated and limited the issue under discussion the greater the prospects for success; the more comprehensive the goals, the more complete the impasse. Thus in the area of atomic energy the major powers have been able to come to some agreement only on the issues of an international atomic energy agency dealing with the peaceful exchange of atomic materials and knowledge and a cessation of nuclear tests. Both these issues will be considered separately below. On the other hand a Soviet demand for the total prohibition of nuclear weapons has proven to be a fairly good indication that the purposes of discussion are more propagandistic than for agreement.

There are four different facets to the problem of nuclear weapons control: (1), unconditionally banning the *use* of nuclear weapons; (2), destroying the *past* production of nuclear weapons stocks; (3), prohibiting the *future* production of fissionable materials for weapons purposes (commonly known as a "cut-off" in atomic weapons production); and (4), a cessation of nuclear weapons tests. Of these four only the latter two are susceptible to verification by means of some type of a control system. As far as the Western powers have been concerned since the mid-1950s, an isolated agreement prohibiting unconditionally the use of atomic weapons or calling for a destruction of all accumulated stocks has been out of the question. They cannot be controlled and a disarmament agreement without controls remains unacceptable. This leaves a cut-off in weapons production and a test ban as the only areas open for possible agreement on nuclear weapons. (Those negotiations concerning a limited "atomic-free zone" in Europe are not considered here because of their close connection with other disarmament issues and political questions.)

The Western powers have decided to put a greater stress on a cut-off in atomic weapons production than on a nuclear test cessation. President Eisenhower first proposed a cut-off agreement in a letter to Premier Bulganin dated March 1, 1956. The United States, he said, "would be prepared to work out, with other nations, suitable and safeguarded arrangements so that future production of fissionable materials anywhere in the world would no longer be used to increase the stockpiles of explosive weapons." [4] Without specifying any details, the president expressed confidence that an effective system of safeguards could be devised. That same month the British and French submitted a plan before the Disarmament Subcommittee which included in one of its stages a cut-off in the manufacture of nuclear weapons. France, in particular, stressed the importance of a cut-off. Her representative warned that without such an agreement the French would proceed with making and testing their own nuclear weapons. [5]

Western suggestions for a cut-off did not meet with a favorable Soviet response. In fact, in its counterproposals of March 27, 1956, [6] the Soviet Union totally ignored the problem of controlling nuclear weapons. Apart from a cessation of nuclear tests this proposal dealt only with conventional armaments. Mr. Gromyko defended his government's omission of nuclear disarmament on the grounds that the problem was too controversial for big-power agreement. Not since the first discovery of atomic weapons had the Soviet Union failed to press for some type of nuclear disarmament. One can only speculate on the reasons for this dramatic reversal in Soviet policy. Quite

[4] UN, Disarmament Commission. *Third Report of the Sub-Committee of the Disarmament Commission.* Document DC/83, May 4, 1956, Annex 1. Previously a proposal for a cut-off had been included in the Anglo-French Memorandum of June 11, 1954. This was part of the second phase of a three-phased general agreement. See *U. S. Documents,* p. 333.

[5] Anthony Nutting, *Disarmament: An Outline of the Negotiations* (London, 1959), p. 23.

[6] See UN Document DC/83, May 4, 1956, Annex 5, pp. 8-11.

possibly the Soviets were on the threshold of catching up in
nuclear weapons development with the United States and felt
that any agreement reached might jeopardize their achieving
equality. Certainly the period between 1954-1958 witnessed
an intensive development of nuclear weapons, if tests are any
indication. In at least one important development they achieved
an atomic "first" over the United States: the Soviet Union successfully tested a deliverable hydrogen bomb dropped from an
aircraft November 23, 1955, whereas the United States did not
detonate an H-bomb in an actual drop from an airplane until
May 21, 1956.[7] This Soviet achievement was the culmination of
a series of tests begun in August, 1955. In 1956 another extensive
test series was conducted in the Soviet Union, some of the tests
having as their object the perfecting of atomic warheads for
tactical purposes. Through March, 1958, the Soviet test program accelerated to such a pace that in the early part of that
year there were several instances of more than one test being
conducted on the same day. When the Geneva conference to
ban tests began in November, 1958, the Soviet Union had already
developed a wide range of nuclear weapons.[8]

Later in 1956, following the failure of the Disarmament Subcommittee to reach agreement on any disarmament measure,
Mr. Gromyko did announce Soviet willingness to accept a
cut-off, but this concession was tied in with a demand for the
destruction of already accumulated nuclear stockpiles as well
as an unconditional ban on the use of nuclear weapons.

The last major effort of the United Nations Disarmament Commission to work out a comprehensive disarmament agreement
including nuclear weapons took place in the spring and summer
of 1957. Initially a mood of optimism prevailed as the Subcommittee began its fifth and longest session in March. The
frequent resort to name-calling and invective which had so

---

[7] Arnold Kramish, *Atomic Energy in the Soviet Union* (Stanford, Calif.,
1959), pp. 125 and 127.

[8] *Ibid.*, pp. 126-29. The Soviet announcement on May 14, 1956, of a reduction in its armed forces by 1,200,000 over and above the 640,000 reduction
announced in 1955 was probably an indication of the developing nuclearization
of its armed forces.

much characterized the Subcommittee sessions from 1954 through 1956 was noticeably absent at the London sessions. Moscow's initial position on nuclear weapons was a two-stage plan proposed March 18, 1957. In the first stage all states, *inter alia*, would assume a solemn obligation not to use atomic and hydrogen weapons. In a second stage the prohibition would be complete, including the destruction of past stockpiles and a cut-off on future weapons production. The only guarantee of observance proposed was a control organ empowered to inspect on a permanent basis.[9]

Again the West found the Soviet atomic prohibition too sweeping for any proposed or even known control system. In reply Valerin Zorin introduced a new set of Soviet proposals for partial disarmament April 30, 1957. They included no suggestion for nuclear weapons control. They called for a formal declaration renouncing "the use for military purposes of atomic and hydrogen weapons of all types . . ." and singled out a test cessation as the one problem requiring solution "without delay." [10] Throughout this session Mr. Zorin placed the highest priority on a test ban agreement. All four Western powers insisted that a cut-off must accompany any test ban. A test ban without a cut-off, they argued, would leave those nations farthest advanced in nuclear development with a permanent military advantage and free to go on increasing their advantage by piling up stocks. In reply the Soviet delegates refused to accept any cut-off agreement that was not accompanied by an unconditional ban on the use of nuclear weapons and the destruction of all stocks. The diplomats were arguing in circles.

Much of the good will that had opened the 1957 subcommittee session in March disappeared during the summer. Mr. Zorin's temper grew noticeably shorter in August. He complained of the slowness of the proceedings and attacked the sincerity of Western intentions to negotiate. Finally on August 27, 1957,

[9] UN, Disarmament Commission. *Fourth Report of the Sub-Committee of the Disarmament Commission.* Document DC/112, August 1, 1957, Annex 1. These stages, of course, included provisions for conventional disarmament.
[10] *Ibid.*, Annex 7.

he in effect terminated all serious negotiations with a blistering attack upon the Western positions. "In all this time," he said, "the subcommittee has not advanced one inch towards the solution of the problems referred to it."[11] He accused the NATO powers of using the discussions as a "cover" while they armed themselves with atomic weapons. Two days later the Western powers introduced a revised set of proposals. Mr. Zorin promptly rejected them on the same day, and for all practical purposes the Disarmament Commission went out of business.

Since then the propaganda ploy of all disarmament negotiations has become more blatant than ever. A prime objective of Soviet nuclear policy has been to encourage opposition within Europe to the nuclear armament of NATO, particularly West Germany. The dangers of a nuclear war in Europe have been repeated incessantly, particularly after the NATO Council decided in December, 1957, to accept American nuclear weapons and have them at NATO's disposal.[12] Having found the Subcommittee with its private talks an unsuitable sounding board for its propaganda efforts, the Soviet Union has continuously pressed for a larger negotiating forum. In addition it has demanded one in which the communist powers would be represented in equal numbers.

Soviet Russia gave notice before the Twelfth General Assembly that it would no longer participate in the Disarmament Commission and its subcommittee as then constituted.[13] What it wanted was a commission composed of the full United Nations membership (then eighty-two nations). A compromise with the Western preference for a small body composed of those principally concerned was effected, enlarging the Disarmament Commission to twenty-five. This failed to satisfy the Soviet bloc. True to their threat, they boycotted the Commission in 1958. At the Thirteenth General Assembly in November, 1958,

[11] UN, Disarmament Commission. *Fifth Report of the Sub-Committee of the Disarmament Commission*. Document DC/113, September 11, 1957, Annex 4, p. 2.
[12] Nutting, *op. cit.*, p. 44.
[13] UN, *ORGA*, 12 sess., 1st Com. 890th meeting, November 4, 1957, par. 2, 7.

the Commission was expanded to include the full UN membership; but to date it has not functioned as a negotiating forum.

Other than the debates before the General Assembly all disarmament negotiations since 1957 have been conducted between
the two sides, outside the United Nations. And with the exception of the question of a nuclear test cessation (to be considered below) these conferences have not been principally
concerned with international control over atomic energy. Three
conferences were held or initiated in 1958. Two concerned the
banning of nuclear tests. A third meeting in Geneva from November 10 to December 18, 1958, sought to study possible
measures to prevent surprise attack. It could not so much as
agree on an agenda.[14]

The last group to consider some form of nuclear weapons control was the ten-nation committee created at the Foreign Ministers' Conference in the spring of 1960. At Soviet insistence the
group was composed of an equal number of communist and
Western powers. Representatives of Bulgaria, Canada, Czechoslovakia, France, Italy, Poland, Rumania, the Soviet Union, the
United Kingdom and the United States comprised the group. The
purpose of the foreign ministers' meeting which set up the group
was to lay the groundwork for an anticipated summit conference
of the Big Four heads of governments. Disarmament and German
reunification were the two principal items on the agenda. By
setting up another high-level conference—as the ten-nation
group—the major powers hoped possibly to delineate those
areas of agreement and disagreement for reconciliation at a
summit conference or to have the heads of government ratify
whatever agreement was reached. As it turned out, the summit
meeting collapsed before commencing and the ten-nation group
disbanded after less than three months' work.

When the ten-nation group convened March 15, it had before
it Premier Khrushchev's plan for general and complete disarmament introduced originally before the Fourteenth General
Assembly. It called for the usual complete prohibition of all

[14] See UN, General Assembly document A/4078 (S/4145) January 5, 1959
for the Conference Report.

atomic and hydrogen weapons. While it proposed a control over this and other measures, it offered no details as to that control.[15] The five Western nations proposed only that joint East-West studies be undertaken immediately to determine measures guaranteeing a cut-off in the manufacture of fissionable materials for weapons and to determine ways to transfer the fuel from weapons to peaceful purposes. Both the cut-off and transfer would be effected as soon as the controls were agreed upon.[16] On June 2, 1960, Mr. Zorin offered a Soviet counterproposal. In the nuclear area it revealed some accommodation to the Western demands. It too provided for joint studies for a cut-off and the destruction of nuclear stockpiles. At the same time it offered a control plan that significantly advanced beyond previous Soviet offers. The Soviets agreed to a control organization authorized to make on-the-spot inspections of all atomic enterprises from extraction to final use. Subject to further agreement, *fixed* control teams might be established at "some" enterprises and installations.[17] The "joker" in this proposal, however, was the Soviet demand that the West agree to all stages of the control plan, including an ultimate total prohibition, even before the joint studies were undertaken to determine whether control was feasible. Also they demanded as one of the first-stage measures that any state having nuclear weapons refrain from transferring such weapons to states not possessing them; and nonnuclear powers were to refrain from manufacturing atomic weapons.

What the Soviets were seeking within the ten-nation group was a Western commitment to total disarmament before any of the details of control were agreed upon. Clearly they were not going to get such a commitment. During June Mr. Zorin and his Eastern European colleagues set the stage for a termination of negotiations. They displayed irritation with the slowness of the American response to the proposals of June 2. Then sud-

[15] 86th Congress, 2nd sess. US Senate. *Hearing before the Subcommittee of the Committee on Foreign Relations.* June 10, 1960. The text of the Soviet proposal is contained in the Appendix, pp. 37-39.

[16] *Ibid.*, pp. 39-41.

[17] *Ibid.*, pp. 41-45.

denly on June 27, repeating a Soviet performance of two years previously, the Soviet delegates broke up the conference and walked out just as the West was about to make a counter-proposal. Their pretext was the charge that the West was stalling and had no genuine desire for disarmament. Premier Khrushchev called the talks "just a waste of time." [18] The first year of the new decade thus closed with no meeting of the minds nor with even a meeting of the diplomats.

TOWARD A CESSATION OF NUCLEAR TESTS

A cessation of nuclear tests is considered separately because the issue has developed somewhat differently from other nuclear disarmament problems. The most significant difference has been Soviet willingness to accept genuine controls, which if implemented would limit its freedom of action. In no other area of all postwar disarmament negotiations have the major powers been closer to an agreement. This issue too is one of the few in which the Soviet Union has taken the initiative. These observations must be qualified by the fact that an agreement has not yet been reached even here and there is no guarantee to date that one will be consummated. If one is, it will be a marked exception to Soviet atomic energy policy. Then, too, a test cessation, however important, is the most minimal goal of all those considered in connection with international control over atomic energy. Finally, those tactics of delay, dividing the Western powers and utilizing propaganda that have characterized all Soviet atomic energy and disarmament proposals, have been fully evident in their test ban negotiations.

Nuclear testing first became an international issue in 1954, following the thermonuclear explosions carried out by the United States in the Pacific Ocean in March, 1954. Disturbed and moved by the possible "after-effects" of the thermonuclear test explosions, India in April, 1954, asked the Disarmament Commission and its subcommittee to consider a "standstill agreement" on testing, "even if arrangements about the discontinuance

[18] *New York Times*, June 29, 1960.

of production and stockpiling must await more substantial agreement . . ." India's call received the wide support of Asians in general and was reiterated by the Asian-African conference held in Bandung in April, 1955.[19] Japan, whose citizens had been not only the first wartime victims of an atomic attack but also the first serious casualties of the testing program, expressed particular concern.

Soviet Russia made effective use of the world-wide concern, seizing the initiative in proposing a discontinuance of nuclear weapons tests. In its May 10, 1955, proposals the Soviet Government included a test cessation as one of the first measures to be carried out in the first stage of a comprehensive disarmament program. Later, on March 27, 1956, the USSR called upon all states "to discontinue forthwith tests of thermonuclear weapons" independently of the attainment of agreement on other problems of disarmament.[20] Premier Bulganin continued to press for an independent test cessation in his correspondence with President Eisenhower. On September 11, 1956, he wrote:

> I should also like to direct your attention, Mr. President, to so important and pressing a problem—one which is a part of the atomic problem—as that of discontinuing tests of atomic and hydrogen weapons. It is a known fact that the discontinuation of such tests does not in itself require any international control agreements, for the present state of science and engineering makes it possible to detect any explosion of an atomic or hydrogen bomb, wherever it may be set off. In our opinion this situation makes it possible to separate the problem of ending tests of atomic and hydrogen weapons from the general problem of disarmament and to solve it independently even now, without tying an agreement on this subject to agreements on other disarmament problems.[21]

Premier Bulganin's assertion that controls to detect a test violation were unnecessary was flatly denied by the West. Anglo-French proposals of March 19, 1956, agreed to a test ces-

---

[19] *U. S. Documents*, pp. 246-49 and 258.

[20] UN Document DC/83, May 4, 1956, Annex 5. Also *U. S. Documents*, p. 386.

[21] The White House Disarmament Staff, *Reference Documents on Disarmament Matters*, Background Series D-1 through D-42 (Washington, n.d.), D-36, p. 220.

sation, under controls, only as part of the third stage of a comprehensive disarmament agreement. United States Ambassador Lodge in January, 1957, added a cut-off, under an agreed control system, as a second Western condition before accepting a test ban. He defended this requirement on the grounds that without a cut-off the stockpiling of atomic weapons and the manufacture of additional weapons would continue. These would be weapons with a high radioactive fallout since there would be no tests to perfect low radioactive fallout weapons. To the French a test cessation without a cut-off in the production of nuclear war materials was undesirable because, as Jules Moch warned the Subcommittee, such a cessation would allow:

unlimited stockpiling of the deadliest weapons in the arsenals of three States—and three States only—and would create between Powers equal in law a *de facto* difference which might in the long run have very serious consequences. None of the Western Powers wants the world to be divided into three.[22]

The Western insistence on the need to continue testing until a cut-off agreement and a control plan were negotiated encountered strong criticism not only from the Soviet bloc in the United Nations but many of the leading neutralist nations as well. What particularly concerned many of the delegates at the Eleventh, Twelfth, and Thirteenth General Assemblies was the pollution of the atmosphere with radioactive fallout.

The first significant break on the question of a test cessation took place in the lengthy fifth session of the Disarmament Subcommittee in the spring and summer of 1957. Because of the strong feelings expressed in the General Assembly the Subcommittee gave it first priority. Initially both sides became bogged down on the old issue of control. The Soviet Union on April 30 repeated its demand for singling out the problem of a "discontinuation" of nuclear tests from the general problem of nuclear weapons, and solving it "without delay."[23] Mr. Zorin insisted that a test ban was self-policing and required no control machinery to supervise it because all explosions could be detected

[22] United Nations Document DC/SC.1/PV.149, August 21, 1957, p. 12.
[23] United Nations Document DC/112, August 1, 1957, Annex 7, p. 10.

at any distance. On May 6 the United Kingdom submitted a memorandum on nuclear test explosions which repeated the two Western conditions of a control system to police a ban and a cut-off in weapons production. It suggested the formation of a committee of technical experts to work out a system of control.[24]

A major barrier was suddenly eliminated in principle when on June 14 Mr. Zorin announced his government's willingness to accept controls over a test ban. In return for a two- or three-year moratorium on tests the Soviet Union agreed to "the establishment, on a basis of reciprocity, of control posts in the territory of the Soviet Union, the United States of America and the United Kingdom and in the Pacific Ocean area . . ."[25] There remained now only the question of a weapons production cut-off. In a move to compromise, the West offered to suspend tests under control for twelve months and to renew the suspension another twelve months, if satisfactory progress was being made in devising a control system for the production of fissionable fuel for military purposes. If at the end of this twenty-four-month period the cut-off had not been put into operation, tests might be resumed. Mr. Zorin rejected the compromise and with that the Subcommittee negotiations collapsed entirely.

The Soviet June 14 concession on controls for a test ban permitted it to seize the propaganda initiative to an extent previously unavailable to them. No single issue has served the USSR better than that of a test cessation in repairing the propaganda defeat it suffered in the United Nations Atomic Energy Commission. At the Twelfth General Assembly it capitalized upon the anxiety felt throughout the world over increased radiation in the atmosphere. The Western demand for a cut-off as a condition for a test ban was looked upon by many as an unnecessary obstacle toward obtaining an agreement. Further pressure was exerted against the American position when on March 31, 1958, the

[24] *Ibid.*, Annex 8. It also proposed that the three nuclear powers register in advance all test explosions with the United Nations.
[25] *Ibid.*, Annex 12.

Soviet Union announced a unilateral cessation of testing and called upon the other nuclear powers to do the same. Some of the impact of this announcement was lessened by the fact that the Soviet Government had just completed an intensive series of nuclear tests and the United States was about to begin a test series in Nevada.

Without abandoning the cut-off as a precondition for a test ban,[26] President Eisenhower proposed to Premier Khrushchev in the spring of 1958 that technical talks be held to determine the specific control measure for a test cessation. Premier Khrushchev's concurrence opened the way for the first Geneva conference on ending nuclear tests. Between July 1 and August 21, 1958, a group of twenty-three experts from East and West met in closed session to work out the details of a control system that would effectively guarantee a test ban. In exactly thirty official sessions the conference completed its work. In so doing it became the first postwar disarmament group to reach agreement. It reported that "it is technically feasible to establish . . . a workable and effective control system to detect violations of an agreement on the world-wide suspension of nuclear weapons tests." [27]

In order to detect any illegal nuclear explosion the conference recommended the establishment of 160 to 170 land-based control posts and ten posts on ships. The land-based posts would be distributed as follows: twenty-four in North America; six in Europe; thirty-seven in Asia; seven in Australia; sixteen in South America; sixteen in Africa; four in Antarctica; and sixty in various oceanic islands. Each post would be staffed with about thirty specialists. In addition aircraft would constantly fly along north-south routes over the oceans, taking air samples. Four principal techniques were specified as means of detecting a nuclear explosion: collecting samples of radioactive debris; recording seismic, acoustic and hydroacoustic waves; receiving

---

[26] This condition was dropped early in 1959.
[27] United Nations document A/3897, August 28, 1958, p. 20. Concise summaries of the work of this conference are contained in "Issues Before the 13th General Assembly," *International Conciliation* (Carnegie Endowment for International Peace), September, 1958, pp. 18-22 and "Issues Before the 14th General Assembly," *ibid.*, September, 1959, pp. 12-23.

radio signals; and on-site inspection of suspected and unidentified earth tremors. This system, it was agreed, was capable of detecting explosions of five kilotons (one kiloton = 1,000 tons TNT) and over. An international control organ would supervise and co-ordinate the whole system.[28]

This conference established the technical basis for a test ban control system. To the United Kingdom and the United States the logical follow-up was a second conference to decide upon the political and administrative basis of such a system. A proposal to that effect was made August 22, 1958. The Soviet Government assented, although Premier Khrushchev insisted that in the light of the conclusions of the first conference there was no justification for not immediately stopping all nuclear tests. President Eisenhower, in order to facilitate the work of the second test ban conference, declared a one-year moratorium on all United States nuclear tests. The second conference, also held at Geneva, began its work October 31, 1958. It is limited to representatives of the Soviet Union, the United Kingdom and the United States.

The Geneva Conference on the Discontinuance of Nuclear Weapons Tests, as it is formally known, is now in its third year. Its sessions, numbering over 275 to date, have witnessed the most intensive negotiations on disarmament ever conducted between the Soviet Union and the West. In some ways this conference has been a microcosm of all postwar disarmament conferences: it has alternated between periods of great activity and near agreement and stalemate accompanied by propagandistic accusations. Perhaps the most significant difference is that the group has been able to maintain a forward momentum, so that the prospects of an eventual agreement have never died. One major factor behind this momentum is the feeling expressed by US Senator Hubert Humphrey, "If these negotiations fail, then there is real doubt that any negotiations on arms

[28] United Nations document A/3897, August 28, 1958, pp. 20-25.

reduction and control can be successful." [29] He is absolutely
correct. It is more than doubtful, however, that a more substantial agreement will follow even a consummated test ban.
For the reasons which impel the Soviet Union to give serious
consideration to an agreement on a test ban are unique to this
issue.

There is first the major emphasis that a negotiated test ban
would give to the idea, already popular among millions throughout the world, of banning the use of nuclear weapons. This has
been the foremost Soviet objective in all disarmament negotiations and its attainment would be a supreme Soviet victory. The
importance of nuclear weapons in the Western defense establishment barely needs emphasis. Of course, in the governments of
the United Kingdom and the United States a clear distinction
between banning tests and banning the use of bombs is made.
But this distinction will very likely be blurred by Soviet propaganda, if an agreement is reached. By propagandistic means
directed toward Western as well as neutralist public opinion
the Soviets will undoubtedly seek to achieve that inhibition
toward the use of nuclear weapons which they cannot obtain
at the diplomatic conference table.[30] Along the same lines, a test
ban which curtails the development of small tactical weapons,
the so-called clean atomic bomb and anti-missile missiles, will
tend to stifle the means by which atomic weapons can more
effectively be used by the United States as a deterrent and in
fighting limited nuclear wars.

An oft-mentioned factor spurring the test cessation is the
possible spread of nuclear weapons to lesser powers—the "*nth*
nation*" problem. It may well be in the Soviet (as well as

[29] 86th Congress, 2nd sess. US Senate. Disarmament Subcommittee of the
Committee on Foreign Relations, *Conference on the Discontinuance of
Nuclear Weapons Tests* (Washington, October, 1960), p.v.

[30] Henry A. Kissinger, "Nuclear Testing and the Problem of Peace,"
Foreign Affairs, XXXVII, No. 1, October, 1958. In March, 1960, Valerian Zorin,
Soviet representative at the ten-nation disarmament conference, indicated that
the signing of a nuclear treaty would, in effect, be the acceptance of an obligation to renounce the use of nuclear weapons. *New York Times*, April 1, 1960.

Western) interest to limit this spread. No nation is likely to accumulate a weapons stockpile until the weapon is tested for operational use. Already the technology of atomic weapons production is relatively widespread. The 1955 Conference on the Peaceful Uses of Atomic Energy revealed that no less than five countries had developed independently the same techniques for the extraction of uranium from certain essential ores. Late in 1960 the United States Joint Committee on Atomic Energy announced that recent advances in centrifuge technology had brought the capability of producing weapons-grade material within the reach of many nations. Germany, for one, has developed a gas centrifuge (the Degussa model) which separates fissionable U-235 from nonexplosive U-238 at a greatly reduced cost over the standard diffusion apparatus. France, in February, 1960, became the fourth atomic possessor. Reports indicate that in the near future at least eleven other countries will be technically able to embark on programs of their own.[31]

Politically such a dispersion of atomic weapons can profoundly alter the present balance of world power. It could seriously weaken the influence that the United States and the Soviet Union now exercise within their own alliance systems. Smaller nations able to produce such weapons would be capable of exercising a form of "atomic blackmail" to which even the largest nation would not be immune. Quite possibly, for example, it may be in the Soviet interest to retard the independent production of atomic weapons by the Peoples Republic of China. It may well be that an agreement on a cessation of testing would provide the USSR with an excuse to deny information to its ally. At any rate, it would certainly slow down communist Chinese development of a nuclear weapon and make that ally more dependent upon the Soviet Union.

But the Soviet Union has balked at paying the price for a test cessation, namely control. Between the agreement in principle

[31] The countries include Belgium, Canada, China (communist), Czechoslovakia, East Germany, West Germany, India, Italy, Japan, Sweden and Switzerland. See Howard Simmons, "World Wide Capabilities for Production of Nuclear Weapons," *Survival* (Institute for Strategic Studies), I, No. 4 (Sept.-Oct. 1959), 127.

and the application in fact the Soviet determination not to permit foreign intrusion of its internal affairs remains. In almost every issue at dispute the Soviet Union has sought to weaken the control system. This is evidenced in its demands for fewer control posts and fewer inspections than the West wants; in limitations on the authority of the control organ; and in its demands for staffing the posts with nationals of the nation under inspection. As of late 1960 the principal areas of agreement and disagreement could be summed up under three headings: (1), the composition and voting procedure of the control organization; (2), the staffing of the control posts; and (3), the number of on-site inspections to be permitted annually.[32]

Early in the negotiations agreement was worked out on the rudiments of a control organization. Both sides agreed to the establishment of a seven-nation control commission, to be headed by an Administrator. The United Kingdom, the United States and the Soviet Union would be permanent members and elect four other nations to serve on a rotating basis. But agreement is lacking on who the four non-permanent members should be, as well as the voting procedure of the commission as a whole. The USSR wants the four non-permanent members to include two Soviet allies, one Western ally and one neutral—thus giving the over-all composition a 3-3-1 ratio. The West seeks a commission composed of one Western ally besides the United Kingdom and the United States, one Soviet ally with the Soviet Union and two neutrals—an over-all 3-2-2 ratio. On the question of voting the old problem of the veto rears its head. Consistent with all its past positions the Soviet Union insists that each of the three powers have a veto over all substantive decisions of the commission including such vital questions as the dispatch of inspection teams and financial and budgetary questions. The West wants majority rule. In December, 1959, a Soviet compromise was offered to end the impasse on both questions. If the

---

[32] A detailed description of the twenty-five unresolved issues as of August, 1960, is contained in *Conference on the Discontinuance of Nuclear Weapons*. For a concise summary of the work of the conference up to September, 1960, see "Issues Before the 15th General Assembly," *International Conciliation*, Sept., 1960, pp. 20-30.

United States accepted the Soviet formula for representation on the control commission, the USSR would permit all substantive decisions to be taken by a two-thirds vote. In theory the veto was abandoned, but in practice no decision under that arrangement could be taken without the concurrence of the three Soviet bloc members. The proposal has not been accepted.

A second major point of contention is the staffing of the permanent control posts. Initially the two Western powers insisted that all the members of the control posts be nonnationals of the country in which the post was located. The Russians wanted all inspecting personnel to be nationals of the country under inspection with the exception of a few foreign "observers." Gradually a partial compromise has been hammered out. It is agreed that each post would contain approximately thirty people. According to a Western proposal made in July, 1959, ten would be from the United States and United Kingdom combined, ten from the Soviet Union and ten from nonnuclear nations. This has been accepted by the USSR on the understanding that, of the ten nonnuclear representatives, a third should be allies of the Soviet Union, a third allies of the West, and a third neutrals. This acceptance, however, was made as a part of its December, 1959, compromise on the composition of the control commission. Agreement on this issue has not been ratified.

Finally there is the complex issue of the number of on-site inspections to be permitted. Whenever a control post records an upheaval which may either be an atomic explosion or some natural event, such as an earthquake, and there is doubt as to which of the two it is, there would be need for an inspection team to examine the locality to verify that it was not an illegal test explosion. A problem of considerable magnitude is posed by underground explosions of low kiloton yield, because their signals, as recorded on seismic instruments, closely resemble the signals caused by earthquakes. To guarantee compliance with a test ban the control agency would have to send an on-site inspection team to the locality of a certain percentage of these unidentifiable explosions. According to United States sources there might have to be as many as 75 to 150 inspections on

Soviet soil annually.[33] The idea of roving teams inspecting Soviet territory is extremely repugnant to the Kremlin, which has repeatedly charged that these teams would be used by the West for espionage purposes.

In an effort to break out of this deadlock, President Eisenhower proposed April 13, 1959, that only atmospheric tests up to fifty kilometers in the atmosphere be prohibited, inasmuch as these could easily be detected without on-site inspection. Premier Khrushchev rejected this proposal "as a dishonest deal" but in return suggested an alternate solution: a complete ban with the establishment of a fixed number of inspections under a quota system. "It is understood," he said, "that such inspections would not be numerous." [34] Rather than determine the number of inspections by scientific means, the Soviet Union would settle the issue by "political" compromise. On February 11, 1960, President Eisenhower offered an alternative compromise, again in the nature of a limited treaty. He called for a treaty halting aboveground tests, tests in the atmosphere, tests in outer space up to 175,000 miles, oceanic tests and underground tests of a seismic reading of 4.75 or higher—in short, a ban on all those tests wherein violation could be detected by known scientific means. If accepted, this would reduce the number of on-site inspections for doubtful underground explosions in the Soviet Union to about twenty. The proposal suggested a research program to find means of verifying tests deep in outer space and of a low kiloton magnitude underground. The Soviets agreed in principle to the limited treaty and the program of research on condition that a voluntary four- or five-year moratorium on tests below a 4.75 reading accompany such a treaty. Later they let it be known that twenty annual inspections in the Soviet Union were too many. Three, they feel, will suffice.

Two problems remain in the forefront barring an agreement on a limited treaty: one is the question of the duration of voluntary moratorium on underground tests of less than 4.75

[33] New York Times, March 20, 1960. This figure was for an unlimited treaty banning all tests.
[34] United States Department of State Bulletin, XL, No. 1038 (May 18, 1959), 705.

seismic reading. As of late 1960 the West is reluctant to go beyond a year. The other is the scope and nature of the research program that would be carried out for low kiloton tests while the moratorium was in effect. Both sides recognize that nuclear devices must be used in improving seismic detection; but the Soviet Union has disavowed any intention of carrying out any research program utilizing nuclear devices of its own. The United States has announced that its research program will involve nuclear explosions. But it is at a loss as to how to assure the Soviets that these test explosions will not involve weapons development. The USSR wants to examine the interior of any devices used by the United States, but this type of inspection is prohibited by the United States Atomic Energy Act. If this problem is not resolved, the United States must face the issue of conducting its research program without Soviet approval. What the consequences of that will be are not now known.

THE INTERNATIONAL ATOMIC ENERGY AGENCY

Three and a half years after President Eisenhower's proposal before the General Assembly the International Atomic Energy Agency (IAEA) became a reality. The statute officially entered into force July 29, 1957, with the requisite number of ratifications including the five major powers: Canada, France, the Soviet Union, the United Kingdom and the United States. It is today primarily concerned with the peaceful uses of atomic energy. Two of the Agency's most important functions are (1), to encourage and assist research on the application of atomic energy for peaceful purposes throughout the world, including the exchange of scientific and technical information; and (2), to provide materials and facilities for the practical application of atomic energy, including the production of electric power.[35]

Neither of these functions is directly related to disarmament; and, in truth, disarmament was at best only a secondary element of President Eisenhower's atoms-for-peace proposal before the United Nations in 1953. Nevertheless, the IAEA was created

[35] IAEA Statute, Art. III.

with an eye to reducing "the potential destructive power of the world's atomic stockpiles." [36] While international control over all existing fissionable fuel is impossible, the Agency might serve as a useful instrument for siphoning off some of this fuel from military stockpiles to peaceful purposes. Of course, the four atomic powers are under no obligation to reduce their military stockpiles by selling or donating the fuel to the Agency.

Nor does membership in the IAEA obligate any of the atomic producers to accept any form of international control. The safeguards designed to assure that fissionable material and equipment are not used for military purposes are applicable only to those nations receiving Agency assistance. For all practical purposes the Soviet Union in the foreseeable future will be in the category of provider rather than recipient.

Those nations which do receive fissionable materials from the Agency must submit to controls which are extensive indeed. Each nation-recipient must conclude a special agreement with the Agency giving it the right to examine the design of the equipment and facilities used and "to approve it only from the viewpoint of assuring that it will not further any military purpose . . ." The Agency must approve the means used for the chemical processing of irradiated materials for the same purpose. It can require the observance of health and safety measures. Any fissionable materials recovered or produced as a by-product in excess of what is needed for the project must be deposited with the Agency. In order to ensure the accountability for all fissionable materials the Agency requires the maintenance of operating records. By far the most significant control of the Agency is its power to send into the recipient state inspectors "who shall have access at all times to all places and data and to any person who by reason of his occupation deals with materials . . . which are required . . . to be safeguarded." [37]

Though neither the United States nor the Soviet Union are bound by any of these safeguards today, the IAEA does provide

[36] Statement by President Eisenhower quoted in Bernhard G. Bechhoefer, "Negotiating the Statute of the International Atomic Energy Agency," *International Organization*, XIII, No. 1, 1959, 42.

[37] IAEA Statute, Art. XII.

the framework for extending limited international control of atomic energy on a world-wide basis. It may *at the request* of any of its members extend these safeguards "to any bilateral or multilateral arrangements" or "to any of [a] state's activities in the field of atomic energy." [38] In view of its consistent opposition to internal inspection in practice, the Soviet Union is not likely to accept this control in the foreseeable future. But its very membership in and support of the Agency has made the principle of international inspection a living reality.

The negotiations leading to the formation of the IAEA were carried out during the years 1954 to 1956.[39] Initially the Soviet response to American suggestions for an exchange of ideas on the creation of an Atoms-for-Peace agency was entirely negative. Between March and September, 1954, the United States submitted six confidential memoranda to Soviet Ambassador Zarubin outlining ideas for a proposed statute for an international agency. All were rejected. Soviet Foreign Minister Molotov rejected the entire concept of world-wide co-operation in the peaceful uses of the atom until a solution was found to the problem of nuclear disarmament. To him the two issues were inseparable. The Soviet Government took the same position on Atoms-for-Peace that it was taking before the parallel negotiations in the Disarmament Subcommittee, namely, that the first order of business was the complete prohibition of nuclear weapons.

Meanwhile the United States decided to go ahead with the negotiations with or without the Soviet Union. Invitations were sent to seven other nations, each important as a supplier of source material or technological know-how, to discuss in private the formation of an Atoms-for-Peace agency. Representatives of Australia, Belgium, Canada, France, Portugal, the Union of South Africa and the United Kingdom joined the United States in Washington in the summer of 1954. The door remained

[38] IAEA Statute, Art. III, par. 5.
[39] This summary of the Soviet role is taken primarily from the analysis by John G. Stoessinger entitled "Atoms for Peace: the International Atomic Energy Agency" in *Organizing Peace in the Nuclear Age*, Report of the Commission to Study the Organization of Peace, Arthur N. Holcombe, Chairman (New York, 1959), pp. 117-58. See also Bechhoefer, *loc. cit.*

opened to the Soviet Union. On September 22, 1954, the USSR dramatically reversed itself and agreed to discuss the issue of an international agency separate from disarmament. Quite probably by the fall of 1954 the Kremlin foresaw the eventual creation of the agency and realized that Soviet interests would better be served by being involved in its formation rather than being an outsider at the beginning. Formal Soviet entry into the negotiating group was not effected until July 29, 1955, when the United States enlarged the eight-nation group to a twelve-nation group with the addition of Brazil, Czechoslovakia, India, and the USSR. The twelve-power negotiations were carried out in Washington between February 27 and April 18, 1956.

Soviet Russia's participation in this group was unusually cooperative in view of its past behavior in international negotiations with the West. By and large the essential conflicts within the group were between the atomic powers and the atomic have-not powers rather than between East and West. The Soviet delegation did seek to assume the role of champion for the underdeveloped nations but it was by no means consistent in that role. In the end the twelve-nation group was able to come up with a proposed statute acceptable to all.

Several of the Soviet suggestions for revisions of the work previously accomplished by the eight-nation group were propagandistic only, and several were worthy of serious consideration. In the former category Mr. Zarubin made a determined, but unsuccessful, attempt to have Communist China admitted to the initial membership of the Agency. He also sought the inclusion of statements in the statute stressing the "sovereign rights of states."

Much more significant was the position of the Soviet Union on issues concerning the Agency's structure. The eight-power negotiators had provided for three principal organs: a Board of Governors, a General Conference, and an administrative staff headed by a director general. One of the tasks of the twelve-nation group was to formalize agreement on the composition and authority of each. Since the Board of Governors was the highest authority, having the power to make most of the Agency's decisions, membership on the Board became a controversial issue. The original eight-power proposal was for a sixteen-member Board, five of whom would be given permanent seats and special voting privileges. The Soviet delegate supported Indian criticism of this arrangement as denying adequate representation of the underdeveloped nations. A compromise solution was eventually worked out creating a twenty-three-member Board which insured larger representation of nations from the Middle and Far East and Eastern Europe.

Similarly, a compromise was worked out on the Soviet demand for increasing the authority of the General Conference vis-a-vis the Board of Governors. It was agreed that the number of Board members elected by the Conference be raised from six to ten and that the Conference be given the authority to "take decisions" (rather than make recommendations) when the Board was unable to arrive at a decision. On the other hand, the Soviet and Indian position that the director general be equally responsible to the Board and the Conference was denied. The majority felt that sound administrative principles required the chief executive (*i.e.*, the director general) to be responsible primarily to the Board. Two other Soviet suggestions, one concerning the vote required for budgetary matters and one on the jurisdiction of the International Court in settling disputes of interpretation, also were settled by compromise. On the latter issue the Soviet Union obtained the assurance that it would not be brought before the Court without its consent.

Having successfully completed its work, the twelve-nation group submitted the draft proposals to an International Conference convened to draft the statute in its final form. Eighty-one states met for this purpose at the United Nations Headquarters in New York from September 20 to October 26, 1956. The success of this conference was assured by the consensus established within the twelve-nation group. One contentious issue stood out among all others: the question of the safeguards to assure that fissionable materials not be used for military purposes. It was primarily a struggle between the underdeveloped countries led by India against the atomic powers. India argued that the proposed safeguards constituted a dangerous interference in the economic growth of those nations which would be most likely to avail themselves of the Agency's aid. Although a member of the atomic "haves" and not likely to be subjected to these safeguards, the Soviet Union sided with the underdeveloped countries. Again the Soviets stressed the necessity for observing the sovereign rights of states. A compromise was worked out retaining the safeguards but providing reasonable assurance that they would not be utilized to curb the economic development of those nations submitting to them.[40] On October 23, 1956, the Conference unanimously adopted the statute.

For the Soviet Union ratification entailed no problem because it implied only one clearly defined legal obligation: the responsibility to pay the assessed share of the Agency's administrative budget.[41]

[40] Bechhoefer, *loc. cit.*, p. 57.
[41] Stoessinger, *loc. cit.*, p. 153.

Part Two

Evaluation of the Soviet
Negotiating Methods

9: THE SOURCES OF SOVIET OPPOSITION TO INTERNATIONAL CONTROL OF ATOMIC ENERGY

THE OUTSTANDING FEATURE OF SOVIET ATOMIC ENERGY POLICY has been its consistent and emphatic opposition to international control. Amid the myriad fluctuations in the procedure of negotiations, throughout the continuous changes in minor concessions offered, during the kaleidoscopic propaganda charges hurled against the Western powers, this opposition remained constant. It was intimated in Premier Stalin's noncommittal attitude on first learning of the bomb; it was suggested during the Soviet silence on the subject from Hiroshima until the Atomic Energy Commission's convocation; and it was confirmed by the record of Soviet negotiations in the Atomic Energy Commission, General Assembly, Security Council and Disarmament Commission.

Soviet opposition to international control was manifest first in the Kremlin's refusal to offer a detailed and workable plan for control. Had the Soviet Government considered international control of atomic energy desirable, it would have recognized the advantage in seeing control established as soon as possible after the American announcement (November, 1945) agreeing to promote such control. The refusal of the Russian representatives to elaborate on their own plan in 1946 and 1947 indicates that they neither expected nor desired acceptance of the Soviet proposals. A second reflection of Soviet hostility to control *per se* was the refusal of the Soviet delegations to acknowledge even the basic scientific facts circumscribing the types of practical control plans. Throughout the negotiations the Soviets continued to maintain that there was no connection between the production of nuclear fuel for peaceful uses and for atomic bombs.[1] It is difficult to imagine that the Soviet leadership was so totally ignorant of the processes involved in nuclear fuel production to believe all of their own statements discounting the relation between production and control. Even if one discounts the information available to the Soviet Union through its own scientific achievement or espionage in 1945, there remains the fact that the United States Government itself published enough information on the technical nature of the Manhattan project to prove the need of a very comprehensive control system.[2] Thirdly, the hostile tactics of the Soviet negotiators in the United Nations demonstrated their basic unwillingness to explore the possibilities of agreement with the Western powers.[3]

On its face the record revealed three principal points of opposition between the majority and minority positions: the veto questions, the priority of prohibition or control and the nature of the control plan. However important they were, the first two issues were clearly subsidiary to the third. Logically the

[1] See, for example, the speech of Andrei Vyshinsky in *A/C.1/SC 18/SR.2*, 2nd meeting, p. 10. This assertion had been made repeatedly before. As late as 1951 such an assertion could not be defended on the grounds of ignorance since the Soviet Government had exploded its own bomb in 1949.

[2] This information was published by the War Department on August 16, 1945, and is known as the "Smyth Report." See Henry DeWolf Smyth, *Atomic Energy for Military Purposes* (Princeton, 1945).

[3] Margaret Coit in her biography of Bernard Baruch records the following conversation between Ferdinand Eberstadt, a member of Baruch's staff, and Andrei Gromyko early in August, 1946. Eberstadt called on Gromyko in his rooms and was received with courtesy. Eberstadt wasted no time on pleasantries. "If you are prepared to accept a plan [for international control of atomic energy], the details are not really important. If not . . . , our only problem is when to quit." Gromyko looked shrewdly at his visitor and finished the sentence. "And how," he said. It was the answer Eberstadt had expected. He reported Gromyko's answer to Bernard Baruch. (Coit, *op. cit.*, p. 595). Miss Coit, who had access to Baruch's official files, does not cite a source for this interview. There is some credibility for the conversation in the fact that Bernard Baruch gave his personal approval of this biography.

question of punishment of violators of a control agreement should have been considered after agreement on a control plan. If a working control system had been established, the major security problem would have been solved. No veto in the Security Council would have prevented the treaty-abiding nations from taking effective action against a violator whether under Article 51 of the Charter or independent of the United Nations. The important consideration was the existence of a foolproof warning system, and it would have been comparatively easy for any nation to give warning that it would not tolerate any unauthorized seizure or production of nuclear fuel.

Similarly, the question of the priority of prohibition over control was a peripheral issue. Both the Soviet Union and the Western powers sought the prohibition of the manufacture and use of atomic weapons as an ultimate objective. At various stages in the negotiations each nation had indicated a willingness to have prohibition go into effect simultaneously with the beginning of the control plan. This agreement was more verbal than real inasmuch as the beginning of a control plan was never agreed upon; but it is not unreasonable to assume that had there been sufficient agreement on the nature of a control system and motivation to implement it, the prohibition question could easily have been compromised. Jules Moch's proposal for a tentative prohibition did at a late stage in the negotiations receive approval from the Russian representatives.

At the heart of the controversy stood the Russian determination to resist internationalization of its future atomic industry. Within the governing elite of the Soviet Union the harmful expectations that would result from placing its atomic energy resources under international control exceeded the threat inherent in an atomic arms race and the possibility of a war involving atomic weapons. These expectations made it impossible for the Soviet leadership to see the problem of control in the same light as the majority of nations represented in the United Nations. To the Russians the objectives of the negotiations were in themselves potentially more harmful than the status quo. The Soviet evaluation of the relatively greater threat of international control over national control was a compound of two views: (1), the Soviet belief that the atomic bomb would not be the most decisive factor in winning future wars; and (2), a fear that if any segment of the Soviet economy were placed under noncommunist control, communism in the Soviet Union would be threatened.

Between these two beliefs the first was of considerably less significance. Its importance in Soviet thinking lay in its de-emphasis of the atomic bomb as a threat to national security. Where the non-Soviet world in 1945 hailed the discovery of the atomic bomb as presaging a new era in armed combat, Soviet spokesmen described the atomic bomb as just another, albeit more powerful, weapon in man's continually improving arsenal of destructive explosives. Soviet spokesmen expressly denied that the atomic bomb could have a decisive effect on the outcome of a war. Premier Stalin's first public statement on the atomic bomb in September, 1946, included a denial that atomic weapons could "determine the fate of war." This view was maintained even after the Soviet Government exploded its own bomb.[4]

Soviet military doctrine in the postwar years combined the lessons of the Second World War with Marxist theory.[5] The successful Russian defense against Hitler's armies was attributed to the size and fighting qualities of the Red armies as well as the support given to them, in terms of weapons, supplies and behind-the-lines aid (guerilla warfare) by a loyal populace. Strategic bombing and the use of weapons of mass destruction were considered to be at best only a supplement to large land armies supplied by an industrial base.[6] Stalin, who until his

---

[4] *Pravda*, September 25, 1946. O. V. Trakhenberg, " 'Sotsiologiya' Atomnoi Bomby," (The Sociology of the Atom Bomb), Voprosy Filosofii, III (1948), 295. See also Kissinger, pp. 264-68.

[5] Dinerstein, *loc. cit.* The following description of Soviet military doctrine is taken primarily from Dinerstein's article and Raymond Garthoff, *Soviet Military Doctrine* (Glencoe, Ill., 1953). After the death of Stalin in 1953 Soviet military doctrine changed radically. This is clearly shown in Dinerstein, *loc cit.*, pp. 243-46. See also H. S. Dinerstein, *War and the Soviet Union* (New York, 1959), chap. I, and Raymond L. Garthoff, *Soviet Strategy in the Nuclear Age* (New York, 1958), chaps. I, II, and IV.

[6] P. M. S. Blackett, *op. cit.*, p. 75 and chap. II entitled "Air Power in the European War, 1939-1945."

death dominated Soviet postwar military thinking, looked upon modern war as necessarily a combat of attrition. Those factors which determined victory or defeat in war, said Stalin in 1942, were the stability of the rear, the morale of the army, the quantity and quality of divisions, the armies' weapons, and the organizing ability of the commanding officers.[7] Such elements of combat as the use of "blitzkreig" attacks or military surprise were condemned as "adventurist" or ignored as useless. Stalin refused to admit that nuclear weapons might compress the effects of years of normal attrition into a few days. Soviet commentary on atomic weapons acknowledged the atomic bomb's tremendous destructive power but denied its practicality on the front line on the grounds that the atomic bomb would kill one's own as well as enemy troops.[8]

This brief summary of the Soviet attitude toward the atomic weapon is relevant here only to the extent that it sheds light on the Soviet leadership's conception of the bomb as a threat and hence on its evaluation of the need for international control of atomic energy. Compared to the Western evaluation of the atomic bomb, the Soviet leadership tended to minimize the bomb's importance. This is not to say that the leaders in the Kremlin failed to see in American possession of the atomic bomb a potentially serious threat to the Soviet Union. They saw, however, in internationalization of Russian future atomic industry an even greater threat, the threat of foreign penetration of its economy. Behind the efforts to ward off this threat lay the cause of the eight-year deadlock on negotiations for international control of atomic energy.

[7] Dinerstein, *loc. cit.*, pp. 241-42.

[8] *Pravda*, June 24, 1946. Different interpretations have been given as the source of the Soviet attitude toward atomic weapons. Edward Shils argues that the central element in the Russian attitude toward the bomb was ignorance of its significance, Shils, "American Policy and the Soviet Ruling Group," *Bulletin of the Atomic Scientists*, III, No. 9 (September, 1947), 239; Shils, "The Failure of the United Nations Atomic Energy Commission: an Interpretation," *ibid.*, IV, No. 7 (July, 1948), 208; P. M. S. Blackett, a noted scientist and military analyst, argues that the Soviet doctrine is based upon a correct assessment of the facts, Blackett, *Fear, War, and the Bomb*, p. 5; Henry Kissinger argues that Soviet statements on atomic weapons were designed primarily for internal and external propaganda purposes, Kissinger, *op. cit.*, pp. 372-73.

International control of Russia's atomic industry was held to be intolerable by the Soviet leadership because it felt that any noncommunist control over the Russian economy would be used to curb Russia's economic growth. This belief sprang from a more basic conviction that the communist and capitalist systems of economy were irreconcilably opposed to each other. In Soviet eyes there was no permanent middle ground between the two; nor was it possible for neutral representatives to arbitrate political and economic conflicts between communism and capitalism. It was apparent throughout the first half decade of the atomic age that the only producers of atomic energy then and in the immediate future would be the largest and most industrially developed nations which included the major communist and capitalist powers. The Acheson-Lilienthal Proposals, Baruch Plan and United Nations Plan, by putting all atomic energy industries under joint control, would have placed the Soviet Union and the major Western powers in a position where innumerable problems of conflict of interests would have had to be resolved continuously.

Both the United States Government and the members of the majority in the Atomic Energy Commission insisted that the international control agency must substantially own and operate all national atomic energy industries, even those concerned with the production of power for peaceful pursuits, if security against the manufacture of bombs was to be assured. This was required because of the scientific conclusion that "There is an intimate relation between the activities required for peaceful purposes and those leading to the production of atomic weapons . . ." [9] As has been described above, the powers allotted to the international agency included ownership of the world's supply of uranium and thorium; ownership and managerial control over nuclear, chemical and metallurgical refineries and all primary and secondary reactors; and ownership of all fissionable fuel, as well as powers of inspection, accounting and licensing. With these powers the control agency would have been able to

[9] *AEC First Report*, Part II, p. 11.

determine the extent of nuclear production and its distribution in every nation having atomic facilities.

Of the problems of military security and economic development the latter posed by far a greater number of unanswered questions. There were, for example, the complex problems involved in pricing. How much was the agency to pay for raw material? By what system were labor costs of miners, skilled labor, technicians and scientists to be computed? How was the cost of plants and refineries and reactors to be determined? And what was the price mechanism to be used in computing the value of fissionable fuel licensed to different nations and individual power companies? A competitive price mechanism was not possible where some of the participating nations operated under a centrally controlled economy. An arbitrary determination of prices would inevitably favor some economies over others. Too high a price for raw materials would favor the suppliers of raw materials over the consumers. Too low a price charged for the use of fissionable fuel would discriminate against the conventional suppliers of power.

Depletion of resources raised another set of questions. From which nation's supply of uranium and thorium was the agency to draw? In which nations was prospecting to be encouraged and in which discouraged? Would principles of cost, need or security determine the location of refineries and reactors? From which nations would scientific talent be drawn? Toward what type of needs would the research efforts of the agency be directed? What codes would labor standards follow?

Unquestionably the knottiest set of problems involved the final allocation of fissionable fuel for peaceful purposes. Who would receive the final product of the internationalized industry? Would fissionable fuel be allocated according to the power needs of individual nations or equally throughout the world? How was a power need to be evaluated? Were less developed nations to be favored for having a greater long-term need for power or highly industrialized nations because they could put the power to more immediate productive use? What was to be the balance between long-term and short-term needs? And what was to be the basis of need in the first place: population, natural resources, standard of living, gross national product?

None of these questions was insoluble. Conflicts of interests were involved, but conflicts of interests could be resolved. Prime requirements for resolving these conflicts were an organization with decision-making authority, an accepted operating procedure for the organization and a general set of principles to guide the agency.

A partial set of guiding principles was provided by the second Atomic Energy Commission report. Four important guides were established by this report to help the proposed agency fulfill its function. First, the report recommended that at least initially the agency keep the production of nuclear fuel to "the minimum required for efficient operating procedure necessitated by actual beneficial uses . . ." For the time being that meant that the production of nuclear power was to be discouraged. Insofar as the Soviet Union had not then begun the production of nuclear fuel for actual beneficial uses, the Soviet Government could legitimately presume that the agency would not be a positive spur for the promotion of atomic power in the Soviet Union—at least for the time being. Secondly, the report recommended that national deposits of atomic raw materials be depleted "proportionately." Thirdly, stockpiles of fissionable fuel and production facilities were to be distributed throughout the world on a strategic basis. That is, there was to be no concentration of fuel or facilities in any one nation or region; so that no one nation could seize a major portion of the world's supply of fuel at one stroke. Fourthly, and most important, the second report recommended that the treaty establishing the agency define in advance the production policy of the agency and that, as far as possible, specific quotas be written into the treaty specifying for each nation its share of ores to be mined, production facilities to be constructed and fissionable fuel to be received.

These guides were recommended to the future signatories of the treaty. They were not established as the only or the definitive principles circumscribing the control authority. Of the four, only the proposal for a quota system received even so much as a tentative agreement from Soviet spokesmen. The Soviet representatives particularly condemned the proposal that the peaceful uses of atomic energy be postponed in order to facilitate control.[10] The proposals for a quota system to guide the agency at first met with Gromyko's approval. Originally the Soviet view was that a quota system was the best method of protecting the interests of all atomic-producing nations. A year after indicating its agreement, however, the Soviet Government sharply reversed itself and condemned the quotas as an American plot to place the Soviet Union on a "starvation ration" of atomic fuel.

As important as these guides were, even if accepted, they would have left to the agency itself a wide area of decision making. The personnel of the agency would have been endowed with a power and a responsibility unique in the history of international organization. A completely new field of administrative law would have developed. The decisions of the control agency would have a binding authority over individual member nations far greater than the authority of any existing specialized agencies of the United Nations. Where national law conflicted with the decisions of the atomic authority, the former would have to give way.

Almost no formal consideration was given to the composition and procedural rules of this most important authority. In May, 1947, Committee Two of the Atomic Energy Commission did establish a Working Group to consider the "Organization and Administration of the International Agency," but no report was ever submitted by the group. The group convened again in January, 1948, and again abandoned its efforts as "premature." In both instances the group failed to pursue its objective because its members felt that agreement on the agency's structure was meaningless until prior agreement on the agency's powers and functions was established.

No proposals, therefore, were formally made as to the voting procedure of the Board of Directors when such a Board would

[10] M. Rubenstein, "The Atomic Age as American Scientists Picture It," *New Times*, March 15, 1946, pp. 27-28. See also *Izvestia*, March 29, 1950.

come into existence. There was no doubt, however, but that the major portion of the Board's decisions would be by majority vote. This determination was expressed only obliquely in the Atomic Energy Commission's first report, which stated that ". . . the rule of unanimity of the permanent members, which in certain circumstances exists in the Security Council, shall have no relation to the work of the international control agency." [11] Soviet spokesmen as early as December, 1946, acknowledged that majority rule would predominate in the control agency. V. M. Molotov conceded majority rule in the "day-to-day" operations of the agency before the General Assembly and Andrei Gromyko admitted the same rule "in appropriate cases" before the Atomic Energy Commission. Only in cases involving sanctions against violators was the subject of majority rule in dispute.

As to the composition of the Board both the Soviet Union and the United States were agreed that its personnel should be selected "on an international basis." Nothing more explicit was ever specified as to the basis of selection. It was clear, however, that the members of the Board would be composed of representatives of the states which were the principal atomic-producing powers and most industrialized states capable of future atomic production. Probably the representatives of smaller nations would have been included to give regional representation to the Board. The Soviet expectation was that the Board would be composed of the representatives of states-members of the Atomic Energy Commission. The Acheson-Lilienthal Report had suggested that the agency might take the form of a United Nations Commission—in which case the composition of its Board of Directors would not have differed significantly from Soviet expectations. In any event, the representatives of noncommunist states would have predominated on the Board.

The question presented to the Soviet leadership, then, was whether it could safely entrust a potentially important segment of its economy to the control of a Board, a majority of whose

[11] *AEC First Report*, Part III, "Recommendations," p. 18.

members represented capitalist nations. Could it depend upon the impartiality of a group whose education and values had been conditioned in a political system which it considered inherently opposed to communism? The leaders in the Kremlin felt they could not. As the control agency was—and would have to be—devised, conflicts of interests would be resolved according to a procedure of representatives voting as national units, with the majority making the ultimate decisions. In Soviet eyes the more basic social and economic conflicts involved not so much those among nation states, but those among classes: between communism as a system and capitalism as a system. Representation in the control agency was inequitable to the Soviets because the capitalist nations together would have considerably more votes than the one or few communist nations on the Board. It was assumed that on all major decisions the capitalist nations would vote as a bloc.[12]

In the final analysis the atomic energy deadlock resulted from two widely divergent conceptions of the source of law. To the Western powers every nation has its own interests which it must defend, sometimes at the expense of and sometimes in conjunction with the interests of other nation-states. The national interest is expressed in the laws and policies of its government. To the Soviet leadership economic groupings or class interests are the basic and most dynamic source of law and political policy. Nation-states are the facade for class interests. The most im-

[12] An example of the same type of deadlock was the Soviet refusal at the Twelfth General Assembly session to participate in the United Nations Disarmament Commission because its membership was "weighted" in favor of the Western powers. In the hopes of securing Soviet participation the Western powers agreed to increase the Disarmament Commission membership from ten to fourteen and finally to twenty-five nations. In the new Commission every major power, region, and political system is represented, but the Soviet Union still considers the over-all balance unfavorable to it. This Soviet objection could not be met even if a system of weighted voting were established; because even under such a system the communist nations could be outvoted. The only system that would suffice for the Soviet Union would be that which gave it an equal vote to that of all the capitalist powers. This was obtained by the Soviet Union in the ten-nation disarmament group which met at Geneva from March through June, 1960. Five nations represented the Western powers and five the Soviet bloc. The group broke up in deadlock.

portant arena of legal and political antagonism is not interstate rivalry, but interclass rivalry.[13]

In the view of the Soviet leadership the Western powers were attempting to create a limited world government in a world which lacked a consensus of values upon which a system of law acceptable to both sides could be devised. Inevitably some pattern of law would emerge to guide the control agency, and the communist leaders were convinced it would not be favorable to the promotion of communism either in the Soviet Union or throughout the world. Andrei Gromyko subtly expressed this fear before the Security Council when the majority plan first came before the Security Council in March, 1947, when he said:

> In any system of government short of tyranny, the personalities of the leaders and administrators must have a sociological source of nourishment which energizes their aims. If there is no 'world community,' then the leaders must rely for their moral strength upon the communities that do exist.[14]

Other Soviet spokesmen raised this problem repeatedly in more direct fashion. Andrei Vyshinsky asked the General Assembly at its 253rd meeting, "If it was acknowledged, as the supporters of the United States plan did acknowledge, that evidence of bad faith might possibly be given by the governments, why not acknowledge that such bad faith might equally well be shown by the staff of the control agency in its administration?" [15]

Questions of good and bad faith were not related to the individual moral character of the administrators, nor to personality behavior. They were above all questions of political judgment. Between representatives of communism and capitalism the Soviet leadership did not believe political neutrality on major questions

---

[13] Modest Rubenstein said of P. M. S. Blackett's pro-Soviet book, *Fear, War and the Bomb*, that "for all its merits [Blackett's book] suffers from one serious defect. It avoids all attempts at social and economic analysis, which alone can furnish an understanding of the complex military and political problems examined in the book. *Blackett analyses the antagonism of states, but he does not see . . . the antagonisms and the struggle of classes . . .*" Rubenstein, "Policy of the Atomic Imperialists," *New Times*, January 26, 1949, p. 30. (Italics added.)

[14] Quoted from Joseph Neyer, "Is Atomic-Fission Control a Problem in Organizational Technique?" *Ethics*, LVII, No. 4 (July, 1947), 292.

[15] UN, *ORGA, Fourth Session, Plenary Meetings . . . Summary Records of Meetings 20 September-10 December 1949*, 253rd meeting, p. 336.

was possible. *Pravda* offered as one of its defenses for rejecting the United Nations plan the argument that it would be impossible to find "independent people" who would be above political considerations to run the control agency.[16] This disbelief in the impartiality of states and statesmen when questions of differing economic systems are involved has been a consistent feature of Soviet foreign policy. In one international conference after another Soviet delegates have opposed the idea of compulsory arbitration of disputes by third parties.[17]

Although essentially a political problem, the debate on international control of atomic energy was often expressed in theoretical terms. To this debate the governing Soviet elite brought a theoretical framework of international law and international organization which stressed hostility and conflict. The Soviet Union's objection to the United Nations plan for control of atomic energy was not an isolated instance of its refusal to co-operate in an international venture. Co-operation with noncommunist states is as alien to the Soviet Union ideologically as it has been practically.

Had a control treaty been agreed upon and signed, it would have become positive international law binding equally upon all its adherents. For the Soviet Union as well as all the treaty's signatories it would have involved a voluntary limitation of national sovereignty in the sphere of atomic energy production. This demand ran counter to the Soviet concept of the inviolability of national sovereignty and the legitimate role of international law in regulating interstate behavior.

In Soviet legal doctrine the chief characteristic of international law is national sovereignty. International law—or as it is commonly designated in Soviet jurisprudence, interstate law—is the result of the process of conflict and co-operation among states and comes into being only on the basis of voluntary agreement. It is "the sum total of legal norms governing rights and

[16] *Pravda*, October 5, 1948. See Nathan Leites, *A Study of Bolshevism* (Glencoe, Ill., 1953), p. 43.
[17] C. Dale Fuller cites only two exceptions to this pattern. Fuller, "Soviet Policy in the United Nations," *The Annals* of the American Academy of Political and Social Science, CCLXIII (May, 1949), 143-44.

duties of collectivities of the ruling classes . . ." [18] International law, thus, has a class base. Insofar as there is constant conflict between classes, there is naturally bound to be conflicts between the legal norms of capitalist and socialist states as products of a different class structure. Thus the area of real and full agreement between socialist and capitalist states is bound to be very limited. E. A. Korovin, one of the Soviet Union's foremost international legal theorists, even denies that there is or has ever been a uniform general international law valid for all the states of the world. Such a world-wide general international law he calls a "myth." The importance of absolute national sovereignty is that it leaves every nation free to reject legal norms devised by a state or group of states of a different (and hence hostile) class structure.

This does not mean that the lack of ideological solidarity between capitalist and socialist states precludes all international legal relations between the two types of states. It only means that such relations are limited. According to Korovin there are three spheres of interests within which international legal relations are possible:

(1) Humanitarian interests independent of political intentions. These would include agreements for the prevention of epidemics, for the preservation of historic monuments, works of art and the like.

(2) Material economic interests of a merely technical character. Such, for instance would include postal, telegraphic, river, railway and communications treaties and agreements.

(3) Material interests of social or political importance. Here would be included the conventional commercial treaties and customs unions.

---

[18] D. B. Levin, "Falsification of the Concept of International Law by Bourgeois Pseudo Scholarship," *Current Digest of the Soviet Press,* IV, No. 22 (April, 1952), 3. With the exception of other sources specifically cited the following description of the Soviet theory of international law is taken from Hans Kelsen, *The Communist Theory of Law* (London, 1955) and Mintauts Chakste, "Soviet Concepts of the State, International Law and Sovereignty," *American Journal of International Law,* XXXIX, No. 3. Both authors rely primarily upon the writings of E. A. Korovin, the most prominent Soviet international legal theorist.

Agreement on matters in the first category is not considered difficult. Essentially it would be based on ideals and values common to any social system and hence beyond politics. Issues of a technical economic nature come closer to the source of political and economic conflict inherent in class conflict. However, agreements on such matters are possible if there is a substantial harmony of interest between the contracting parties. Such agreements may be and often are of a long-term nature.

Legal relations between socialist and capitalist states involving economic interests of political importance can never be permanent and are rarely of long duration. They are based solely on the exigencies of the moment and usually involve a compromise between the class interests of competing social systems. It is here that international law is described as "the area of the struggle of two opposing tendencies." [19]

International control of atomic energy would, of course, have fallen within the third category. In view of the potentially important role of atomic energy in the Soviet Union's economy and security and the extensive abnegation of sovereignty required by a control agreement, it is possible that a control treaty might have been put by the Soviets in a fourth category—a category of matters involving the question of a nation's very existence.

The emphasis placed by Soviet jurisprudence on national sovereignty is not as contradictory as would seem in view of the Marxist doctrine of the state as the product of the irreconcilability of class antagonisms and the prophecy of the eventual demise of the state after the destruction of the exploiting capitalist class. When the atomic age began, the Soviet Union was the only major power espousing a socialist classless society. The Soviet leadership looked upon the Soviet Union as a communist nation beleaguered in a world of hostile and strong powers. The emphasis on sovereignty was for it a means of national self-defense.

Sovereignty has been defined by Soviet authorities as the legal and actual independence of a state in carrying out its functions.

[19] Chakste, *loc. cit.*

It serves, in their eyes, as a protection from imperialistic states—
a protection for the USSR and weak and poor states who might
be exploited by capitalist nations. Just before the Soviet Government offered its June, 1947 proposals E. A. Korovin wrote in
Pravda:

> Sovereignty in its Soviet sense is a weapon in the fight of pro-
> gressive-democratic forces against the reactionary-imperialist forces.
> Sovereignty under contemporary conditions has the mission to serve
> as a legal and international political barrier for the defense against
> the imperialistic encroachments and for guaranteeing the opportunity
> for the greater construction of progressive social and state forms—
> socialist and popular democratic; it serves as a guarantee of the
> liberation of the oppressed colonial peoples and of the independence
> of nations from the imperialist yoke.[20]

This view was fully consistent with what he had written in
1924, that any limitation of national sovereignty, as long as the
capitalist encirclement exists, is incompatible with the interests
of the Soviet state, since such a limitation would mean the
victory of capitalism over socialism.[21]

National sovereignty in Soviet theory includes the primacy
of national over international law. Those in the West who
postulate the existence of a world law or advocate a world government are viewed as using such ideas to promote aggression
against the Soviet Union. Such ideas are seen as weapons in
the constant battle between the Soviet and non-Soviet world.
The concept of "supra-national" law is considered to be a reactionary conception which has its purpose to serve as a "screen
for the tendencies of the large imperialist powers." Similarly,
advocates of a world government err in assuming "universal
interests of mankind" which transcend the interests of individual
states. Some Soviet writers found considerable grounds for
suspicion in that many of the proponents of the Baruch Plan
were also advocates of some form of world government.[22]

---

[20] *Pravda,* May 3, 1947.

[21] Kelsen, *op. cit.,* p. 158.

[22] "The excessive praise for the Baruch Plan from advocates of 'world government' clearly shows that . . . the preaching of the cosmopolitan 'theory'
of 'world government' has as its aim the founding of a policy of interference

In practice the Soviet doctrine of the supremacy of national sovereignty has been carried through in the United Nations by the Soviet insistence that all international disputes be settled only by unanimous agreement of all nations concerned. For this reason the Soviet Government has consistently insisted that only the Security Council was the proper organ for the resolution of important international conflicts; and the Soviet Government has equally consistently resisted all efforts to eliminate the "veto" in the Security Council's voting rules.

Soviet jurists have recognized the importance of General Assembly decisions, but emphatically deny the validity of General Assembly decisions as binding. In the Soviet view the resolutions of the General Assembly have "political and moral" significance; but even the "political and moral" injunctions of those decisions are limited to those nations which voluntarily subscribe to the General Assembly decisions. Andrei Vyshinsky, a Russian legal theorist as well as a diplomatic representative, described this function of General Assembly resolutions before the First Committee during one of the disarmament debates. He said:

Recommendations by the Assembly had often been described as mandatory from the moral and political viewpoint, and rightly so, but no one could deny with regard to a specific recommendation that those moral and political obligations were binding on all the delegations *which had not opposed them*. To maintain that a formal declaration prohibiting atomic weapons and weapons of mass destruction was only a piece of paper not binding on anybody because it provided for no enforcement measure would be tantamount to denying the force of any recommendation adopted by the General Assembly. That would be the height of political cynicism. Such an attitude would undermine the very foundations of the work of the United Nations, the authority of which was based on political and moral facts and obligations which each government undertook to

---

in the affairs of different states, including subversive, diversionary, and spying activities, practiced by the American imperialists and their hired hands," quotation from O. E. Polentz, "World Government, a Weapon of the American Imperialists in the Struggle for World Hegemony," in Elliot R. Goodman, "The Soviet Union and World Government," *The Journal of Politics*, XV, No. 2 (May, 1953), 240. See Levin, *loc. cit.*, p. 3.

respect *when its delegation voted in favor of a particular recommendation.*[23]

By limiting the applicability of a moral force to those General Assembly decisions which a nation supported, of course, the Soviet Government absolved itself from being bound by the numerous General Assembly resolutions which its delegation had opposed. Any suggestion that the General Assembly's or any United Nation's organ's decisions might have or should have the character of international legislation has been condemned in Soviet thinking as a falsification of international law.[24]

A natural corollary of Soviet insistence upon the principle of unanimity in the solution of international disputes has been the Soviet Union's objection to the practice of majority voting both in the United Nations and at international conferences. Those nations which have advocated the use of majority voting at international conferences have been critized by Soviet spokesmen as advocating this voting procedure to promote anti-Soviet policies. *Pravda* commented in 1949:

A question of international significance—in which the aggressive tendencies of American imperialism against the sovereignty of peoples and states and in which its pretensions toward world-wide hegemony are displayed—had been the question of the order (procedure) of voting in international conferences and international organs. Both in the United Nations and the Paris Peace Conference the representatives of the American bloc asserted the principle of an arithmetical solution to the international problems—according to majority vote.[25]

[23] UN, *ORGA, Eighth Session, First Committee, Summary Records of Meetings 16 September-7 December 1953*, 664th meeting, p. 211. (Italics added.)

[24] Levin, *loc. cit.*, p. 4. Writing in *Sovetskoye Gosudarstvo i Pravo* Levin adds "representing the decisions of the United Nations, along with decisions of other international organizations, as 'international legislation' directly suits the predatory interests of the American imperialists who, in a number of the United Nations bodies and other international organizations, possess an assured majority and, with the mechanical voting of their satellites, can railroad through any decisions they please in the guise of decisions of 'international bodies' . . . ," *ibid.*, p. 4. See also M. Rubenstein, "The Atomic Age as American Scientists Picture It," *New Times*, March 15, 1946, p. 29.

[25] E. Korovin, "Amerikanskii Imperializm—Ugroza Suverenitetu Narodov" (American Imperialism—Threat to Popular Sovereignty), *Bolshevik*, VIII (April, 1949), 53.

The Soviet objection to the use of majority vote has a theoretical and a political basis. Theoretically, Korovin has argued that: "Genuine democracy and judicial levelling have nothing in common, and the organization of international relations on formal and levelling principles would be a crying violation of the most elementary equality . . ." [26] Judicial leveling is rejected because in the Soviet view not all the national units are equally "democratic" hence deserving of equality of the vote. Only the Soviet Union among the major powers has a real "sovereignty of the people." The nations of the West have a "sovereignty of the bourgeoisie" and hence do not genuinely represent the people. As sacred as is the principle of national sovereignty, even that principle—in theory at least—must be subordinated to the principle of democracy, i.e., the dictatorship of the proletariat. If the principle of majority rule were exercised in international politics, the interests of governments and not necessarily the people would receive primary consideration.[27]

One of the political arguments against the use of majority vote takes into consideration the unequal strength and power of the nations of the world. Greater power involves greater responsibility. The veto power is viewed as necessary for the great powers to exercise their responsibilities for guarding the peace as well as ensuring their rights. To decide international issues by majority vote with every state voting as a unit, would, in Soviet eyes, place the Soviet Union in the same category as Nicaragua or Guatemala.

Another Soviet objection to majority voting stems from the minority position vis-a-vis the United States in which the Soviet representatives often found themselves at the negotiating table. In part this situation exists, in Soviet eyes, because the representatives of smaller and weaker capitalist nations are compelled to vote as the United States dictates. Where the class interests of a larger capitalist nation conflict with those of a smaller nation the former has resorted to exercising political and economic

[26] Korovin quoted in Kelsen, op. cit., p. 170.
[27] E. Korovin, "Amerikanskii Imperializm—Ugroza Suverenitetu Narodov," p. 53; Chakste, loc. cit. For qualifications of this doctrine see Kelsen, op. cit., pp. 173-76.

pressure on the latter. Because of their small size, proximity to the United States and close economic ties, the Latin-American republics, for example, have been looked upon as semi-wards of the United States. This relationship has, however, not been considered limited to nations that are small or in the Western hemisphere. During the period of postwar American aid to Europe *Pravda* charged that the United States was using the "ill-famed 'voting machine' of the Marshallized countries" to block all the Soviet proposals for atomic energy.[28]

Fifty or one hundred years ago, commented Korovin in 1947, suggestions to solve international problems by a simple majority vote might have appeared as progressive; "today it is reactionary." [29]

As proposed by the United States, international control of atomic energy ran directly counter to Soviet Russia's traditional attitude toward the outside world. This attitude, emphasizing the suspicion, hostility and conflict among nations, is reflected in Soviet thinking by its description and normative judgments on the nature of international relations as described above. The Soviet leadership evaluated the several proposals for international control of atomic energy urged upon them. Its evaluation was strongly negative. On balance the negative expectations resulting from acceptance exceeded the anticipated benefits. There were five principal negative expectations which the Soviet Government saw inherent in the American proposals. These five threatening elements were:

(1) Effective domination of the control agency would be exercised by the United States.

(2) The early stages of the control plan would lessen Soviet security vis-a-vis the United States.

[28] Ya. Victorov, "Kto Sryvaet Delo Mari i Mezhdunarodnovo Sotrudnichestva" (Who Is Frustrating the Matter of Peace and International Cooperation), *Pravda*, November 28, 1948.
[29] Korovin, "Sovetskaya Kontseptsiya Suvereniteta i Kritika burzhuaznykh teorii mezhdunarodnovo prava" (The Soviet Concept of Sovereignty and Critique of the Bourgeoisie Theory of International Law), *Pravda*, May 3, 1947.

(3) The development of atomic power for peaceful uses would be retarded by the control agency.

(4) National research on the peaceful uses of atomic energy would be curtailed by the control agency.

(5) International control of atomic energy would be used as a pretext for hostile interference in the internal affairs of the Soviet Union—including possibly military intervention.

Mention has been made above of the Soviet conception of the dominant-subordinate relationship existing between the larger capitalist powers and the smaller ones. Actually the Soviet Union looked upon the United States as the most dominant capitalistic nation in the world and the obvious leading force in the future agency. In effect, the United States would be given "unlimited rights and opportunities" by the control organ because it would always have a majority vote since every other nonsocialist representative in the control organ is "economically and politically dependent upon the United States." [30] Soviet spokesmen in the Atomic Energy Commission candidly and categorically rejected the American contention that the United States would be as controlled by the agency as the Soviet Union. Said Semen K. Tsarapkin before the Atomic Energy Commission's Working Committee:

Further, the representative of the United States . . . appeared, with a candid air, to present matters as if the control organ could not be ruled by the United States inasmuch as every country participating in the membership of such organ would have only one vote at its disposal, and this would include the United States. This naive explanation by the United States can only be considered as a joke, since we know full well the dependence on and the subordination to the United States of many countries who are members of the Atomic Energy Commission. This is obvious from the Atlantic Pact, from a political point of view, and from the economic point of view it is seen in the Marshall Plan.[31]

Of the several negative Soviet expectations, this fear ranked foremost because it explained the means by which the remaining four could be implemented.

[30] *Pravda*, November 12, 1949.
[31] *AEC/C.1/PV.49*, 49th meeting, p. 41.

One of the major blocks to Soviet-Western agreement was the question of the stages by which the plan would be brought into operation. The device of a system of stages was an American innovation designed to guarantee that an effective plan of control was in operation before the United States revealed its secrets of atomic production and ceased producing the bomb. No detailed plan of stages was ever discussed during the period of negotiations, but the American proposals clearly provided that one of the earliest stages must include a world-wide geographic survey of the sources of uranium and thorium. While the plan accepted by the United Nations did not state any particular sequence of stages, it did empower the control agency "to determine when a particular stage or stages have been completed and subsequent ones are to commence."

This authority to determine the sequence of stages would, in the Soviet view, be abused through American domination of the agency. Mr. Naszkowski, the Polish representative, expressed this fear before the General Assembly's *ad hoc* political committee as follows:

> The well-known theory of stages had been invented so that the international agency, or rather the super-trust visualized in the United States plan, might first and foremost obtain full possession of atomic raw materials and investigate the sources of atomic raw materials throughout the world. Only then would provision be made for controlling the facilities for the production of nuclear fuel and, eventually, for the prohibition of atomic weapons; but the plan did not specify the length of time which would be allowed to elapse between stages. Obviously, the first stage alone would require many years, if not decades; it would involve long scientific research, investigation, sending of expeditions and the gradual process of appropriations of atomic raw materials by the international agency.[32]

The latent fear behind the Soviet objection to stages was that the United States never intended to go beyond the first stages, with the consequence that the United States would have an unlimited survey of the mining establishments and raw materials in the USSR and hence a fairly complete target map of the

[32] UN, *ORGA, Fourth Session. Ad Hoc Political Committee. Summary Records of Meetings 27 September-7 December 1949*, 31st meeting, p. 177.

Soviet Union. It was thought not improbable by the Kremlin that a comprehensive survey of Soviet raw materials would reveal to the West a wide range of nonatomic military secrets such as the location of Soviet Russian industry and airfields. Considering the over-all greater secrecy of Soviet society in comparison to that of the United States, the net security loss for the Russians would have been greater than the Americans, if the control agreement never went beyond its initial stages.[33]

Unquestionably the problem which raised the most persuasive doubt in the Soviet mind concerned the peaceful uses of atomic energy. Adoption of a control plan would have placed the direction of the Soviet Union's atomic industry in the hands of an international body. As the uses of nuclear fuel for power and other industrial uses developed, the role of the international body in the Kremlin's centralized planning for the whole Soviet economy would increase proportionately. Not only did the Kremlin mistrust the potential influence of this international body in promoting or discouraging the use of atomic power among the several sectors of the Soviet economy, but it feared that a deliberate effort would be made by the agency to deprive the Soviet Union of the benefits of atomic power. V. Matveev, in *Izvestia*, expressed this idea somewhat bluntly when he wrote: "The American monopolists sleep and see in their sleep the visions of countries placed on starvation rations

[33] A considerable circle of non-Soviet opinions agreed that initially the Soviet Union would suffer a greater degree of security loss than the United States by the American plan of stages. The most eloquent English spokesman for this argument was P. M. S. Blackett, *Fear, War, and the Bomb*, pp. 152-54. Also "British Atomic Scientists' Proposals for International Control of Atomic Energy," *Bulletin of the Atomic Scientists*, II, No. 2 (February, 1947). Even a member of Truman's Cabinet felt that the Russians had a legitimate reason to reject the American plan because of the use of stages. Henry Wallace, Secretary of Commerce, wrote that the Baruch Plan had a fatal defect: "That defect is the scheme, as it is generally understood, of arriving at international agreements by 'many stages,' of requiring other nations to enter into binding committments not to conduct research into the military uses of atomic energy and to disclose their uranium and thorium resources while the United States retains the right to withhold its technical knowledge of atomic energy until the international control and inspection system is working to our satisfaction." Henry Wallace, "Letter to the President" (July 23, 1946), *Bulletin of the Atomic Scientists*, II (October 1, 1946), 2. See Bernard Baruch's "Memorandum to the President (September 24, 1946)," *ibid.*, p. 2.

for the production of atomic energy for peaceful purposes." [34]

More than just foreign influence in the domestic economy was involved. With its hand on the pulse of the Soviet atomic industry, the international agency would in time have a considerable knowledge of the working strengths and weakness of the Soviet Union. The Soviet economy would have been exposed to foreign observation to an extent which had no precedent in Soviet history. In view of the secrecy with which the Soviet leadership clothes so much of its activity, it is not unreasonable to assume that the Kremlin would have found the demand to reveal its economic policies as intolerable as the control which would have been exercised over those policies.

This negative expectation on the part of the Soviet leadership was often verbally expressed by exaggerated accusations against the majority powers. For example, Modest Rubenstein, one of the Soviet Union's leading commentators on atomic affairs, charged that the control agency envisaged by the Baruch Plan would establish "according to its own discretion" (*i.e.*, the "will of the United States monopolies") quotas for the various nations for the extraction of raw materials and the production of atomic energy, giving to individual states licenses for the right to use their own human and material resources. Rubenstein's accusation could hardly be squared with the clear statement in the Atomic Energy Commission's Second Report that the quotas would be determined by treaty in advance of the assumption of power by the agency.

Another charge leveled by Rubenstein was that the control agency would not limit its authority over the immediate production of atomic energy but would extend its authority over "other basic branches of industry" and would "completely subordinate the economic life of other states." [35] The recommendation in the Atomic Energy Commission's First Report that the control authority was to "interfere as little as necessary with the operations of national agencies for atomic energy or

[34] *Izvestia*, March 29, 1950.
[35] Rubenstein, "Proval Atomnoi Diplomatii Amerikanskikh Imperialistov," p. 43.

with the economic plans and the private, corporate, and state relationships in the several countries" was inadequate assurance for the Soviet Government.

What is important in these charges is not the specific Soviet misinterpretations of the majority proposals but the strong Soviet disinclination to believe that the majority plan could be implemented fairly and honestly. One of the major Western efforts to meet the Soviet objections was the quota system. Even when these proposals were under discussion in 1947, the Soviet delegates took almost no part in the debate. This was because their objection to the majority plan stemmed from a hostility to the basic idea of international control and not alone to any specific features of the plan. No modifications or softening of the majority plan could make it acceptable to the Soviet Union.

A few features of the majority plan did specifically run counter to Soviet aspirations in the field of atomic energy; and some of the legitimate problems raised by the Soviet representatives were inadequately covered by the plan. In the area of peaceful application of atomic energy the Atomic Energy Commission's Second Report did tend to minimize the possibilities for future national development of atomic industries. This it did in the interests of security, and the limitation applied equally to the atomic industries of every nation. To the Soviet leadership this de-emphasis of the potential peaceful uses of atomic energy was both unwarranted and undesirable.

Nor were the Soviet representatives convinced of the adequacy of the quota system in equalizing the existing possibilities for atomic development among the nations of the world. Even if the quota plan were agreed upon before the establishment of control, there remained the problem of change. Presumably every nation's quota would be based upon the known resources and industrial potential at the time of the initial quota agreement. But industrial capacity changes and new sources of raw materials are discovered. There exists always the problem of differential rates of growth. Andrei Vyshinsky alluded to this problem of differential rates of growth when in criticizing the proposal for comparable national depletion of the thorium and uranium resources throughout the world, he remarked:

> . . . any given State which had been assigned a definite quota could not obtain additional quotas even if its needs for atomic energy were growing constantly as was the case in the Soviet Union which had tremendous need for atomic energy and was utilizing it to the maximum extent and exclusively for peaceful purposes.[36]

Essentially the Soviet leadership recognized that atomic development was capable of dynamic strides. Whatever quota provisions might have been given at any one time would have been based upon the conditions existing at the time of agreement—*i.e.*, on the status quo. Change would have been inevitable and the Soviet leadership was not persuaded that once it had relinquished its sovereignty on atomic energy it would be in a position to obtain the necessary quotas desired in a changing situation.

Another set of provisions in the majority plan which violated Soviet expectations in atomic development were those concerned with research. National research in atomic energy under the plan was seriously circumscribed. Only the international control agency was permitted to engage in research involving "dangerous quantities" of fissionable materials and "dangerous activities" (*i.e.*, those concerned with nuclear explosions). National atomic research agencies were to be permitted to engage in small-scale atomic research, particularly that associated with medical uses of atomic energy. For this purpose nondangerous quantities of fissionable materials would be allotted to national agencies by the control board. However, no set standards could be determined as to what constituted "dangerous" quantities and so the final determination of what amounts of nuclear fuel were to be allotted was left with the international agency. The power of an external agency to give or withhold the materials which the Soviet Government would utilize in research was looked upon

[36] UN, *ORGA, Fourth Session, Ad Hoc Political Committee, Summary Records of Meetings 27 September-7 December 1949*, 35th meeting, pp. 208-209.

as "frank interference in the internal affairs of independent governments . . ." [37] Not only would the Soviet Union be stopped
from ever matching the accomplishments of the Western powers
in developing an atomic bomb, but it could not, without agency
approval, develop nuclear explosives for large scale excavating
and leveling work.

The majority plan presumed some sort of agreement among
nations as to what constituted legitimate peaceful uses of atomic
energy and, thus, in what direction research could be permitted
to go. Soviet spokesmen questioned the existence of this common
understanding. The use of nuclear explosives for leveling was
a case in point. Shortly after the first Soviet explosion in 1949,
Andrei Vyshinsky announced that the Soviet Union was using
atomic energy for leveling work, including "razing mountains."
When the Western representatives pointed out to him that
nuclear explosions used to destroy mountains could also be
used to destroy cities, Vyshinsky objected to considering such
work as destructive. "Some had not failed to stress that leveling
work was in fact destructive," he told a General Assembly subcommittee; but he insisted that in the Soviet Union the use of
nuclear explosions for leveling work was considered strictly a
peaceful pursuit.[38]

Finally, the Soviet leadership saw in the control agency a potential instrument for noncommunist interference in the internal
affairs of the Soviet Union. This expectation was a generalized
one which found expression frequently with reference to many
phases of the majority plan. The Soviet reaction to the agency's
potential influence on economic planning has already been mentioned. Reference has been made, too, to the Kremlin's fear that
the geological survey teams and the international inspectorate
would gather information which would ultimately find its way
into the intelligence offices of hostile Western nations. The
Soviet belief that the control agency would adversely affect
Russia's military security included even the possibility that the

[37] V. Kudriastsev, "S SH A i atomnoe oruzhie" (The USA and the Atomic
Weapons), *Izvestia*, August 2, 1947.
[38] UN, *ORGA, Fourth Session, Ad Hoc Political Committee, Summary
Records of Meetings 27 September–7 December 1949*, 35th meeting, pp. 208-209.

agency would serve as an instrument for military intervention reminiscent of Allied intervention against the Bolsheviks in 1918. Andrei Vyshinsky in 1948 outlined before the General Assembly the logic for such a use of the control agency:

. . . what has been completely lost sight of was that the right of ownership required appropriate means for its defense. That in turn would involve a police force to safeguard the control of nuclear energy raw material from dangers such as those feared by the majority of the Atomic Energy Commission: attempts at evasions or the seizure of atomic plants by a country secretly preparing for aggression. However, the idea of placing at the disposal of the international control agency armed forces capable of action against a sovereign country would be completely unrealistic and inadmissible. It would, in fact, only foment new possibilities of armed conflicts. What if the international force were so weak as to be incapable of defending that ownership? Could that not be used as an excuse for importing into that particular State, under the guise of defending the interests of international security, additional armed forces? That would equal military intervention.[39]

How seriously the Kremlin envisaged ultimate foreign invasion as a result of adoption of a control plan can only be guessed. At the very least, Soviet policy toward international control of atomic energy can be summed up as a struggle to resist what the Soviet elite considered to be a threat to the national interest of the Soviet Union.

[39] UN, *ORGA, Third Session, Part I. Plenary Meetings . . . Summary Records of Meetings 21 September-12 December 1948*, 156th meeting, p. 413. See also *Pravda*, November 12, 1949.

10: THE GAMESMANSHIP

OF INTERNATIONAL NEGOTIATION

ONE OF THE MOST IMPORTANT FEATURES OF SOVIET POLICY TO-
ward international control of atomic energy was its duration
and consistency. Given the deep-rooted nature of the Soviet
aversion to internationalizing any segment of Russia's economy,
it remains a question why the Soviet Government did not reject
the proposals *in toto* in 1946 instead of engaging in an eight-year
debate with the object of defeating the proposals? In other
words, why was the Soviet rejection of international control
of atomic energy an indirect instead of a direct one? To broaden
the question, of what importance was the prolonged series of
negotiations in the Atomic Energy Commission, General Assembly and Disarmament Commission in the promotion of
Russian national interests?

Just as the analysis of the Soviet objection to international
control began with the expectations involved in control as held
by the Soviet elite, so an analysis of the Soviet objectives and
tactics in negotiating control must begin with the Soviet conception of the challenge posed by the American-British-Canadian
proposal (the Truman-Attlee-King declaration of November,
1945) to negotiate international control of atomic energy in the
United Nations.

The devastating effect of the American bombs dropped on
Hiroshima and Nagasaki stirred in the imagination of peoples

throughout the world a vision of incalculable destruction and carnage in a future war involving the use of atomic bombs. Almost immediately a world-wide popular demand arose that such weapons never again be used. Part of this demand, of course, was an outcry against war itself. A weariness of war and armed conflict was a natural and inevitable reaction to the titanic struggle between the Allies and Axis powers which ended in August, 1945. The negative reaction to fighting that took place in 1945 included the weapons used in the war—particularly atomic bombs. Demobilization and disarmament rivaled the restoration of peacetime economies as the principal world-wide national objectives following Japan's surrender.

This world-wide reaction against the use of atomic weapons found expression in the speeches and actions of the representatives of the nations at the convocation of the First General Assembly in January, 1946. Without a dissenting vote the membership of the First General Assembly approved the creation of the Atomic Energy Commission to bring atomic weapons under international control.

Along with the leaders of every major nation, the Soviet elite recognized the world-wide pressure of public opinion for some form of control against use of atomic bombs. Premier Stalin himself commented that "the desires and conscience of people demand that the use of atomic energy for war-like purposes be prohibited." [1] Andrei Gromyko gave expression to this same force in his opening speech before the Atomic Energy Commission when he said:

If we continue to use these discoveries for the production of weapons of mass destruction we may intensify mistrust between states and keep the peoples of the world in continual anxiety and mistrust. Such a position would work against the aspirations of the peace-loving peoples who are thirsting for the establishment of a solid peace and who are making every effort to endure that their aspirations shall be transformed into reality.[2]

The Soviet Union, which purported to base its foreign policy upon popular aspirations for peace and security could no more

[1] Interview with Harold Stassen on April 9, 1947. *Izvestia*, May 8, 1947.
[2] UN, *AECOR*, No. 2, 2nd meeting, June 19, 1946, p. 24.

afford to neglect world opinion on this subject than could any other major nation. At the very least it had to pay lip service to this popular expression. More than that, however, the Soviet Government had to take into consideration the attitudes of the major Western powers—particularly the United States— which then possessed the secret of atomic fission. In American hands the bomb presented a potential threat; and it was necessary that the Soviet Union not adopt a policy which might provoke the United States into a program of building up an atomic stockpile for use against the Soviet Union. A strong negative reaction to control by the Soviet Government would in all likelihood have had that effect.

The negotiating techniques of the Soviet Union in the United Nations were, however, considerably more complex than merely paying lip service to a universally accepted ideal. And Soviet objectives in negotiating control of atomic energy were more ambitious than solely digging the grave for international control. Considerable attention, in fact, was given by the Soviet Government to the United Nations debate to promote Soviet interests. While Soviet atomic energy policy did vacillate at times and appeared at moments confused and inconsistent, there was a broad pattern of objectives and tactics which over the eight-year period of atomic energy negotiations was both consistent and positive. Over the past decade, as negotiations for disarmament replaced negotiations for international control of atomic energy, these same objectives and tactics have dominated Soviet diplomacy.

The over-all motivation of Soviet behavior in atomic energy negotiations was to mobilize world public opinion favorable toward the Soviet Union. For their purposes the Soviet leadership divided world opinion into roughly three segments: the communist world, the Western world and that segment not encompassed by either, which can be labeled neutral public opinion. Each segment, of course, required the use of a different set of tactics, or more accurately, a stress of one particular technique over another to meet the requirements of the different objectives for the communist, Western and neutralist segments.

Broadly speaking, the Soviet objective in atomic energy negotiations vis-a-vis the communist world was to reinforce anti-Western feeling by emphasizing the aggressive intention of the United States and England. Toward the Western nations the Soviet representatives were more concerned with using the negotiations to put pressure on the United States to renounce use of the bomb. Soviet efforts to influence the neutralist nations were primarily aimed at justifying the Soviet proposals and seeking United Nations approval—at least in principle—of Soviet atomic energy policy.

Some of these objectives and the tactics used to achieve them were incompatible and there were times when Soviet policy did not seem to be consistently seeking any recognizable objective. For example, many of Molotov's or Vyshinsky's vitriolic speeches, which were directed primarily to the ears of the pro-communist world, so irritated the vast majority of United Nations representatives that some neutralist nations which might have given some support to the Russian proposals were alienated; and, some of the Soviet propaganda charges against the United States were so palpably untrue that they had the effect of discrediting some of the more reasonable Soviet claims.

The major proposals advanced by the Soviet Government were not meant to be taken literally. They were too extreme to be accepted by the majority. They exceeded even Soviet expectations. Their purpose was to put the Soviet Union in a position from which it could bargain—i.e., in a position from which it could gain concessions by offering concessions. Many of the Soviet resolutions and speeches had no relevance at all to negotiating in the conventional sense of a give-and-take in negotiation. These were designed only to convey and reiterate a propagandistic theme—e.g., that the Soviet Union stood for the absolute prohibition of atomic weapons or that the United States was planning to attack the Soviet Union. The Soviet representatives were not directly concerned about the truth or falsity of their statements before the various United Nations commissions and committees. What concerned them was the effect of what they said on the attainment of their objectives. They were interested in creating attitudes. They were not interested in sounding out the extent of Western demands and then attempting to reconcile these demands with those of the Soviet Government.

The distinction between communist, Western and neutralist areas of opinion which the Soviet representatives sought to influence is partially arbitrary. Rarely were Soviet propaganda efforts at ony one time directed at only one area. The differing demands of each area had to be met continuously in every organ of the United Nations where international control of atomic energy was under debate.

One of the important features of the way Soviet atomic policy in the United Nations was carried out was the general uniformity of presentation before all the various organs where the subject was debated. In general, there were no significant differences in the content and tone of Soviet speeches made before the General Assembly and its committees, the Security Council or the Atomic Energy Commission and Disarmament Commission and their various working committees.

One might have expected a difference in approach to correspond with the different functions of the various United Nations bodies. The smaller working committees of the Atomic Energy Commission and Disarmament Commission, for example, were designed to facilitate an exchange of information and to reconcile conflicting points of view. When issues came before the larger United Nations organs—including the Atomic Energy Commission and Disarmament Commission—these objectives ordinarily gave way to attempts to enlist general support for or to justify a nation's policy. However, the general procedure for the Soviet representatives was to present the same kind of speeches before every body, large or small. Wherever they had the opportunity, the Soviet representatives utilized the smaller working groups to give the same long, tendentious, and hostile speeches that they gave before the Security Council or General Assembly.

It is, therefore, possible to analyze the over-all objectives sought by the Soviet representatives without identifying these objectives with a particular United Nations body or limiting them to a particular period of time. Soviet representatives used the atomic energy negotiations principally for the attainment of five objectives. They were:

(1) To reject the American atomic energy proposals without appearing to do so.

(2) To link Soviet policy with popular aspirations throughout the world.

(3) To portray the policies of the Western bloc—and the United States in particular—as aggressive.

(4) To prevent the United States Government from using its atomic superiority to gain political advantages.

(5) To stall for time.

Toward the attainment of each of the objectives the Soviet representatives utilized a specific set of tactics which they considered most relevant. Often one particular tactic served more than one objective. One such case was the Soviet use of parliamentary tactics of diversion which served not only to stall for time, but fitted in with the Soviet goal of rejecting proposals without appearing to do so.[3] As noted above, some of the tactics designed to facilitate one particular objective hindered the attainment of other objectives.

Unquestionably the most important of the Soviet objectives was to reject the United States—later the United Nations—plan without directly incurring the responsibility for the failure of the negotiators to reach agreement. This was not only the most important but the most difficult objective to attain because the United States, in effect, posed a challenge to which the Soviet Union had to respond.

Logically there were only three alternatives open to the Soviet Government: to accept the Western plan, reject it, or propose a more viable alternative. None of the choices fully

[3] For an analysis of these tactics as applied to all postwar disarmament negotiations see Joseph L. Nogee, "The Diplomacy of Disarmament," *International Conciliation*, January, 1960, pp. 277-89.

suited Soviet needs. Consequently the Soviet response fitted none of the alternatives dictated by pure logic. Politically, the Soviet response had a logic of its own.

Three major tactics were employed by the Soviet representatives to defeat the Western plan discreetly. First, the Soviet delegations in the United Nations attempted to compel the Western delegations to reject formally as many Soviet resolutions as possible. Secondly, the Soviet representative sought to force the Western powers to compromise their plan for atomic energy control. Thirdly, the Soviet delegation strove wherever possible to divert consideration of the majority proposals. Each of these tactics was applied by a varied assortment of methods and techniques which can in themselves be considered sub-tactics.

The purpose of compelling the Western powers to reject as many Soviet proposals as possible was twofold: first, a large number of Western rejections of Soviet proposals would serve to balance the numerous rejections the Soviet delegation was compelled to make. In so doing the Soviet delegation was partially able to deny the charges of negativism made against them. Secondly, nearly every Russian resolution was so framed that it contained a general proposal acceptable to all and one or more not acceptable to the Western powers. So when the Western representatives rejected a Russian proposal the Soviet delegates were able to claim that the United States, Britain and France were opposed to everything in the Russian proposals.

In order to provoke negative reactions from the Western representatives the Soviet delegations resorted to many different tactics. The most common of these were: (1), attaching unacceptable conditions or provisions to the Russian proposals; (2), continued introduction of the same proposals; (3), defending their proposals with long and repetitive speeches; and (4), accompanying their proposals with hostile anti-American or anti-Western propaganda.

Throughout the negotiations on atomic energy the one condition which the Russian representatives attached to every one of their major proposals and included in almost every resolution they offered was the immediate, unconditional prohibition of atomic weapons. It was the most effective condition they could attach to incur an American veto. They were well aware that the United States would never agree to a prohibition without some prior assurance of an effective control system. But other conditions were used, too. One was the insistence upon the retention of the veto system in cases involving sanctions. When in 1952 the Atomic Energy Commission was merged with the Commission for Conventional Armaments into the Disarmament Commission, the demand for a blanket one-third reduction of all armed forces became another condition which was included in all Soviet atomic energy resolutions. Both demands were effective conditions because both were totally unacceptable to the United States, which the Russian government knew.

One of the most irritating features of the Soviet negotiators was the plethora of identical resolutions introduced by the Soviet delegates. Not only were similar or identical resolutions introduced year after year before the same United Nations organs but they were introduced in every committee, subcommittee and working committee of each organ. And where a representative of the Ukraine, Byelorussia or one of the Eastern communist nations was a member of the group, the number of similar resolutions introduced was often multiplied by two or three.

A typical pattern for Soviet resolutions was as follows: a Soviet resolution would be offered before the Atomic Energy Commission (or later the Disarmament Commission) in plenary session. It would be referred first to a working committee and then to either a subcommittee or working group. After lengthy debate the average Soviet proposal was rejected by a subcommittee or working group. The same proposal would then be introduced before the working committee and would again be rejected. This procedure continued before the plenary session of either the Atomic Energy Commission or Disarmament Commission. Annually the subject of atomic energy came before the General Assembly, and the typical thrice-defeated Russian proposal would again be introduced. From the General Assembly the issue was always referred to the First Committee and thence to either a special subcommittee or working committee. At each level the Soviet resolution would be defeated only to be re-introduced at a higher level. Every Soviet resolution rejected by each General Assembly then had usually already been re-jected a minimum of six times previously. In actual fact, the number of rejections of a Soviet resolution previous to that of each General Assembly was usually far greater than six because of duplicating resolutions of "satellite" nations and the practice of the Soviet representatives to introduce a defeated resolution often more than once before the same body which had just re-jected it.

As tactics to induce a negative reaction from the Western delegates the Soviet practice of giving long and repetitive speeches and including anti-Western propaganda in these speeches operated in a slightly different manner from the above-men-tioned tactics. The latter were designed to put the Anglo-American representatives on record as voting "no" to specific Soviet proposals. Much of the presentation and content of the Soviet speeches was concerned with paralyzing the debate and forcing the majority to terminate it. For over eight years with almost no letup, the majority delegates had to endure a Soviet talkfest of staggering proportions. Representatives Gromyko, Molotov, Vyshinsky, Malik, Tsarapkin, Manuilsky and Tara-senko all gave the longest speeches on record before the nego-tiating bodies. Their prepared speeches were invariably long and repetitious and their impromptu talks were rarely short. It was not at all uncommon for the Russian representative to deliver a lengthy speech to be followed by an almost identical speech delivered by a representative from one of the Eastern European nations or Soviet Republics. In all, the Soviet dele-gates talked as much as or more than the delegates of Great Britain, France, Canada and the United States combined.[4]

[4] This observation is based upon my impression from reading all of the debates on record. Dr. Lilian Wald, who studied the verbatim records of the AEC's committees in 1947 and the General Assembly in 1949 reported that the time taken up by the various delegations in the meetings was as follows:

Of the four total breakdowns in atomic energy negotiations (May, 1948, July, 1949, January, 1950 and May, 1952) three resulted from Western impatience with Soviet tactics and, of course, the feeling of futility caused by the Soviet Union's refusal to accept a plan of control. Only once was the Soviet Government directly responsible for stopping the talks. That was in January, 1950, when Jacob Malik led a Soviet walkout of the major United Nations organs. After each of the breakdowns in negotiations Soviet spokesmen in and out of the United Nations charged the United States with responsibility not only for failure of the talks, but for the refusal of the majority to continue negotiating.

Exerting pressure on the majority to compromise was a second important Soviet technique for covertly rejecting the majority plan. Unlike many of the Soviet tactics, it was not a very subtle one. The majority plan, constructed on the lines necessitated by the scientific and technological facts of nuclear fuel production, was for all of its radical nature, as minimal a plan as Western scientists thought possible. It could not be compromised in its essentials, and Bernard Baruch made this clear from the beginning. In effect, a demand for compromise was a negation of control. Two features of the majority proposals which could have been compromised were the provisions for elimination of the veto in the application of sanctions against violators and for establishing control by stages. However, neither of these features were integral elements of the control plan itself.

A threefold pattern of operation comprised the Soviet tactic

	1947	1949
Four Powers	36%	21%
USSR	37%	21%
Remaining delegations	27%	58%
	100%	100%

These figures do not take into account the speeches of the Eastern European communist nations who invariably repeated the Russian speeches. If they are considered, it is estimated that the Soviet bloc speeches consumed as much time as the resulting forty-eight members of the United Nations. The figures are quoted from Osborn, "Negotiating on Atomic Energy, 1946-1947," *Negotiating With the Russians*, p. 231.

of compromise: (1), initially the Soviet representatives adopted a totally uncompromising position; (2), after a period of futile debate the Soviet representatives would offer a compromise from their previous proposals; (3), and finally, the Soviet delegation would condemn the United States for not agreeing to meet it halfway.

During the six-year period when negotiations were being conducted within the Atomic Energy Commission the Soviet representatives made four significant concessions which they attempted to utilize as bargaining points for comparable Western concessions. These concessions provided for: (1), day-to-day decisions of the control agency to be made by a majority vote (December, 1946); (2), periodic inspection (February, 1947); (3), simultaneous conclusion of prohibition and control treaties (October, 1948); and (4), continuous inspection (June, 1949).

These modifications of the Soviet position were "concessions" only in the sense that they marked a departure from the original extremely negativistic Russian position toward the Baruch Plan. From the Western point of view, some were less concessions than recognition of the basic realities involved in any workable control plan.

During the summer of 1946, when Bernard Baruch made public the American plan of control, Andrei Gromyko completely rejected almost every element of the Baruch Plan and went so far as to intimate that the only control over atomic energy acceptable to the Russians was national—not international—control. He specifically rejected inspection as "not in conformity with the sovereignty of states." Thus, when in the fall of 1946 the Soviet delegation agreed to consider inspection and in February, 1947, included inspection in its amendments before the Security Council, the Soviet Government was actually taking a belated first step toward control. This step was welcomed by the United States, England and France; but it hardly constituted a *quid pro quo* for agreement to abandon international ownership and management of atomic raw materials, plants and fissionable fuel, which was the concession demanded by the Soviet Union. Inspection was, in the majority plan, only one of several necessary provisions to make the control plan a success.

This refusal by the Western powers to grant a comparable *quid pro quo* for Russian agreement to inspection was used by the Soviet representatives to prove that the United States did not genuinely want to come to agreement on a control plan. Typical was Andrei Vyshinsky's sarcastic commentary before the General Assembly Committee in 1948 on the "inconsistency" of American policy. The United States, he said, at first insisted on inspection; but after the Soviet Union agreed to inspection, the American representative "had said that inspection was not really so important and could be an effective means of control only when connected with other measures." [5]

A similar pattern of Soviet behavior followed the Western refusal to accept the many Soviet resolutions asking for agreement on the simultaneous conclusion of conventions prohibiting atomic weapons and establishing control over them. Admittedly, the Soviet willingness to establish prohibition and control at the same time marked an advancement from Gromyko's original demand (June, 1946) that a prohibition agreement must precede a control agreement. However, the United States adamantly refused to acknowledge even so much as the principle of prohibition until assurance existed that a control plan would work. When in October, 1948, Vyshinsky called for the simultaneous draft conventions there existed not the slightest Soviet-American consensus on the nature of a control plan. To the American government an agreement approving in principle the simultaneous establishment of prohibition and control could only support the Russian goal of a declaration of prohibition with or without controls. The Western refusal to welcome the Soviet concession was used by the Soviet delegation to prove "to the world that the Anglo-Americans are not interested in the prohibition of atomic weapons; nor are they interested in setting up controls." [6]

[5] UN, *ORGA, Third Session, Part I. First Committee, Summary Records of Meetings 21 September-8 December 1948*, 145th meeting, p. 27.

[6] UN, *ORGA, Fourth Session, Plenary Meetings . . . Summary Records of Meetings 20 September-10 December 1949*, November 23, 1949, pp. 334-41.

When, in June, 1949, the Atomic Energy Commission had decided to cease its work, Jacob Malik made a long and impassioned speech denouncing the Atomic Energy Commission's decision. In this speech Malik stated what was to be one of the Soviet delegation's principal rebuttals to the four-power charge that Soviet refusal to accept a workable control plan was responsible for the Commission's failure. Malik charged:

We are asked on what basis, since no new basis has been presented, we make our proposal. Let us try to work on it; let us try to prepare a convention; let us try to find an agreed decision which will be acceptable to all, not only to one particular group of states. We are constantly being threatened with the need for something new. You demand something new, but what have you presented that is new, you of the majority? I have heard nothing from you that is new. We agreed with the imposition of immediate strict control. We agreed not only to periodic inspection, but to constant inspection. We agreed to the immediate implementation of the convention on prohibition and control. You insisted on this, and you gave us to understand that you were categorically against having the prohibition convention put into effect first, and only after that, the convention on control. We always supported the position that only the conclusion of the convention on the prohibition of atomic weapons can and should be the first step towards the establishment of control and for various measures of control that would in turn realize properly the implementation of the first convention. We were always of that opinion and we continue to support it. Trying to meet halfway the opinion of the majority, trying to find an agreed decision at the last session of the General Assembly, we did arrive at a compromise. We conceded the immediate establishment of the implementation of the two conventions. This was something you asked for and you got it. We took a decisive step towards meeting you halfway. But what have you done? Nothing. You have grasped the Baruch Plan and you do not wish to deviate one step from it. It is not control; it would mean ownership, but it is in accordance with the desires of the United States monopolists who would like to own everything on this earth and probably everything on Mars.[7]

Another technique utilized by the Soviet delegation to reject the majority proposal was to divert consideration of these pro-

[7] *AEC/C.1/PV.46*, pp. 44-45.

posals through parliamentary tactics. These tactics will be considered below in connection with the Soviet objective of stalling for time.

A second important objective of the Soviet Government in negotiating international control of atomic energy was to establish a connection between Soviet atomic energy policy and popular aspirations; in other words, to convince world public opinion that the Soviet Union stood for peace and security and was opposed to atomic war and an atomic arms race. To achieve this objective Soviet policy makers relied principally upon two techniques: (1), the constant reiteration of propaganda statements emphasizing the peaceful motivations behind Soviet policy; and (2), a simplification of the issue of atomic energy control.

Before the Soviet Union made its own atomic explosion in 1949 it was possible for the USSR to establish a partial identification between itself and the majority of the United Nations membership as nonatomic powers. Utilizing this potential source of identification, Soviet representatives sought to exploit an "us - them" dichotomy: the "us" including all the nonatomic powers and the "them" comprising the United States and Great Britain and Canada, which shared in the development of the atomic bomb. Soviet spokesmen described the Russian people as a peace-loving people like the majority of common people throughout the world. They described the Soviet desire for the absolute prohibition of atomic weapons as conforming to the best interests of not just the USSR, but every nation in the world which was the potential object of an American atomic attack. In the Soviet view not just the USSR, but every nonatomic power was threatened by the mere possession of atomic weapons by the United States.

After the Soviet atomic explosion in 1949 a change of emphasis was made in Soviet propaganda. No longer was the "us-them" dichotomy possible because the Soviet Union as an atomic power then belonged in the "them" category. No longer could the mere possession of atomic bombs be interpreted as constituting a threat. Beginning with Andrei Vyshinsky's famous speech of September 23, 1949,[8] Soviet spokesmen sought to emphasize the peaceful ends to which the USSR was directing and would continue to direct, its atomic energy resources. Russian publications and United Nations spokesmen described irrigation projects, excavation works and developments in medicine in connection with atomic energy, but they rarely publicized either the actual or the potential use of atomic weapons as a part of the Kremlin's military arsenal.

Simplifying the problem of control was another means by which the Soviet Union sought to appeal to world opinion. No single theme was repeated more regularly than the deceptively simple "ban the bomb" theme. Here was, argued the Soviet representatives, the one panacea for the terrible prospect of atomic death. No one, the argument went, who honestly opposed the use of atomic bombs could fail to agree to a declaration forbidding their manufacture and use. Soviet speakers likened such a declaration to the Geneva Protocol against gas and bacteriological warfare (1925) and reminded their listeners that the Second World War was fought without the use of either gas or bacteriological weapons.

Soviet publicists ignored the connection between prohibition and control which the Western powers insisted was essential. The basic Western contention was that only an effectively working control plan could guarantee the security sought by a declaration of prohibition. Prohibition without control would, in Western eyes, actually increase international tension because no nation could be positive that another nation was not secretly violating the prohibition agreement.

Vyshinsky, Molotov and Gromyko all disputed this. They asked instead only for an agreement "in principle" on prohibition. Their view was that such an agreement "in principle" would alleviate international tension and " . . . a recommendation made by the assembly for the prohibition of weapons of mass destruction," as Andrei Vyshinsky said, "would have . . . moral and political force." He admitted such a recommendation would not constitute a legal obligation, but

[8] See p. 152 in chap. VI.

The fear that such a decision might be violated by a State which secretly manufactured atomic weapons was a completely specious argument for such violations would always be discovered. Modern scientific techniques were sufficiently advanced so that the world could always know what was happening in the field of atomic energy or hydrogen weapons. Moreover, there would be a control body which could before long discover all violations. States which were not discouraged by moral obligations would hardly be disturbed at being thus exposed, but States which believed that moral obligations should be fulfilled and which assumed responsibility for their actions, would not allow themselves to be shamed in that way.[9]

Questions of detail, such as how one nation would have means of discovering violations abroad until control was established, how long after prohibition a control plan would take effect, or how were states exposed as violators to be restrained, were never answered by the Soviet delegation. Soviet propaganda in the United Nations operated on the assumption that easily understood generalizations repeated endlessly would have a greater impact upon world opinion than a more involved analysis proving the Soviet argument factually or logically.

A third objective of Soviet negotiators was to create an image of the United States as an aggressive nation. To accomplish this Soviet negotiators resorted to a vast propaganda campaign both within and outside of the United Nations. More time and words were devoted by Soviet spokesmen to hostile accusations against the United States and the Western bloc than were actually spent in proposing and defending the Soviet position. One variant of the propaganda tactic was the Soviet practice of deliberate misinterpretation of the United States proposals and the majority plan. It is likely also that the Soviet delegation hoped to discredit American policy by putting the American delegates in the position of defending America's retention of its atomic monopoly until the Soviet Union acceded to a control plan.

Two of the most frequently used anti-American propaganda

[9] UN, *ORGA, Eighth Session. First Committee, Summary Records of Meetings 16 September-7 December 1953*, 664th meeting, p. 211.

themes were that the United States was opposed to international control of atomic energy and that the real purpose of the Baruch Plan was to establish an international atomic supertrust under American domination. According to Soviet spokesmen the American government opposed atomic energy control in order to preserve its own monopoly of atomic weapons—a monopoly with which it was threatening the world and which it was using to gain political advantages. Another reason for American opposition to control, according to the Soviet Union, was the fear among suppliers of conventional fuel that if the United States abandoned its monopoly, profits from the sale of these fuels would in the long run be threatened.

American opposition to international control was deduced from the refusal of the United States to accept Soviet Russia's proposals and from the deliberate obstacles (*e.g.*, elimination of the veto, international ownership of national industries and the like) created by the United States to prevent Russia from accepting the majority plan.

At the same time as they accused the United States of not wanting control, the Soviet representatives championed the idea that the United States promoted the Baruch Plan in order to create a world atomic "supertrust" dominated by the United States. Soviet propagandists saw the United States policy for this "supertrust" motivated by (1), the desire to acquire the world sources of uranium and thorium; (2), the desire to interfere in the internal economy of the Soviet Union; and (3), the desire to obtain intelligence information about the USSR.

Logically these imputed objectives of American policy would appear to be in contradiction. Mr. de Rose, the French representative in a speech before the Atomic Energy Commission pointed out the contradiction of the oft-repeated Soviet claim that the United States did not want agreement on a control plan and at the same time wanted adoption of the plan to create an American-dominated supertrust. Mr. de Rose noted, "One cannot at the same time wish to prevent the adoption of a plan of control and try to establish one's own supremacy by setting up that plan of control." Tsarapkin's reply to this contention was that, "In fact, there is no contradiction whatsoever. The United States is agreeable to either of the alternatives." [10]

Much of Soviet propaganda had no immediate relation to the subjects under discussion by the United Nations organs. The Atomic Energy Commission, General Assembly and Disarmament Commission were utilized by Soviet diplomats for attacks on all aspects of American foreign policy. The most common accusations were that United States foreign policy was in general aggressive and, in particular, the United States was planning an attack on the USSR. To support these charges, Soviet representatives cited statements and articles in the American press. Reference was made to statements from such leaders as Generals Bullene, Bradley, Waite, Creasy, McAuliffe, and Eisenhower and Secretaries Forrestal, Lovett and Johnson to show that "the security of all other States would be jeopardized by the aggressive policy of the United States." [11]

Actual quotations were infrequently used; but when given they were invariably taken out of context. As a rule Soviet spokesmen preferred to refer to anonymous general statements which had no basis in reality but were devised to stir up anti-American feeling. Such, for example was Andrei Vyshinsky's claim before the General Assembly in plenary session that "Statements to the effect that atomic bombs must be used against the Asian people are made quite openly; this means against the Chinese people, against the peoples of Burma, Indonesia, Malaya, Vietnam and so on. 'Those are the peoples that must be dealt with first!' That is what certain gentlemen [in the United States] are saying, gentlemen who cannot be described otherwise than as cannibals." [12] Sometimes articles from popular American magazines such as the *Saturday Evening Post, United States News and World Report* and the *New York Times Magazine* were quoted as official American policy proving that the United States was planning to attack the Soviet Union.

[10] UN, *AECOR, Fourth Year No. 5, 21 Meeting 25 March 1949*, p. 6 and *AEC/C.1/PV.45*, p. 61.
[11] *DCOR Second Report*, pp. 15, 40.
[12] UN, *ORGA, Fifth Session. Plenary Meetings, Verbatim Records of Meetings*, Vol. I, 321st meeting, p. 616.

Soviet "hate-America" propaganda within disarmament talks reached its apogee during the Korean War. From 1949 until the death of Stalin in 1953 propagandistic tactical maneuvers took precedence over every other aspect of Soviet activity related to atomic energy control. This emphasis on propaganda to discredit the United States during this period can be explained partially by the fact that by 1949 the Soviet Government had achieved as much success as was possible toward the attainment of at least three out of five of its primary objectives—viz., it had skillfully rejected the majority proposals; it had succeeded in identifying the Soviet Union with a "ban the bomb" policy; it had stalled for enough time to enable the Soviet Union to explode its own atomic device. Portraying the United States as an aggressive power became an objective of particular importance after 1950 in order to counteract the bad light in which the Soviet Union was placed as a result of its support of the North Korean attack on South Korea.

This intensive propaganda campaign began during 1949. Outside of the United Nations it started with the "First World Congress of the Partisans of Peace" which convened in April, 1949, in Paris and Prague and led to the creation of a permanent committee and a secretariat.

Almost a full year before the outbreak of the Korean War the Soviet press was ready to condemn the United States for using bacteriological and radiological weapons. One Soviet social scientist wrote in 1949: "Bourgeois sociologists, mercenary servants of the warmongers, are ready to hail bacteriological warfare and plans for infecting residential areas by spreading radioactive substances." [13] In the United Nations every effort was made to convince public opinion that in American hands the atomic bomb would only be used for evil purposes.

Characteristic of the Soviet tendency to rewrite history in terms of current politics, Soviet spokesmen extended their condemnation of America's potential use of the bomb to include the only two times the bomb had been used. In 1949 Andrei Vyshinsky reminded the General Assembly that, "History would

[13] *Current Digest of the Soviet Press*, I, No. 27, 4.

record . . . the name of the country which had been the first to use atomic energy for the purpose of destroying thousands of human beings, although that had not been necessary either for the conduct of the war or for the achievement of victory." [14]

After the outbreak of the Korean War Soviet diplomats used the disarmament talks primarily to supplement their propaganda line in the United Nations as a whole. At the Sixth General Assembly the Soviet proposal for prohibition and a formal condemnation of the "aggressive Atlantic bloc" were formally combined in a resolution entitled "Measures to combat the threat of a new world war and to strengthen peace and friendship among the nations." The disarmament provisions of this resolution were referred to the newly created Disarmament Commission where the Soviet representatives continued to bring up their charges that the United States had used bacteriological weapons against the North Koreans and Chinese.

In addition to making statements about the aggressive intentions behind the Western proposals, the Russian representatives attempted to discredit the Western nations by misquoting and misinterpreting the contents of the majority proposals. When the Security Council began its debate on the three completed Atomic Energy Commission reports in 1948, the Soviet delegate twisted that feature of the majority plan which provided that control must *begin* at the mines to signify that the plan provided for no control whatsoever over plants producing fissionable fuel. In spite of the specific recommendations contained in Part II, Chapter 4, of the Second Report providing for control over nuclear plants and reactors, Andrei Gromyko informed the Security Council that ". . . it became quite evident that the United States Government would like the establishment of control to be limited to the sources of raw materials." [15]

This patently untrue description of the American position was maintained before the General Assembly that year. Andrei Vyshinsky summarized the Soviet Government's position on

[14] UN, *ORGA, Fourth Session. Ad Hoc Political Committee, Summary Records of Meetings 27 September-7 December 1949,* 35th meeting, p. 208.
[15] UN, *SCOR, Third Year No. 85, 321 Meeting 16 June 1948,* p. 10.

controls as follows: "The USSR maintained that a properly organized international control body should exercise control over the production of atomic energy in all its stages, beginning with the production of raw materials up to and including the output of manufactured goods." This was precisely the essence of the majority proposals, but Vyshinsky added: "The Governments of the United States, the United Kingdom, France and other powers could not agree with that position." [16]

Similarly, Andrei Vyshinsky presented an entirely inaccurate description of the quota provisions of the majority plan. Part II, Chapter One, of the Second Atomic Energy Commission Report stipulated that the principles governing the policy of the control agency with regard to the production and use of atomic energy "should be established by international agreement" and that the treaty establishing the agency should "in certain cases . . . prescribe a numerical quota" where questions of distribution of atomic fuel were involved. Yet Andrei Vyshinsky maintained that he could not find any statement in the majority plan that the quotas for atomic energy would be allocated with the agreement of the governments concerned.

In order to discredit the quota features of the plan, he resorted to reading portions of the Second Report which related to the quotas for the mining of ores, based on the relative size of the mines ("proportional deletion") and attacked the Western powers for proposing similar quotas for peaceful uses. In defense of the majority plan, the Western representatives pointed out that the quotations used by the Soviet delegate referred to matters related to mining, not to the quotas assigned for peaceful uses, but their refutation had no effect upon the tactics of the Soviet representatives.

A fourth objective of Soviet atomic energy negotiators referred not to the non-Western world, but to American public

[16] UN, ORGA, Third Session, Part I. Plenary Meetings . . . Summary Records of Meetings 21 September-12 December 1948, 143rd meeting, p. 126. See also speech of Andrei Vyshinsky, UN, ORGA, Third Session, Part I. First Committee, Summary Records of Meetings 21 September-8 December 1948, 145th meeting, p. 27.

opinion and the United States Government itself. The Soviet Government sought to weaken the will of the American government from using or considering using the atomic bomb.

This tactic of encouraging the American inhibitions toward use of atomic weapons was manifest in two forms. One was the Soviet campaign to "ban the bomb." By emphasizing the extremely cruel aspects of this weapon and placing it in a special category of weapons, the Soviet Union sought to foster a worldwide revulsion against the bomb. It was expected that if enough pressure from world public opinion could be exerted on the United States, the American government would be extremely reluctant ever to use the bomb. This pressure, which can be called an external pressure, was fostered by the numerous speeches in all the United Nations organs citing the atrocious nature of atomic weapons. Outside of the United Nations, this pressure was generated by the "World Peace Movement" which the Soviet Union claimed received the support of over 500 million people.

A second manifestation of this pressure was the Soviet effort to obtain outright condemnation of the bomb by the American representatives themselves. The greater the condemnation that could be elicited from American spokesmen, the more difficult it would be for American leaders to justify to the American people a policy of reliance upon atomic weapons. To achieve this result Soviet speakers constantly challenged the United States representatives to accept the Soviet proposal for prohibiting atomic weapons. When the American representatives refused, the Soviet diplomats claimed to have proof of America's aggressive intentions and glorification of the atomic bomb. They charged Americans with worshipping "the cult of the atomic bomb."

Constantly confronted with these accusations, the American representatives were compelled to respond and deny them. In denying these accusations the American representatives frequently had to explain that America's retention of the bomb was necessitated by the prospects of Soviet aggression. Nevertheless,

Soviet expectations of weakening the American resolve to build atomic weapons were raised by the possibility that those denials might, over a period of time, be accepted by American public opinion without the qualifications that usually accompanied them.

Soviet propagandists, in other words, appealed to the moral values and preconceptions of the American people and did everything possible to encourage that element of American thinking which opposes the use of force and weapons of mass destruction. In this sense the pressure encouraged by Soviet negotiations was an internal one.

The fifth major Soviet objective was to stall for time. Stalling was, of course, a technique of rejection; but, in addition, it was an end in itself. As the weeks of fruitless negotiation passed into months and these into years, the Soviet Government was able to mobilize its scientific knowledge and industrial capacity toward making its own atomic stockpile. And with the passing of time the majority plan became increasingly obsolete.

There is no question but that the Soviet Union placed a high priority on the creation of its own atomic bomb. Prestige, an increased military posture, and a stronger political position were all at stake. A homemade atomic bomb was of importance to the Soviet Union not only for the military and political benefits it brought, but for its own sake.

Militarily, a Soviet nuclear stockpile meant that in the event of a conflict with the West, the war could be brought to the United States. While Stalinist military doctrine may have depreciated the value of the bomb as an "ultimate weapon," it is not likely that he and his military staff ignored the benefits of the greater firepower per ruble cost of delivery made possible by atomic instead of conventional bombs. Nor is it likely that the importance of the bomb in fostering European neutralism (particularly in Germany) was ignored. Politically the possession of the atomic bomb put the Soviet Union in a stronger bargaining position.

Even without the more tangible benefits of atomic weapons, the creation of an atomic bomb would have had a high priority for the Russians. It served to vindicate Soviet science; it gave the Russians a feeling of equality—if not superiority—in the ability of the Soviet Union to duplicate the American accomplishment without the aid of allies and under the handicap of a weaker industrial base. Most important of all, it provided that greater feeling of absolute security which is so essential to the Bolshevik mentality.

Parliamentary tactics of delay were among the principal means of stalling for time. Many of these tactics have been mentioned above; long, repetitious speeches, a constant reintroduction of similar or identical proposals, evading the issue and refusing to answer questions. One of the most persistent of the Soviet techniques was insistence upon a very strict application of the rules of procedure in the Atomic Energy and Disarmament commissions. Foreshadowing the behavior of the Soviet representatives in the Atomic Energy Commission was Gromyko's demand in the opening days of the Commission's work that all decisions on matters of substance be taken by a two-thirds vote instead of a majority vote. His argument for a procedure making Atomic Energy Commission decisions more difficult to obtain was that a two-thirds vote would give greater weight to the Commission's decisions. This contention was rejected by the majority in favor of a procedure making possible more expeditious action.[17]

During the course of the Commission's work, the majority frequently attempted to lighten the Commission's labor by eliminating the preliminary statements (often very lengthy) to the numerous proposals before the group, or by dispensing with consecutive translations of the speeches. These efforts were stoutly resisted by the Soviet representatives who stood in their rights under traditional rules of United Nations procedure. The use of these rights was often carried to extreme

[17] UN, *AECOR, No. 4. Fourth Meeting 3 July 1946*, pp. 64-67. Note that this point of contention essentially involved the question of the Commission's taking its decisions by a vote of seven or eight, since the number of the full Commission was only twelve.

length so as to prolong debate even on the most trivial items.

It is traditional practice in United Nations negotiations to permit a delegation to make preliminary remarks on every resolution or proposal submitted and then later to make a more definitive statement when the delegation's government has been consulted. To shorten the time interval the Western representatives often gave advance copies of their impending proposals to the Soviet delegation so that it would have time to consult authorities in Moscow. This procedure achieved very little success. Soviet spokesmen still insisted on making long preliminary remarks and the time lag between Lake Success and Moscow was almost invariably longer than that between Lake Success and London and Paris. What irritated the majority spokesmen even more, however, was the inflexibility of the Soviet position. Soviet diplomats were given very little leeway in accepting modifications of their government's proposals. Thus the many questions of the majority, as well as suggested compromises, had to wait days and even weeks before they received any sort of response whatsoever.

Nor was the majority very successful in saving time by resorting to informal discussions or informal meetings. Shortly before the Atomic Energy Commission drew up its Third Report acknowledging a deadlock, Frederick Osborn, the American delegate, asked Mr. Gromyko to join with representatives of the majority to consider the problem of control informally. Gromyko refused this request, as had other Russian delegates, on the grounds that he would have no way of knowing whether the opinions expressed were those of the delegates personally or those of their governments. During one period of informal committee sessions the Soviets did send an observer only. That was in 1947 in connection with the working papers comprising the Commission's Second Report. Even as observers only, the majority delegates found that the Soviet representatives consumed more time in raising questions of procedure than any of the delegations engaged in the actual work on the papers.[18]

[18] See Frederick Osborn, "The Russians Delay Action on Atomic Control," *Bulletin of Atomic Scientists*, III, No. 10 (October, 1947), 299.

These five objectives, then, constituted the esoteric goals of Soviet atomic energy negotiators in contrast to the exoteric[19] goals stated on the face of the Soviet proposals. It is not likely that these objectives were formulated at one time in any systematic manner; but the postwar record of atomic energy negotiations reveals that the Soviet representatives worked primarily and consistently toward these ends. Moreover, it is quite clear that these same tactics have been an integral element of all Soviet disarmament negotiations over the past fifteen years. With the changing subject matter, of course, some goals have changed. No longer, for example, do the Soviets need to stall for time to build an atomic stockpile. New objectives have replaced some of the old. More recently Soviet negotiations have been directed toward a weakening of the NATO alliance system by encouraging dissension among the Western powers and by preventing the arming of NATO forces with nuclear weapons. It is clear that the lessons of the first eight postwar years apply to the past decade and a half.

"Gamesmanship" is perhaps too facetious a term to describe the intensely serious contest in propaganda and psychological warfare that characterized Soviet-Western negotiations toward international control of atomic energy. But it does serve to emphasize several elements of this contest. Like most contests atomic energy negotiations were undertaken for stakes. In this case the stakes were political gain. Also like most contests there were certain rules to the game. The rules of atomic energy negotiation correspond roughly to the tactics and techniques described above. Unlike most contests, the rules by which this diplomatic contest was carried on were rarely—if ever—publicly delineated. Nor were the Soviet objectives ever publicly described.

If the Soviet Union had announced that its primary objectives were not prohibition and international control of atomic energy, but a rejection of control proposals, a discrediting of the United States and a stall for time, the attainment of these unexpressed

[19] See Gabriel A. Almond, *The Appeals of Communism* (Princeton, 1954), pp. ix-xvii.

goals would have been jeopardized.[20] The Soviet "game" then, was for the most part subtly played. It had to be subtle to be convincing. Where Soviet tactics were not subtle, they risked exposure and thus the defeat of the Soviet objectives.

[20] An incident reported by Frederick Osborn, concerning America's atomic energy negotiations during 1947-1949, provides an interesting example of the Soviet attitude toward atomic energy negotiations. Before Andrei Gromyko was scheduled to return to Moscow in 1949, Osborn asked him if the two of them could not sit down together and go over atomic energy matters before Gromyko left, in order to break the deadlock that had developed over the past few years. The American representative expressed the opinion that Gromyko was sincere in his desire to find a solution and that the Soviet representative trusted Osborn's sincerity. Together, said Osborn, they might be better able to explore both their governments' positions than in the public debates on the Atomic Energy Commission. Gromyko looked at Mr. Osborn quietly for a moment and replied, "Mr. Osborn, you may be sincere, but governments are never sincere." They never had their talk. Osborn, "Negotiating on Atomic Energy, 1946-1947," in *Negotiating With the Russians*, p. 230.

BIBLIOGRAPHY

I. Sources in the Russian Language

a. *Books*

Korsunskii, M. I. *Atomnoe Yadro.* Moscow, 1952.

Potemkin, V. P. *Istoriya Diplomatii.* Vol. 3. Moscow, 1954.

Tolchenov, M. P. *Problema Vseobshchevo Sokrashcheniya Vooruszhenii* (Stenograma Publichnoi Lektsii Prochitannoi 19 Dekabrya 1946 Goda v Lektsionnom Zale v Moskve). Moscow, 1947.

b. *Articles*

Korovin, E. "Amerikanskii Imperializm—Ugroza Suverenitetu Narodov," *Bolshevik,* VIII (April 30, 1949).

"Krakh Diplomatii Atomnovo Shantazha," *Bolshevik,* XVII (October, 1949).

Leonidov, A. "Voennive Monopolii Protiv Razoruzheniya," *Kommunist,* January, 1960. No. 1.

Morev, V., "Amerikanskie Atomshchiki," *Bolshevik,* XIV (July, 1952).

Otvety Tov. Stalina I. V. na Voprosy Prezidenta Agentstva Yunaited Press G-na Khyu Beili, Poluchennye 23 Oktyabrya 1946 Goda," *Bolshevik,* XIX (October, 1946).

"Otvet Tovarischa I. V. Staline Korrespondentu 'Pravdy' Naschet Atomnovo Oruzhiya," *Bolshevik,* XIX (October, 1951).

Rubenstein, M. "Proval Atomnoi Diplomatii Amerikanskikh Imperialistov," *Bolshevik,* VI (March, 1950).

Trakhenberg, O. V. " 'Sotsiologiya' Atomnoi Bomby," *Voprosy Filosofii,* III (1948).

c. *Newspapers*

Izvestia, Moscow, issues from 1945 to 1960.
Pravda, Moscow, issues from 1945 to 1960.

II. UNPUBLISHED MANUSCRIPTS

Brodie, Bernard. "The Atomic Bomb and American Security." Yale
   Institute of International Studies, Memorandum No. 18, Novem-
   ber 1, 1945.
Committee on Social Aspects of Atomic Energy of the Social
   Science Research Council, "Public Reaction to the Atomic Bomb
   and World Affairs" (A Nation-wide Survey of Attitudes and
   Information). Cornell University, April, 1947.
Corenetz, Helen. "Views of Pravda and Izvestia on International
   Control of Atomic Energy." Master's thesis, Columbia University,
   September, 1952.
Fuller, Sterling Hale. "The Foreign Policy of the Soviet Union in
   the League and in the United Nations." 2 vols. Doctoral disserta-
   tion, University of Texas, June, 1952. Available at the United
   Nations Library in New York.
Jacobson, Harold Karan. "The Soviet Union and the Economic and
   Social Activities of the United Nations." 2 vols. Doctoral disserta-
   tion, Yale University, 1955.
Ruggles, M. J. and A. Kramish. "The Soviet Union and the Atom.
   The Early Years." Rand Research Memorandum, RM-1711, April
   2, 1956. Available at Yale University Library.

III. UNITED NATIONS MATERIALS

The bibliography of United Nations material used in this study
is too extensive for a complete listing. For the period 1946 through
1949 the complete *Documents* and *Official Records* of the Atomic
Energy Commission are indispensable for a thorough understanding
of the politics of atomic energy control. In addition all General
Assembly *Documents* and *Official Records* for 1946 through 1953
pertaining to international control of atomic energy were consulted.
The same is true of all *Disarmament Commission Documents* and
Official Records for the period 1952 and 1953, as well as for
Security Council *Documents* and *Official Records* for the period
1946 through 1949. More specific references to this general listing
can be found in the footnotes.

As bibliographic aids the following are recommended:

An International Bibliography on Atomic Energy: Political, Economic and Social Aspects. United Nations Document AEC/INF/7 rev. 2, 1949-1951; 2 vols.

Check List of United Nations Documents, Part 3: Atomic Energy Commission, 1946-1952. United Nations Document ST/LIB/ser. F. Library, New York, 1953.

Index to Documents of the Disarmament Commission, General Assembly, Committee of Twelve and Security Council on the Subjects of the International Control of Atomic Energy and the General Regulation and Reduction of Armaments, 1 May 1951 to 31 October 1952. United Nations Document DC/INF, 2, 25 June 1953.

Index to Documents of the Disarmament Commission, the Subcommittee of the Disarmament Commission and the General Assembly on the Regulation, Limitation and Balanced Reduction of all Forces and all Armaments and Related Matters, 1 November 1952 to 31 December 1954. United Nations Document DC/INF. 3, 1 May 1956.

Index to the Three Reports of the Atomic Energy Commission. United Nations Document AEC/C.1/80.

United Nations Yearbook, Secretariat, Department of Public Information.

Of the several special reports published by the United Nations as documents the following are the most important:

First Report of the Atomic Energy Commission to the Security Council, 31 December 1946. United Nations Document AEC/18. Rev. 1.

Second Report of the Atomic Energy Commission to the Security Council, 11 September 1947. United Nations Document AEC/26.

Third Report of the Atomic Energy Commission to the Security Council, 17 May 1948. United Nations Document AEC/31/Rev. 1.

First Report of the Disarmament Commission, 29 May 1952. United Nations Document DC/11.

Second Report of the Disarmament Commission, 13 October 1952. United Nations Document DC/20.

Third Report of the Disarmament Commission, 20 August 1953, United Nations Document DC/32.

Fourth Report of the Disarmament Commission, 29 July 1954. United Nations Document DC/55.

First Report of the Sub-Committee of the Disarmament Commission, 22 June 1954, Annexes 1-9. United Nations Document DC/53.

Second Report of the Sub-Committee of the Disarmament Commis-

sion, 7 October 1955, Annexes 1-25. United Nations Document DC/71.

Third Report of the Sub-Committee of the Disarmament Commission, 4 May 1956, Annexes 1-12. United Nations Document DC/83.

Fourth Report of the Sub-Committee of the Disarmament Commission, 1 August 1957, Annexes 1-12. United Nations Document DC/112.

Fifth Report of the Sub-Committee of the Disarmament Commission, 11 September 1957, Annexes 1-13. United Nations Document DC/113.

Report of the Conference of Experts to Study the Possibility of Detecting Violations of a Possible Agreement on the Suspension of Nuclear Tests, 28 August 1958. United Nations Document A/3897.

Report of the Conference of Experts for the Study of Possible Measures Which Might be Helpful in Preventing Surprise Attack and for the Preparation of a Report Thereon to Governments, 5 January 1959. United Nations Document S/4445.

IV. GOVERNMENT PUBLICATIONS

United States of America. *Disarmament and Security: A Collection of Documents 1919-1955.* Senate Subcommittee on Disarmament: Committee Print, 84th Congress, 2nd sess. Washington, 1956.

———. *Control and Reduction of Armaments.* Final Report, Senate Subcommittee on Disarmament; 85th Congress, 2nd sess. Report No. 2501, October 13, 1958. Washington, 1958. See especially Annex II, Staff Studies Nos. 2, 3, 4, and 8.

———. *Geneva Test Ban Negotiations.* Senate Subcommittee of the Committee on Foreign Relations; Hearing, 86th Congress, 1st sess. March 25, 1959. Washington, 1959.

———. *Conference on the Discontinuance of Nuclear Weapons Tests.* Senate Subcommittee on Disarmament; Committee Print, 86th Congress, 2nd sess. Washington, 1960.

———. *Disarmament Developments Spring, 1960.* Senate Subcommittee of the Committee on Foreign Relations; Hearing, 86th Congress, 2nd sess. Washington, 1960.

———. Department of State. *A Report on the International Control of Atomic Energy,* prepared by the Secretary of State's Committee on Atomic Energy (The Acheson-Lilienthal Report). Publication 2498. Washington, 1946.

———. Department of State. *The International Control of Atomic Energy: Growth of a Policy.* Publication 2702. Washington, 1946.

——. Department of State. *International Control of Atomic Energy: Policy at the Crossroads.* Publication 3161. Washington, 1948.

——. Department of State. *Disarmament: The Intensified Effort, 1955-1958.* Publication 6676. Washington, 1958.

——. Department of State. *Documents on Disarmament 1945-1959* (2 vols.). Publication 7008. Washington, 1960.

——. White House Disarmament Staff. *Reference Documents on Disarmament Matters.* Background Series D-1 through D-42. Washington, n.d.

The Dominion of Canada. *The Report of the Royal Commission To Investigate the Facts Relating to and Circumstances Surrounding the Communication, by Public Officials and Other Persons in Positions of Trust of Secret and Confidential Information to Agents of a Foreign Power.* Ottawa, 1946.

V. NEWSPAPERS AND JOURNALS

Bulletin of the Atomic Scientists, I-IX. (Vol. I, Nos. 1-6 entitled *Bulletin of the Atomic Scientists of Chicago.*) Chicago, Ill., 1946-1953.

Joint Committee on Slavic Studies, *Current Digest of the Soviet Press,* I-V. Washington, D.C., 1949-1953.

New Times, January 1945-December 1953. (Issues of January 1945-June 1945 entitled *The War and the Working Class.*) Moscow.

New York Times, issues from 1945-1960.

VI. BOOKS

Almond, Gabriel A. *The Appeals of Communism.* Princeton, 1954.

Amrine, Michael. *The Great Decision.* New York, 1959.

Barnet, Richard J. *Who Wants Disarmament?* Boston, 1960.

Biörklund, Ellis. *International Atomic Policy During a Decade 1945-1955.* Princeton, 1956.

Blackett, P. M. S. *Atomic Weapons and East-West Relations.* Cambridge, England, 1956.

——. *Fear, War and the Bomb.* New York, 1949.

Brodie, Bernard (ed.). *The Absolute Weapon: Atomic Power and World Order.* New York, 1946.

Byrnes, James F. *Speaking Frankly.* New York, 1947.

Claude, Inis L., Jr. *Swords Into Plowshares.* New York, 1956.

Coit, Margaret L. *Mr. Baruch.* Boston, 1957.

Connally, Tom. *My Name is Tom Connally.* New York, 1954.

Dennett, Raymond and Johnson, Joseph E. (eds.). *Negotiating With the Russians.* Boston, 1951.

Dhar, Sailendra Nath. *Atomic Weapons in World Politics*. Calcutta, 1957.

Dinerstein, H. S. *War and the Soviet Union*. New York, 1959.

Eichelberger, Clark M. *United Nations: The First Ten Years*. New York, 1955.

Forrestal, James V. and Millis, Walter (ed.). *The Forrestal Diaries*. New York, 1951.

Garthoff, Raymond. *Soviet Military Doctrine*. Glencoe, Ill., 1953.

———. *Soviet Strategy in the Nuclear Age*. New York, 1958.

Goodrich, Leland M. and Simons, Anne P. *The United Nations and the Maintenance of International Peace and Security*. Washington, D.C., 1955.

Holcombe, Arthur N., Chairman. *Organizing Peace in the Nuclear Age*. Report of the Commission to Study the Organization of Peace. New York, 1959.

Kelsen, Hans. *The Communist Theory of Law*. London, 1955.

Kissinger, Henry A. *Nuclear Weapons and Foreign Policy*. New York, 1957.

Kramish, Arnold. *Atomic Energy in the Soviet Union*. Stanford, Calif., 1959.

Leites, Nathan. *A Study of Bolshevism*. Glencoe, Ill., 1953.

Lie, Trygve. *In the Cause of Peace*. New York, 1954.

Martin, Andrew. *Collective Security: A Progress Report*. UNESCO, 1952.

Modelski, George A. *Atomic Energy in the Communist Bloc*. Melbourne, Australia, 1959.

Newman, James R. and Miller, Byron S. *The Control of Atomic Energy*. New York, 1948.

Nutting, Anthony. *Disarmament: An Outline of the Negotiations*. London, 1959.

Rauch, Georg von. *A History of Soviet Russia*. New York, 1957.

Reitzel, William, Kaplan, Morton and Coblenz, Constance. *United States Foreign Policy*. Washington, D.C., 1956.

Royal Institute of International Affairs, *Atomic Energy*. London, 1948.

Stimson, Henry L. and Bundy, McGeorge. *On Active Service in Peace and War*. New York, 1947.

Taracouzio, Timothy A. *The Soviet Union and International Law*. New York, 1935.

Tate, Merze. *The United States and Armaments*. Cambridge, Mass., 1948.

Truman, Harry S. *Year of Decisions, Memoirs*, Vol. I. New York, 1955.

————. *Years of Trial and Hope, Memoirs*, Vol. II. New York, 1956.

Vandenberg, Arthur H., Jr. (ed.). *The Private Papers of Senator Vandenberg*. Boston, 1952.

VII. Booklets and Pamphlets

Collart, Yves. *Disarmament: A Study Guide and Bibliography on the Efforts of the United Nations*. The Hague, 1958.

Frye, William R. *Disarmament, Atoms into Plowshares?* Foreign Policy Association, Headline Series No. 113.

Korovin, Eugene A. "The USSR and Disarmament," *International Conciliation*, No. 292 (Carnegie Endowment for International Peace). New York, 1933.

Masters, Dexter and Way, Katherine, *et al. One World or None*. New York, 1956.

Moor, Carol Carter and Chamberlin, Waldo. *How to Use United Nations Documents*. New York, 1952.

Nogee, Joseph L. "The Diplomacy of Disarmament," *International Conciliation*, No. 526. January, 1960.

Rabinowitch, Eugene (ed.). *Minutes to Midnight, The International Control of Atomic Energy*. Atomic Science and Education Series No. 1 (Published by the *Bulletin of Atomic Scientists*). Chicago, 1950.

Royal Institute of International Affairs. *Defense in the Cold War*. A Report by a Chatham House Study Group. London, 1950.

Salvin, Marina. "Soviet Policy Toward Disarmament," *International Conciliation*, No. 428. (Carnegie Endowment for International Peace). New York, 1947.

Shils, Edward A. *The Atomic Bomb in World Politics*. Peace Aims Pamphlet 45. London, n.d.

Slosson, Preston and Kirk, Grayson. *Swords of Peace*. Foreign Policy Association, Headline Series No. 64.

Smyth, Henry DeWolf. *Atomic Energy for Military Purposes*. Princeton, 1945.

"The Control of Atomic Energy," *International Conciliation*, No. 423 (Carnegie Endowment for International Peace). New York, 1946.

Wood, Alex. *Notes on the Course of Negotiations for Control of Atomic Energy*. Peace Aims Pamphlet 47. London, n.d.

Woodward, E. L. *Some Political Consequences of the Atomic Bomb*. London, 1946.

VIII. ARTICLES

A Foreign Observer. "Russia, the United States and the Atom," *The Atlantic*, April, 1948.

"Symposium on Atomic Energy and Its Implication," Philosophical Society, *Proceedings*, XC, No. 1 (1946).

Arneson, Gordon R. "The Role of the United Nations in Disarmament," *Journal of International Affairs*, IX, No. 2 (1955).

Barghoorn, Frederick C. "The Soviet Union Between War and Cold War," American Academy of Political and Social Science, *Annals*, CCLXIII (May, 1949).

Baruch, Bernard M. "Memorandum to the President" (September 24, 1946), *Bulletin of Atomic Scientists* (hereinafter abbreviated to *BAS*), II, Nos. 7 and 8 (October 1, 1946).

Bechhoefer, Bernhard. "Negotiating the Statute of the International Atomic Energy Agency," *International Organization*, XIII, No. 1 (1949).

Beloff, Max. "The Theory of Soviet Foreign Policy," *Soviet Studies*, III (1951-1952).

Bernard, Stephan. "Some Political and Technical Implications of Disarmament," *World Politics*, VIII, No. 1 (October, 1955).

Benoit-Smullyn, Emile. "United Nations Control of Atomic Energy," *The Antioch Review*, VI, No. 4 (1946-1947).

Berezhkov, V. "World Press Comment on J. V. Stalin's Atomic Weapon Statement," *New Times* (hereinafter abbreviated to *NT*), October 17, 1951.

———. "What is happening in the United Nations Disarmament Commission?" *NT*, June 25, 1952.

Borchard, Edwin. "The Atomic Bomb," *American Journal of International Law*, XL, No. 1 (1946).

Blackett, P. M. S. "Atomic Energy and the UNO Atomic Energy Commission," *BAS*, I, No. 8 (April 1, 1946).

Briggs, Herbert W. "World Government and the Control of Atomic Energy," American Academy of Political and Social Sciences, *Annals*, CCXLIX (January, 1947).

"British Atomic Scientists' Proposals for International Control of Atomic Energy," released by the Council of the British Atomic Scientists' Association on January 20, 1947. *BAS*, III, No. 2 (February, 1947).

Brodie, Bernard. "The Atomic Dilemma," American Academy of Political and Social Sciences, *Annals*, CCXLIX (January, 1947).

———. "The Atomic Bomb as Policy Maker," *Foreign Affairs*, XXVII, No. 1 (October, 1948).

Cavers, David F. "An Interim Plan for International Control of Atomic Energy," *BAS*, VI, No. 1 (January, 1950).

———. "Atomic Power versus World Security," *BAS*, III, No. 10 (October, 1947).

Chakste, Mintauts. "Soviet Concepts of the State, International Law and Sovereignty," *American Journal of International Law*, XXXIX, No. 3 (1945).

Cuthbert, Daniel and Balderston, John L., "A Proposal for an Atomic Armistice," *BAS*, VI, No. 1 (January, 1950).

Cuthbert, Daniel and Squires, Arthur M. "The International Control of Safe Atomic Energy," *BAS*, III, Nos. 4 and 5 (April-May, 1947).

Dinerstein, Herbert. "The Revolution in Soviet Strategic Thinking," *Foreign Affairs*, XXXVI (January, 1958).

Dulles, Allen W. "Disarmament in the Atomic Age," *Foreign Affairs*, XXV, No. 2 (January, 1947).

Eliot, G. F. "Russia and the State Department Report," *BAS*, I, No. 10 (May 1, 1946).

Emerson, Rupert and Claude, Inis L., Jr. "The Soviet Union and the United Nations. An Essay in Interpretation," *International Organization*, VI (February, 1952).

Fox, William T. R. " 'Middle Run' Planning: Atomic Energy and International Relations," *BAS*, IV, No. 8 (August, 1948).

Frase, Robert W., "International Control of Nuclear Weapons," American Academy of Political and Social Science. *Annals*, XCCC (November, 1953).

Fuller, C. Dale. "Soviet Policy in the United Nations," American Academy of Political and Social Sciences, *Annals*, CCLXIII (May, 1949).

Ginsburgs, George. "Soviet Atomic Energy Agreements," *International Organization*, XV, No. 1 (Winter 1961).

Goodman, Elliot R. "The Soviet Union and World Government," *The Journal of Politics*, XV, No. 2 (May, 1953).

Gromyko, Andrei. "A Defense of the Soviet Control Plan," *BAS*, IV, No. 6 (June, 1948).

Haskins, Caryl P. "Atomic Energy and American Foreign Policy," *Foreign Affairs*, XXIV, No. 4 (July, 1946).

Hutchins, Robert M. "Peace or War with Russia?" *BAS of Chicago*, I, No. 6 (March 1, 1946).

Inglis, David R. "The ADA and the Veto Power," *BAS*, I, No. 12 (June 1, 1946).

Kissinger, Henry A. "Nuclear Testing and the Problem of Peace," *Foreign Affairs*, XXXVII, No. 1 (October, 1958).

Korovin, Eugene. "The Second World War and International Law," *American Journal of International Law*, XL (1946).

———. "Absolute Sovereignty or Absolute Falsehood?" A letter to the editor, *NT*, October 8, 1947.

Kulski, W. W. "Soviet Comments on International Law and Relations," *American Journal of International Law*, XLVI, No. 2 (1952).

Lapitsky, I. "Atomic Imperialism," *NT*, July 9, 1952.

Lilienthal, David E. "How Atomic Energy Can Be Controlled," *BAS*, II, Nos. 7 and 8 (October 1, 1946).

Lysenko, T. D. "A Warning to the Atom Cannibals," an interview, *NT*, March 29, 1950.

McNaughton, A. G. L. "National and International Control of Atomic Energy," *International Journal*, Winter, 1947-1948.

Millis, Walter. "The Absolute Weapon?", *The Reporter*, I, No. 3 (May 25, 1949).

Morton, Louis. "The Decision to Use the Bomb," *Foreign Affairs*, XXXV, No. 2 (January, 1957).

Neyer, Joseph. "Is Atomic-Fission Control a Problem in Organizational Technique?" *Ethics*, LVII, No. 4 (July, 1947).

Oppenheimer, J. Robert. "International Control of Atomic Energy," *Foreign Affairs*, XXVI, No. 2 (January, 1948).

———. "Atomic Weapons and American Policy," *Foreign Affairs*, XXXI, No. 4 (July, 1953).

Osborn, Frederick. "The USSR and the Atom," *International Organization*, V, No. 3 (August, 1951).

———. "The Russians Delay Action on Atomic Control," *BAS*, III, No. 10 (October, 1947).

———. "The Search for Atomic Control," *The Atlantic*, April, 1948.

Pollock, H. C. "The International Atom," *The Virginia Quarterly Review*, XXII, No. 4 (1946).

Possony, Stefan I. "The Atomic Bomb," *The Review of Politics*, VIII, No. 2 (April, 1946).

Prince, Charles. "Current Views of the Soviet Union on the International Organization of Security, Economic Cooperation, and International Law: A Summary," *American Journal of International Law*, XXXIX (1945).

"Disarmament: Proposals and Negotiations, 1946-1955," Royal Institute of International Affairs, *The World Today*, August, 1955.

Rubenstein, Modest. "The Foreign Press on the Atomic Bomb," *NT*, September 1, 1945.

———. "Science and Atomic Policy," *NT*, March 15, 1946.

———. "New Energy and Old Illusions," *NT*, December 15, 1945.

———. "The Atomic Age as American Scientists Picture It," *NT*, March 15, 1946.

———. "Monopoly Trusts Control Atomic Energy," *NT*, July 15, 1946.

———. "What Stands in the Way of the Peaceful Uses of Atomic Energy?" *NT*, October 1, 1946.

———. "International Control of Atomic Energy," *NT*, January 24, 1947.

———. "Neanderthal Men of the Atomic Age," *NT*, June 13, 1947.

———. "Once More on the Atomic Energy Commission," *NT*, September 3, 1947.

———. "An Advocate for the Atomic Warmongers," *NT*, March 24, 1948.

———. "Atomic Policy of the American Monopolies," *NT*, August 25, 1948.

———. "Ideology of Atomic Imperialism," *NT*, October 6, 1948.

———. "Atomic Bomb—Weapon of American Imperialist Blackmail," *NT*, October 27, 1948.

———. "The Policy of the Atomic Imperialists," *NT*, January 26, 1949.

———. "American Science and Atomic Energy," *NT*, June 29, 1949.

———. "The Atomites at Loggerheads," *NT*, September 14, 1949.

———. "The New Atomic Blackmail Move," *NT*, March 8, 1950.

———. "Scientists Show Up American Atomic Gangsters," *NT*, April 19, 1950.

———. "Some Political Implications of the State Department Report," *BAS*, I, No. 9 (April 15, 1946).

Rudzinski, Aleksander. "The Influence of the United Nations on Soviet Policy," *International Organization*, V, No. 2 (May, 1951).

Shils, Edward. "The Bolshevik Elite: An Analysis of a Legend," *BAS*, VII, No. 2 (February, 1951).

———. "The Atomic Bomb and the Veto on Sanctions," *BAS*, III, No. 2 (February, 1947).

———. "American Policy and the Soviet Ruling Group," *BAS*, III, No. 9 (September, 1947).

———. "The Failure of the UNAEC: An Interpretation," *BAS*, IV, No. 7 (July, 1948).

Shotwell, James T. "The Atomic Bomb and International Organization," *BAS*, I, No. 7 (March 15, 1946).

Sokoloff, A. "International Cooperation and Its Foes," *NT*, November 15, 1945.

Speransky, A. D. "Ban the Barbarous Atomic Weapons," *NT*, May 1, 1950.

Szilard, Leo. "Can We Have International Control of Atomic Energy?" *BAS*, VI, No. 1 (January, 1950).

Tarle, E. "Peace Vs. Atomic Blackmail," *NT*, November 7, 1949.

Thomson, George. "Hydrogen Bombs: The Need for a Policy," *International Affairs*, XXVI, No. 4 (October, 1950).

Turlington, Edgar. "International Control of the Atomic Bomb," *American Journal of International Law*, XL, No. 1 (1946).

Tolchenov, M. "The Atomic Bomb Discussion in the Foreign Press," *NT*, November 1, 1945.

Van Kleeck, Mary. "Atomic Energy," *Soviet Russia Today* (August, 1947).

Vishniak, Mark. "Sovereignty in the Soviet Law," *Russian Review*, VIII, No. 1 (January, 1949).

Wallace, Henry A. "A Letter to the President" (July 23, 1946), *BAS*, II, Nos. 7 and 8 (October 1, 1946).

Williams, Francis. "Control of the Bomb," *Spectator*, August 17, 1945.

Wolfers, Arnold. "Superiority in Nuclear Weapons: Advantages and Limitations," American Academy of Political and Social Sciences, *Annals*, XCCC (November, 1953).

Wright, Quincy. "Draft for a Convention on Atomic Energy," *BAS*, I, No. 8 (April 1, 1948).

———. "The United Nations Charter and the Prevention of War," *BAS*, III, No. 2 (February, 1947).

Yerusalimsky, A. "The United Nations—6 Years," *NT*, October 24, 1951.

Yemelyanov, V. S. "Atomic Energy for Peace: The U.S.S.R. and International Cooperation," *Foreign Affairs*, XXXVIII, No. 3 (April, 1960).

INDEX

A